Magnify Your Vision For

THE SMALL CHURCH

Magnify Your Vision For

THE SMALL CHURCH

By John Rowell
Pastor,
Northside Community Church

A Publication of
Northside Community Church
Atlanta, Georgia

What Others Are Saying About
Magnify Your Vision for the Small Church

Provocative! God-inspiring! Prophetic! These words come to mind as I reflect on *Magnify Your Vision for the Small Church*. John Rowell's story will bring you to tears as you read how God ministered through his church. What Bruchko illustrated on the impact of a person, this book illustrates on the impact of a local church. I recommend it to any congregation that wants to be mightily used by God. I plan to buy multiple copies of this book to distribute to others who need a model for church-based missions.

— Dr. Bruce K. Camp
Director of District Missions Consultants
Evangelical Free Church of America

Some have said we live in the age of the mega-church. It is commonly supposed that large churches with their vast array of programs, imposing budgets and large staffs will blaze the path toward Christian relevance in the 21st century. John Rowell presents a fresh option. This alternative flows from the crucible of his mid-size church's experience with God and their desire to see Jesus glorified among the unreached peoples of our planet. I have had the privilege of following Northside's pilgrimage through much of the story related in this book. It is all true! I commend this model as an example of what God can do with ordinary people working from a church base that was anything but imposing in size or influence.

— Paul McKaughan
President
Evangelical Fellowship of Mission Agencies

This is one of the most powerful statements on church life I have ever read! It is all the more compelling because it is rooted in committed experience. John Rowell and the community of believers at Northside Community Church are actually living this message out – no sterile theorizing here! Why can't this model be reproduced in thousands of churches?

— George Miley
President
Antioch Network

I have been moved, enlightened and enthused by this book. It communicates effectively and motivationally to pastors and people from smaller congregations. I also think it has much to say for those who are serving larger churches. The book is very practical. Local assemblies that want to become "Great Commission Churches" can use it as a manual. I am praying that our Lord will use it to motivate and mobilize scores – even hundreds and thousands – for the glory of God and the advancement of the Kingdom.

— *Dr. Paul Cedar*
Former President, Evangelical Free Church of America
President, Mission America

This book did something I never expected – it made me cry. Tears of joy and gratitude flowed more than once as I read the story of how God chose ordinary people to make an extraordinary difference in a faraway culture and a very different place than suburban Atlanta. Gone forever is my superior attitude that insists on professionals for the job of world evangelization. Yes, training matters, but heart and grit took this church farther than many would ever venture – even with the best of credentials. This is a story that every pastor should read, then lead his church into similar action.

— *Woody Phillips*
President, United World Mission
Board Chairman, ACMC

John Rowell's book leads the way into new paradigms of missions. He challenges cherished missionary models of the past and presents a positive example of what a faith-filled, local church can do. You don't have to agree with everything John says to be thoroughly stimulated and extremely challenged. I wholeheartedly commend this book to "small" churches who want to make a BIG impact on the unreached peoples of the world.

— *Dr. Rick Love*
U.S. Director
Frontiers

I have had a chance to personally see how the Croatian church leadership views the work undertaken in Bosnia by Northside Community Church. During a consultation in January 1996, these national leaders pointed again and again to John Rowell and his team as a model of the kind of partnership they respected and appreciated most deeply. Clearly, the Northside Community-led initiative in Bosnia has not only captured the attention of other churches in the United States; it has captured the hearts of the indigenous leaders themselves. It is good news that Northside Community Church and their partner churches have managed to avoid the worst and demonstrate the best in partnership efforts with nationals.

—Phill Butler
President and Founder
InterDev

Northside Community Church in Atlanta is a medium-sized church with a giant-sized vision. Reading the account of this church in *Magnify Your Vision for the Small Church* will motivate you to action, the kind of action Pastor John Rowell has led his church to in Bosnia. Be prepared to have some of the passion, faith and vision of the author impact you and your church. Northside Community Church provides us with a reputable model. The Evangelical Free Church Mission cherishes its partnership with Northside Community Church.

—Dr. Benjamin A. Sawatsky
Executive Director
Evangelical Free Church Mission

I could not agree more with John Rowell when he states that: "It is not the size of our resource pool but the limits of our faith and vision that determine our impact for the Kingdom of God." This wonderful story of how the Lord of the Harvest has used one faithful and visionary congregation will stretch your church. I especially recommend the second section of the book which clearly delineates important principles for churches open to being used to reach the lost. I pray that local church leaders will allow themselves to be challenged and motivated by *Magnify Your Vision for the Small Church*.

— William J. Hamel
President
Evangelical Free Church of America

Contents

Part 1
Our Story

Part 2
Principles for Church-Based Missions

With Gratitude

This book has been a collaborative effort, the joint product of the people who make up the small church I serve. I am indebted to more individuals than space allows me to thank personally, but I need to express special appreciation to some of those who have labored in the birth of this book along with me. The finished product could never have been completed without their committed help.

My family has been integrally involved in shaping our church and in seizing the many opportunities that Bosnia has presented our congregation for more than a decade. My wife Ginger has been willing to sacrifice her own priorities to follow me all over the face of this earth as my partner in life and ministry. Her fingerprints are found on every aspect of our philosophy of ministry and her influence fills the pages I have written. Whatever has flowed from my head is in large part a reflection of her heart — for we two are one. Our four sons, John, Jesse, Joseph and James, have also been courageous and eager companions in ministry at home and on the mission field. These young men and their mother have formed my closest support team, keeping me sane and balancing my weaknesses as we share life in our family.

David Lively, Fio Weaver, Becky Coldwell and Stephen Ruff were the pioneers who blazed the trail for our work among Bosnian refugees in Gasinci. Janice Freytag soon followed. Then Kevin and Rahela Conway and Abigajla, their baby and the first biological fruit of our cross-cultural ministry, filled the ranks of our long-term team. God then sent Greg Thelman, Angela Johnson and Lawn Dixon as reinforcements. All these and more now on the field are the real heroes who have done the hard work in Bosnia.

The men on our staff have shared fully in forging Northside Community Church as a living model of the high values we share for small church ministry. Without Neil Flippin, Bill Smith, Tom Conway and our fellow elders, there would be no story to tell!

My dear friend and assistant Mary Magnuson has been tirelessly patient in feeding thoughts from my fingertips to her computer. Every small church pastor would be richly blessed to have a co-worker so well convinced of his vision and so willing to serve.

Dick Sleeper (who is not in our church) deserves a special word of thanks for persistently encouraging me to reduce our journey on the road to Sarajevo to writing. He helped me believe the story was worth sharing and kept me motivated at important intervals along the way.

Lindsay Tucker, Lisa Smith, Sue Dillon and Laurie O'Connor were each vitally important to the editing process. Laurie especially captured the wind of the Spirit for this project and made it one of her major priorities for many months. Gratitude seems too limited a response to repay her for the hours of investment her artistry and expertise lent to the development of the finished product.

Mike Maserjian joined Laurie and me in the design of the cover, lending his engineer's mind and meticulous skill to the effort. What he didn't know about the programs needed to get the job done, he took hours of discretionary time to learn at considerable personal expense and sacrifice.

Jack and Lisa Alexander and Bud Cox's family graciously provided a place to withdraw from the press of pastoral responsibility so that I could focus on writing. The serenity of the sanctuaries these families offered was a timely and priceless contribution to the process.

Steve Kroening came by referral from Kurt Carlson, who is soon to be another of our full-time missionaries in Bosnia. Steve's work in typesetting the manuscript put the finishing touches on the book and allowed it to pass from my desk to his. His professional oversight on the home stretch saved us from the telltale marks of our own amateurism. He was the obstetrician who delivered this book birthed from my heart, through our small church to the world.

To all these folks and more, I want to say thanks for being willing to roll up your sleeves and get your hands dirty with me. May God redeem your time and reward your service to me, to His church and to the Kingdom.

This book is dedicated personally to Dr. Ray and Sue Dillon, faithful friends, fellow workers and fearless warriors for God who have been strong pillars for me and my family through fourteen years of shared ministry.

It is also dedicated corporately to the rest of the Northside Community Church family. These dear folks have loved me, allowed me to grow, and given me freedom to dream. They have also been willing to follow me into warfare on both a spiritual and a natural plane. Being their pastor has magnified my vision for the small church!

Foreword

An International Perspective

By Dr. Peter Kuzmic[*]

As a national leader from former Yugoslavia, I have witnessed the efforts of dozens of organizations and churches that desired to bring relief and hope to millions of desperate people caught in the crossfire of the war in Croatia and Bosnia. Many of God's people around the world responded to the desperate situation in the Balkans. They all deserve special commendation for ministry done in the name of Jesus during this difficult time in our history. Few are more deserving however, than my good friend John Rowell and his congregation at Northside Community Church.

This book is the incredible testimony of God's hand directing this small congregation to become involved in the midst of our mayhem. Beginning in 1992, Northside Community Church allowed itself the freedom to dare "dreaming in the Spirit" as it reached far beyond the limits of its size to sustain a vital contribu-

---

[*]Dr. Peter Kuzmic, President of the Evangelical Church of Croatia, Founder and Director of the Evangelical Theological Seminary in Osijek, Croatia and the Paul E. Toms Distinguished Professor of World Missions and European Studies at Gordon-Conwell Theological Seminary.

tion to our denomination's attempt to serve Bosnian refugees. I commend this congregation for its incarnational approach to ministry, sharing the love of Christ and the gospel message while living among Bosnian refugees during the war. We have come to deeply appreciate this church's faithful service as a valuable long-term partner in ministry.

In a message offered in Northside's mission conference in March 1998, I noted that this church has done more to reach Bosnians with the gospel of Jesus Christ than the rest of America's churches all together. My comments were not an exaggeration! From my perspective the kingdom could be advanced more effectively in many parts of the world if more churches of every size would seize upon this example of partnership and follow it. Northside's story will be invaluable for anyone wishing to better understand the pathways that can lead to effective cross-cultural cooperation in modern missions.

I recommend *Magnify Your Vision for the Small Church* as a must read for anyone involved in missions or in training others for mission service. I am praying that this book will inspire others to take more innovative approaches to ministry on the remaining mission fields of the world. We need the fresh wind of the Spirit to blow as we enter a new millennium of ministry opportunity. May we all follow the example of this relatively small church and commit ourselves to emulate their passion for dreaming in the Spirit!

Foreword

An American Perspective

By Bill Waldrop[**]

This book is the story of a remarkable church. It is remarkable because it is an example of true biblical *effectiveness*. Thus, while it is extraordinary among thousands of ordinary American churches, it is a model of what every church should be. More importantly, it demonstrates what every church *can* be.

Although Northside Community Church is relatively small, by now it could be much larger, even a burgeoning mega-church. Twice it has grown to 450 people, spinning off two other Anglo churches. At the same time it has helped in planting a Farsi-speaking church, which has become perhaps one of the largest Persian congregations in America.

Northside has *chosen* to remain a smaller church. Yet this has not limited its effectiveness. It has adopted its philosophy of ministry and consequent size and structure out of the convictions of its pastor. These convictions were developed over several years before he decided to start Northside Community Church.

[**]Bill Waldrop is the facilitator of international ministries for Mission America. He is also the former president of Advancing Churches in Missions Commitment (ACMC).

I met John Rowell in the early 1980's when we brought him and a colleague to the church I was pastoring for a diagnostic analysis. I had served almost seven years as pastor of a new church in suburban Atlanta, and felt it was time to assess ourselves. I soon discovered that John knew the local church in America better than anyone I had ever known, even though he was a relatively young man in his 30s.

John came by his knowledge of the church honestly. He had served on the staff of one of the best known mega-churches in the country. After this he had been an active member of another well-known mega-church while serving on the staff of a parachurch ministry, Church Resource Ministries (CRM). In his work with CRM, John was often called upon to analyze and evaluate local churches. In this diagnostic role he became familiar with churches of all kinds and sizes.

Along with careful study of the Scriptures to discern God's pattern for the New Testament church, his observation of many local churches brought him to the convictions expressed in this book. More significantly, his convictions have been validated by the planting and development of Northside Community Church, beginning late in 1984.

Although it has been written about, talked about, and earnestly sought for years, few local churches in the United States have developed authentic biblical *community*. Northside has. To experience the worship and fellowship of this congregation as I have on several occasions over the last few years, one is struck by the profound genuineness of its community. The people very evidently care for one another and share their lives on a deep level. This forms the environment and context for all they seek to do beyond their own walls.

Ordering their congregational life through careful teaching of the Scriptures and inspiring worship, they have devoted themselves to prayer at all levels, beginning with the leadership. Out of this has come a corporate understanding of God's direction for the church in both its local and global outreach. Northside's obvious effectiveness in the Atlanta area and in former Yugoslavia prove the soundness of its philosophy of ministry in theory and in practice.

John Rowell's critique of institutional churches is cogent, yet surprisingly thorough and very insightful. Megachurch leaders who are concerned for true effectiveness in the 21st century should unhurriedly reflect on the insights of this book. I believe it can be as helpful to them as to leaders of smaller congregations. Northside's evangelistic and church-planting initiatives among Muslims in Bosnia should also speak to all sizes of churches. The impact of this church should convict many for their relative neglect of cross-cultural outreach beyond the United States. I have never seen a church so blessed in all facets of its congregational life as Northside has been by its overseas mission involvement. If this story can be repeated by other churches, it should be!

Those who research the church find among the younger generation two urgently expressed needs: authentic community and the opportunity to make a difference in the lives of other people. Successful churches in the 21st century will be those that can satisfy these two deeply felt desires. Northside Community Church in Atlanta is already showing the way.

John Rowell has not written this book simply to tell Northside's story, interesting and stimulating as it is. He has written for a much greater, visionary purpose - to convince pastors and lay leaders that God will do incredible things in and through their churches if they will pay the price in prayer and move out in faith to do His revealed will. I am praying that this goal will be achieved as you read *Magnify Your Vision for the Small Church.*

Introduction

"... they had not gained any insight from the incident of the loaves, but their heart was hardened."
Mark. 6:52

"What in the world makes you folks believe a 250-member congregation located half a world away in Atlanta, Georgia, can make a difference in reaching a nation that has steadfastly rejected the gospel for the last 500 years?!!!"

Because they were unexpected, these words carried a powerful jolt. We were stunned as they rang out in the small room where a few of our elders were meeting to discuss our newly formulated plans to reach out to the unreached Muslims of Bosnia-Herzegovina.

Posed by an experienced mission professional, this question immediately made us feel foolish for having thought so boldly about the direction our small church's mission efforts might take. I was not mindful at the time of how this hard question would prove so helpful as time passed.

Only later did I realize the wisdom of this apparently instant opposition to our "God-sized" goal. I know now that the question was not meant so much to change our minds as to challenge our resolve. The intent was not to channel us into some alternative direction turning us away from Bosnia but to check our perspective about our possibilities for success. The words were not fired at us to bring us back to reality but to confirm our conviction that our plan was rooted in a vision revealed to us by the Lord. The force of the question made us recognize even before we began this work that, without God's specific intervention, we had no hopes to effectively see Bosnians come to faith in Christ.

No one needed to tell us we were ill-equipped and under-resourced for the goal we were preparing to pursue. And we didn't need to be reminded that our prospects based on natural reasoning looked grim. We knew we were reaching too far and attempting to do too much given our inexperience and our lack of resources. Silver and gold were obviously in short supply. So were models of other small churches which had dared to tackle an unreached people group target as an expression of their mission commitment. We had no reason to have the slightest confidence in our capacity or our clever planning.

All we had was an optimistic faith, an open door and an overwhelming confidence that God had chosen us out of the expanse of His global family to reach out to the Muslims of what was then Yugoslavia. After we recovered from the initial shock of this question our initial discouragement turned to delight. We were excited to remember how a similar challenge had been used by Jesus to bring faith to the forefront of the disciples' minds in the 1st century when he asked them to feed the five thousand. The incident of the loaves and fishes fueled their vision then, and recalling that story helped us stay our course as we began to plan toward an outreach in Bosnia.

Looking Back Before We Look Ahead

As a first time author I have a concern that some may conclude that I am trying in some way to use the platform of this book to blow my own horn. On that point I want to be crystal clear about my intentions. Sharing this account of our experience in Bosnia is specifically aimed at exciting other church leaders and at inspiring their vision for future ministry. I especially hope to impact leaders of small churches. I do not want in any way to boast.

All the glory for our experience in Bosnia belongs to the Lord and most of the credit goes to national leaders and to others who have helped us along the way. I encourage you to proceed with this book understanding that I write in the same spirit of humility that prompted Paul and Barnabus to share about their first missionary journey in the Antioch church (Acts 14:27). It is my desire to bring honor to God by reporting all the things He has done with us and how he has opened a door of faith for the Gentiles.

To that end, I think it is helpful to offer a summary of our experience as an introduction to the longer story which follows. I have chosen to do so by drawing on a report offered first by Dr. Lewis Wilson in a newsletter published by Global Mission Fellowship. Updated to make his third party report completely current, the following will acquaint you with the road ahead of us.

An Objective Perspective on Our Personal Story

"You give them something to eat!" How these words from Jesus' lips must have rung in the ears of the twelve disciples as they faced 5,000 hungry mouths on the desolate shores of the Sea of Galilee. With a small boy, five loaves and two fish, the master multiplied a limited supply to meet an almost unlimited need. A willing donor, releasing the best gift he could offer, cooperated with the divine intervention of the hands of God to teach the Apostles that they could trust their Heavenly Father to meet extraordinary needs through ordinary means. The importance of this lesson is dramatized by the fact that this is the only miracle story recorded in the Scriptures by all four gospel writers. *Jesus proved by feeding the five thousand with five loaves and two fish that it is not the size of our resource pool, but the limits of our faith and our vision that determines our impact for the Kingdom of God.*

This lesson is not lost on the leaders of Northside Community Church (NCC) as they are involved in a deliberate attempt to take the gospel to Bosnia's Muslims. The story is being relived in the life of a small church, not a small boy, in Gasinci, not in Galilee. With eyes of faith we can see Jesus encountering needy people again with divinely inspired compassion. These people have felt the hot winds of war, not the warm winds of the Holy Land. Meeting their needs today requires the same expressions of faith and vision that the disciples offered when they were walking with Jesus. God will do his part but his followers are the means by which He will supply what was lacking. The leaders at NCC were prepared to fill the shoes of the boy with the loaves and fishes by offering what little their church had to serve Jesus' purposes among far more than five thousand people. Their story may well encourage other small churches to discover the joys and benefits of ministering beyond the obvious limits of their size.

Some time ago NCC, a small *Evangelical Free Church* located in the shadows of far bigger congregations in Atlanta, felt led of God to take on a long-term cross-cultural mission venture. Burdened to reach the Muslim world for Christ, they determined that Yugoslavia held the least evangelized Muslim population in Europe. Consequently, this church adopted the Bosnian Muslims as their "unreached people" mission focus in 1990.

Fine-tuning the vision, the church targeted Sarajevo, a city of 600,000 people with only three churches and a combined Christian population of less than 100 people, as the strategic site to plant a church. The decision to target Bosnian Muslims in Sarajevo was made two years before war broke out in Bosnia-Herzegovina. Nightly news reports of the erupting civil war made the church planting goal seem impossible as the conflict between Bosnia's Muslims and ethnic Serbs escalated. All three pastors in Sarajevo fled the city with their families, and their flocks were scattered across the globe. These fledgling Protestant churches in Sarajevo quickly disintegrated in the war, and Bosnian Muslims were left without a resident witness for the new life available in Christ.

Almost immediately, God intervened to bring the gospel to these people. In the summer of 1992 the Lord divinely directed

NCC's leaders to visit Croatia. There they found a refugee camp filled with 3,500 Bosnians, some of whom were from Sarajevo. These refugees had fled to a resettlement center in Gasinci, a tiny village in northern Croatia, in order to escape the escalating horrors of war and ethnic cleansing in Bosnia.

Upon returning home from visiting the camp, pastors John Rowell and Dan Burton called Dr. Peter Kuzmic, founder of the Evangelical Theological Seminary in Osijek, Croatia, and organizer of the indigenous relief ministry *Agape* to get his advice on the church's emerging vision. They proposed sending a series of two-week teams from Atlanta into the camp. By rotating the teams regularly, NCC's leaders believed they could help meet practical physical needs while having a spiritual impact. It was a monumental task for a small congregation whose membership numbered less than 250 people. In spite of the limited resources the church could offer in the face of such tremendous needs, Dr. Kuzmic enthusiastically supported NCC's vision.

Within weeks, a base team of four inexperienced "missionaries" was mobilized under the leadership of David Lively, a Trinity Seminary graduate and former church planter. David was then working in his father's plumbing business in Atlanta. His base team included a legal secretary, a widow and an 18-year-old high school graduate. These "ordinary people" each agreed to stay for six months and were dispatched to prepare for the series of short-term teams that would visit Croatia on two-week intervals throughout the coming winter and spring. In late October 1992, the first team arrived at the camp in a freezing Croatian rain.

For the next seven months a dozen teams of Americans lived in the refugee camp, first in tents, later in cabins built by the German and Dutch Red Cross. Living conditions were hard: snows came, the winter weather turned cruel, and basic sanitary necessities deteriorated. Still the American teams kept coming.

Food distribution, English lessons and the *JESUS* film in Bosnian were used to establish relationships with both Muslim and Catholic refugees in the camp. These efforts became the platform for sharing personal testimonies and presenting the gospel of Jesus Christ to the beleaguered refugees.

As expected, the team eventually encountered some resistance to this evangelistic effort from the authorities directing this refugee center. However, perseverance, strategic prayer and the power of the gospel prevailed. A number of Muslims in the camp trusted in Jesus Christ. Damir Spoljaric, a national leader in the Evangelical Church of Croatia, has observed that more Bosnian Muslims came to faith in the first six months of this effort in the Gasinci refugee camp than had been converted in all of Bosnia in the previous 50 years!

Missionaries from NCC have remained active in Croatia and Bosnia since this initial project began in 1992. Although NCC's efforts are no longer focused on the camp in Gasinci, the church continues to mobilize several short-term teams from America each year to pursue the goal of evangelizing Bosnia and planting multiplying churches there. David Lively now speaks the Bosnian language and has made a long-term commitment to lead NCC's ministry in Bosnia. He is working full-time with Croatian and Bosnian nationals from the Evangelical Church denomination who established the first churches in the midst of the war in Bosnia-Herzegovina. The Mostar church, founded by a Croatian missionary, has proved to be the "Antioch Church" of Bosnia, spawning other congregations in Sarajevo, Tuzla and Bihac. Each of these infant churches is composed of converts from Serbian, Croatian and Muslim ethnic backgrounds. These new Christian fellowships are proving that Jesus can bring lasting peace and loving reconciliation to warring neighbors within Bosnia.

To date, nearly 400 short-term missionaries have joined this effort being sent by this small church and from a dozen other local fellowships in Georgia, Florida, Tennessee, Pennsylvania, California, Arizona, Connecticut, Illinois and New York. Northside has also mobilized eight long-term missionaries who are working full time with Bosnians.

Presently, David Lively leads this small staff in a partnership with Croatian church planting leaders in Bosnia. His role also involves coordinating Western mission initiatives throughout Bosnia as a service to the new Bible school, which opened in Mostar in October 1996. David has been vitally important in recruiting other Western partners to reach the wounded people of post-war Bosnia with the gospel of Jesus Christ.

The story of NCC's mission adventure in Bosnia is fairly unique. Though small congregations sometimes have a global vision, they often have too little faith to implement their plans. Mission professionals have convinced the leaders of small churches that they lack the networking capabilities, missions expertise or established contacts needed to bring a global vision into reality. But as NCC and its partnering churches have worked together from Atlanta **without the guidance of an experienced mission agency**, they have proved that major missions ministry and meaningful relief efforts are not beyond the reach of small churches. Their success demonstrates that missions ministry is in fact the purview of ordinary people.

This church is also demonstrating that an extraordinary commitment to missions can fuel dramatic growth within a local church. During their years of involvement with Bosnian refugees, for example, NCC has grown from 250 to 450 members. This growth is made more notable because the leaders of this church also have started three other sister churches in Atlanta during this same period. They have mobilized 40 percent of their adults and more than half their teenagers as short-term workers among Muslim refugees, and their total missions and benevolent giving has grown from $89,000 to more than $700,000 on an annual basis! Each of the disciples who carried a full basket of fish and bread away from 5000 satisfied people in Galilee would not be surprised! So why are we?

We need to remember the lesson of the loaves and fish. *It is not the size of our resource pool, but the limits of our faith and our vision that determines our impact for the kingdom of God.*

Conclusion

NCC is putting into practice this insight which Jesus taught two thousand years ago through a small boy, five loaves and two fish. This book tells our story in hopes of encouraging other churches, **especially small ones**, to believe God for a larger participation in the work of world evangelization. Unreached people groups in Bosnia and other dark places on this planet need our workers, our witness for the gospel and our practical help! I have written because I have an abiding conviction that our Master still remains available to multiply everything we will release into His hands to meet human needs.

I believe the story of our small church is not the tale of an isolated instance of effective missions ministry by a local congregation. It is, rather, a typical example of the latent missions potential that lies dormant in the under-mobilized, under-challenged, under-appreciated small churches of the world. Just as He did in 1st century Palestine, the Lord stands ready to increase our faith and our impact in the world as we risk trusting Him. He waits only for us to respond to the opportunities He creates in our own day!

Neither His willingness to move nor His words have changed over the last 2,000 years. In response to pressing human needs found in postwar Bosnia, or in the desperate plight of Rwandan refugees in Central Africa, or in the faces of forlorn children living in makeshift shanties in city dumps from Mexico City to Manila, Jesus' voice now rings in our 20th century ears, "YOU give them something to eat!"

In light of our full awareness of the wonders Jesus worked through His 1st century disciples, we dare not miss our 20th century chance to respond by faith to meet the modern challenge of global missions. It is my hope the chapters which follow will inspire you to offer yourself and your limited resources to the Lord with a genuine expectation that your own "loaves and fishes" can be multiplied as they pass through His hands. Let it not be said of us as it was of the disciples after the feeding of the five thousand, "They had not gained any insight from the incident of the loaves, but their heart was hardened" (Mk. 6:52). It is my prayer that God's Spirit will use this story to magnify your vision for the part you can play in taking the gospel of the Kingdom to the unreached peoples of the earth.

John Rowell
Atlanta, Georgia
November 1998

Part 1

Our Story

The Road to Sarajevo

"The mind of man plans his ways, but the Lord directs his steps."

Prov. 16:9

It was the great Chinese philosopher, Lao Tso, who said, "a journey of a thousand miles must begin with a single step."[1] So it was for our journey as a small church into the complicated arena of world missions. And so it must be for your church as well. Being unsure of where to begin, we all must start by taking that first small step. Our initial steps were neither so bold nor so clever as one might imagine looking at our work today. As we took our first steps by faith, I can pointedly declare we had no idea where this journey would take us. Certainly, we never anticipated the unpredictable path that eventually led us into the war zones of far off Bosnia-Herzegovina.

First Steps

The first step was taken for Northside Community Church (NCC) before we held our initial services as a newly formed Evangelical Free Church in December 1984. Spawned by an independent

Bible Church in Atlanta, our leaders had given careful thought to the vision and the values that we believed should shape the philosophy of ministry for our new congregation. We reduced that philosophy to a written document, declaring our commitment to seven major priorities that we hoped would be reflected in our ministries at every level.

We first made it a stated priority **to build a sense of community** among our 35 adults and 30 children. Weary of institutional expressions of church life, we believed that we were to live in intimate fellowship as brothers and sisters in Christ, trusting God and each other to nurture a deep sense of love and belonging as a part of our witness to the non-believing world (Jn. 13:34-35).

As we gathered for worship, fellowship and prayer, in large groups or small ones, we also wanted our local body to manifest other priorities which seemed essential to church life. We wanted **to be people of prayer** who lived in the reality of our need for the Lord to move in powerful ways overcoming the weaknesses of our flesh (Jn. 6:63), the opposition of the world (Rom. 12:1-2) and the wiles of the devil (Eph. 6:11-12). We desired **to be people of the word**, allowing the Scriptures to serve as our rule for faith and practice (II Tim. 3:16-17). It was, in fact, the testimony of the Word of God which moved us to extend ourselves in an attempt to take the gospel of Jesus Christ to the unreached peoples of the earth (Matt. 28:18-20).

We also wanted to give equal priority to two dimensions of outreach. At the local level, we wanted **to be committed to evangelism** (Rom 1:16). On a global scale, we wanted **to be committed to world missions** (Matt. 28:18-20). From our earliest days of life as a local church, we have firmly believed that every local assembly should be responsibly involved in winning its neighbors from darkness to light. We have also been convinced that an obedient response to the Great Commission required an earnest effort to reach the lost people of other nations.

It seemed to us that God's desire to bless the nations of the earth was clearly expressed in the Abrahamic Covenant. God's mandate made it incumbent on us to be available for Him to use in meeting the needs of others, around the world. In Gen. 12:1-3, God spoke to Abraham saying:

> Go forth from your country, and from your relatives
> And from your father's house, to the land which I
> will show you;
> And I will make you a great nation, and I will bless
> you,
> And make your name great; and so, you shall be a
> blessing;
> And I will bless those who bless you and the one who
> curses you I will curse,
> And in you, all the families of the earth shall be blessed.

Magnifying the impact of this text in our corporate experience, a sixth priority logically followed our commitment to world missions. We had almost no material resources to draw from as our church began. Nonetheless, we fully expected God to enable us **to be a blessing** to others inside and outside the church, at home in the United States and abroad.

Finally, we wanted to make it a priority to minister regularly to the Lord through our offerings of praise and worship, the fruit of our lips expressing thanks to His name (Heb. 13:15). As we gathered in small and large groups alike, when we were alone as individuals or enjoying time together in our families, we desired **to be people devoted to worship.** These seven priorities have shaped our life as a local church from the very start. They have demanded that world missions involvement and efforts to bless the nations remain central to our philosophy of ministry.

Maximizing Limited Financial Resources

Our commitment in this regard was at first expressed exclusively in financial terms. We began to be involved globally by taking responsibility to be a "supporting church."[2] Our initial operating budget as a newly formed church totaled $5,000 on a monthly basis. Of that total we devoted 20 percent, or $1,000 per month, to support missionaries and to fund the development of our mission strategy.

For any small church leader, the frustration of limited financial resources is an all too familiar reality. We looked to leaders in the Association of Church Missions Committees (now Advancing Churches in Missions Commitment, or ACMC) for advice as we faced the problem of trying to make our limited funds count for the kingdom.

From the earliest months of our church's existence, we made it a high priority to send several of our potential missions leaders to ACMC's annual national conference. These gatherings always yielded important fruit in deepening our mission convictions, in directing our initial efforts to encourage missions awareness throughout the body and in offering practical suggestions for the problems we faced year to year. (See Chapter 12, for a more complete explanation of the benefits we derived from our association with this strategic organization.)

We attended the first such meeting in the summer of 1985. The conference introduced us to the advantage of supporting nationals in reaching their own cultures as a "cost effective" alternative to contributing to American missionaries being mobilized to foreign fields at considerably greater expense. We discovered that a commitment of $100 per month could make up as much as one-third of the total support required to keep a national evangelist at work on the mission field. That same amount, to a U.S. missionary with a $3,500 monthly budget, would represent a negligible commitment — less than 3 percent of the total monthly need. Supporting national workers clearly offered a "bigger bang for our missions buck," so we set about developing relationships with Christian leaders from other cultures.

Ambassadors for Christ International,[3] headquartered in Atlanta, Georgia, and Partners International,[4] based in California, became important sources for our divine contacts with some of

God's most devoted evangelists from all over the world. These agencies specialize in identifying credible Christian evangelists serving in unevangelized and unreached cultures, linking them with local churches and supporting agencies in the United States. With their help, we hosted many foreign nationals in our homes in Atlanta before our first full year of ministry ended.

Selecting the ones with whom God eventually allowed us to develop a meaningful rapport, we soon found ourselves praying for and financially committed to key leaders in Burma, Egypt, the Philippines, Pakistan, Bangladesh, India, France and Brazil. What a blessing it was to be involved meaningfully in such a wide range of cultures from the four corners of the earth! Our exposure to the world was great, though the dollars we had to give were small. Still, the level of our limited support was significant to these humble men and women. Partnership with them had a deep impact on our church. We felt fully functional in missions though we had only been a church for a year. Those first small steps in our mission journey seemed like giant steps to us at the time!

Expanding Our Financial Base
Through Faith Promise

For two years (1985-1986) we continued to fund our mission effort through our monthly budget allotment of $1,000. But the support commitments to national workers had quickly consumed our available resources. We were growing as a church, but we were not experiencing a "windfall" of financial blessing in those early years. In fact, we were barely scraping by as we tried to survive the birth and infancy of our local assembly.

ACMC provided needed insight again at this crucial juncture. The training we received at a national conference moved our elders to allow the church to adopt a "Faith Promise Pledge" approach to expanding our financial commitment to missions. Initially, we maintained our monthly budgeted support from the general fund and augmented that with faith promise receipts over the next year. The results were amazing to us!

Faith Promise commitments are simply voluntary pledges by individuals and families who choose to trust God to provide through extraordinary means a designated sum of money to fund our world missions ministry. Having prayerfully determined an amount for a faith promise pledge, two more steps are necessary to see missions funding increased. First, God must prove faithful to do His part by releasing "extra funds" through unexpected gifts, bonuses, commissions, windfall profits, the sale of personal property, and sacrificial lifestyle adjustments among other means. Then, those who make a pledge must also do their part by giving these specially provided sums to support our world missions efforts. Faith promise gifts are contributions made above and beyond our members' regular tithes and offerings. They have never negatively impacted routine giving for other aspects of our church's ministry.

Our congregation enthusiastically embraced this innovative approach to giving. The faith promise pledge program became an exciting faith adventure in stewardship. We agreed corporately to expect God to honor our commitments and we began praying that God would use our local assembly as a conduit to increase His material blessing to the nations — not to us. And so God did!

During the first year we used this approach, the faith promise effort substantially increased our giving by adding more than $8,000 to the $12,000 budgeted allotment for missions. In the second year, faith promise receipts allowed us to more than double our total missions expenditures to a level exceeding $24,000. By the third year, 1989, faith promise receipts alone totaled $25,715, effectively tripling our annual financial investments in missions! We began to fund world missions solely out of faith promise gifts in 1990. To make this possible, we maintained the original budget commitment of $12,000 per year, using it as a reserve fund to supplement our missions giving if faith promise receipts fell short of the total support needed. Sometimes this budget provision also covered timing problems created when faith promise receipts and our monthly funding commitments did not coincide perfectly.

This approach to giving for missions did much to build our faith in God's capacity to provide more finances for global evangelism than we could reasonably expect to generate through the normal budgetary processes. Consistently, faith promise giving allowed us to provide more money for missions than we would ever have seen with eyes of flesh alone. And the faith of our families was stretched in the process! Children pledging half their expected income from birthday and Christmas gifts have seen God double the amount they actually received so that they funded their faith promise pledge in full and still ended up with 100 percent of the gifts they anticipated in a given year. Our young people have learned that we never lose when we give to God!

One professional athlete in our church, a part-time Highland Games competitor, learned a similar surprising lesson. Aging beyond his prime strength years, Larry Satchwell continues to compete in this unusual sport for the conditioning and joy it brings to his life. After making his first faith promise pledge, he worried about how it could be funded out of his modest public school teacher's salary. That year, he set a world record mark in the "sheaf toss," receiving prize money equal to his faith promise pledge. He was delighted at God's "double blessing" of his pledge to support missions through faith promise. Others have received director's fees, insurance reimbursements, unprecedented bonuses and retroactive raises that funded their faith commitments to world missions.

We have rejoiced and laughed and wept together as God has demonstrated His faithfulness to honor our commitment by routinely providing our "extra supply" so that we might give more to global evangelism. We tested the Lord in the early years of ministry as Malachi 3:10 invites His people to do, and we found Him faithful to "open the windows of heaven pouring out blessing until it overflowed." This increased capacity to fund world missions by faith would prove to be a necessary confidence builder for the greater faith demands that lay in store in the days ahead. At this point, we still had no idea we were "on the road to Sarajevo!"

Becoming a Sending Church

In an additional effort to promote missions involvement and to educate our members with respect to modern theories of global evangelism, we began in 1986 to devote all the Sundays in March to an annual mission conference. In 1987, Keith Brown from OC Ministries spoke on one of the Sundays in our "Missions Month," issuing a challenge that ended up taking us to yet another level in our commitment to missions. He challenged us to become a "sending church," mobilizing not just our money but some of our members to serve as missionaries within the ensuing twelve months.

We took his exhortation seriously and began to pray about which of our members might be a candidate to serve full-time as a missionary. By this time, with ever-increasing faith promise funding available each year, we had long since added a number of "member missionaries" to our regular list of workers supported on a monthly basis. But Keith Brown was directing us toward still greater involvement. He was asking us to identify and mobilize our own ordinary people into vocational mission roles. Inexperienced as we were, we had no idea how to respond, but we wanted to be faithful to allow God to extend the boundaries of our vision for mission possibilities.

God answered our prayer in this regard almost immediately. Another speaker that month, Dennis Cochrane, from Wycliffe Bible Translators (WBT) came to acquaint us with the progress of global efforts to make the Scriptures available in every significant language group on earth. As he talked, it was evident that in the modern era of translation work, computer skills were playing an increasingly vital role. It was also a frequent reality that translators needed additional skills to serve their target populations well. For example, many individuals with nursing or medical skills proved effective in tribal situations with WBT teams.

As it happened, we had a member who was a skilled programmer with a strong nursing background. Laurie Nelson did not immediately jump to the conclusion that she should sign on as a WBT missionary, but within weeks God directed her computer career into an unexpected assignment with a United Methodist mission ministry. That assignment brought increased exposure to global evangelism and nurtured her interest in mission service as a career pursuit. Within the year, we were blessed to see Laurie become the first full-time missionary mobilized from our church. She became a member of Wycliffe's translation support staff in Dallas where she still serves today.

Laurie's mobilization proved not to be an isolated event. Our mission conferences were enhancing the global vision of all our members. Many were giving more sacrificially, some were traveling internationally for business purposes, and all were routinely reminded of this important priority in the life of our church. Not surprisingly, within just a few years, we had members serving as new missionaries or tent makers in Russia, Singapore, Germany and Japan. Keith Brown's challenge had moved us forward on the missionary road that would eventually lead us to Sarajevo. This stream of mobilized workers would later become a mighty river as these few missionaries would give way to the short-term involvement of hundreds more!

The Call to Adopt an Unreached People Group

As our local church matured in its mission capacity and vision, our exposure to missionary statesmen from around the world kept us abreast of most emerging developments in "missiology." The urgent need to make sure that every remaining "unreached people group" in the world was formally adopted was among the most widely accepted and pressing issues in the late 1980s. Professional missiologists taught us that as a mission-minded church, we should give priority attention to identifying a specific unreached people group target of our own — one for which we could pray and toward which we could plan to take the gospel.

Over the years, there has been considerable debate over how many such groups exist. By definition, a people group is a significantly large group of individuals who see themselves as having a common affinity for one another. That affinity may be expressed in terms of race, religion, ethnic background, cultural distinctives, language, world view or any combination of these factors. Such a group is recognized as "unreached" if there is no indigenous community of believing Christians with adequate numbers and sufficient resources to evangelize the unbelieving members of the group. By 1990, varying estimates suggested that from 2,000 to 12,000 such groups existed, depending on how missiologists approached their categorization.[5]

In an atmosphere stirred by the urgent pleadings of mission leaders around the world, NCC's elders were convinced that we should participate strategically in this worldwide effort to complete the task of global evangelism by the year 2000 AD. We wanted to do our part by targeting an unreached people group of our own. It was not difficult to choose where to focus our attention.

Prior Experience and Established Relationships Point the Way

As senior pastor of the church, I had traveled to Eastern Europe in 1985 and 1986 on behalf of the Romanian Missionary Society. The contacts established during these visits had led to an ongoing relationship between our church and the Romanian Baptist Church in Atlanta, a congregation of refugees who had fled the Ceaucescu regime seeking political, economic and religious freedom in the United States. Our involvement with Romanians included our sponsorship of Romanian refugees to the states. Many came directly from internment camps in former Yugoslavia. We learned to love these courageous people who had suffered severely under one of the world's harshest communist regimes. We also began to feel comfortable **ministering in a communist context.**

While I was working with Romanians, others in our church were regularly involved in short-term trips to Yugoslavia during the mid-1980s. These trips, sponsored by Campus Crusade for Christ, had offered a very different view of life under communism. Compared to the oppressive and economically deprived environment in Romania, the various Yugoslav republics seemed prosperous and free. Unlike its reasonably evangelized northern neighbor, however, Yugoslavia's evangelical population was extremely small and somewhat stagnant.

The relatively greater need for evangelism and church planting in all the Yugoslav republics seemed to promise greater opportunities as we undertook our fledgling effort to select an unreached people group focus. We needed only to decide where in Yugoslavia we might concentrate our future mission energies.

By early 1990, we had **an ongoing mentoring relationship** with Dr. Peter Kuzmic, president of the Evangelical Church of Croatia and director of the Evangelical Theological Seminary in Osijek. Appealing to him for advice as to where we might direct our efforts, he offered several other criteria for us to consider. He helped us see the wisdom of becoming involved in **a larger urban center** because we were urbanites in our own context in Atlanta. We also knew that we wanted to **work with Muslims** since we saw Islam as the greatest single challenge to completing the great commission worldwide. Dr. Kuzmic was the first to point us toward the millions of Muslims living in Bosnia. Finally, we were encouraged to see the value of laboring in a context from which we might penetrate a **"closed country"** at a later time. Prior to the fall of the Iron Curtain in 1989, communism and Islam were two ideological forces openly and aggressively set against the spread of the gospel. Countries influenced by either or both of these belief systems often established significant barriers to keep missionaries beyond their borders. Sometimes they also established harsh penalties against proselytizing and against converting from accepted national religions. Political jurisdictions showing that kind of "legislated hostility" to Christian witness came to be called "closed countries." In 1990, Yugoslavia's southern neighbor, Albania, was the most closed country in the world to the gospel of Jesus Christ.

These criteria shaped the "selection process" that guided our adoption of an unreached people group. To summarize, we were led to pray for clear direction from the Lord as we made our choice. With the help of Dr. Kuzmic, we eventually determined that we should look for:

> a communist context
> a context where we had existing mentoring relation-
> ships
> a context that represented an urban area like our own
> a context that permitted us to focus on evangelizing
> Muslims
> a context that could later offer the possibility of
> "bridging" our evangelistic efforts into a similar
> people group within a "closed country"

With these parameters in mind, Dr. Kuzmic concluded that Bosnia was the ideal choice for our church. Nearly 40 percent of this republic's citizens were Muslims. More specifically, Peter believed that Sarajevo was the ideal city for us to target. It served as the communist republic's capital, had garnered global attention while hosting the 1984 Winter Olympics and presented a population of more than 600,000. We discovered that fewer than 100 of those residents were evangelical believers and less than that were attending the three small Protestant churches (Baptist, Pentecostal and Independent) which were trying to gain a foothold for the kingdom in Bosnia in 1990. Nearby Albania represented a reasonable future target for mission development — especially in light of the potential for establishing relationships with Albanian citizens living within neighboring republics of Yugoslavia. Kosavo and Macedonia both contained large Albanian populations within easy reach if Bosnian evangelists could later be mobilized for the task.

Getting on the Road to Sarajevo

For these reasons our leaders easily reached a consensus that we should adopt the Bosnian Muslims as an unreached people group target. We went a step further by designating Sarajevo as the first city we would try to serve in church planting. In retrospect, the progress from our first meetings in December 1984, to our decision to adopt the Bosnian Muslims as an unreached people group in March 1989, might seem logical — the result of sound strategic planning on our part — but it was not so.

We were not so farsighted as to have seen this choice when we took our initial steps as a missions-minded church in 1984. Rather than being adept at strategic plans for the long-term future, we were mostly responding to the suggestions of mission leaders who advised us along the way. We followed good counsel systematically, made important decisions without inordinate delay and grew in missiological sophistication almost without realizing it. In effect, we were merely "coloring by the numbers," following sound principles presented to us by a number of mission professionals. And perhaps most importantly, we were covering all of our steps consistently in prayer.

For four years we had roamed the world of missions indiscriminately, yet always with good intentions. We had learned to give beyond our recognizable capacity. We had begun to mobilize our own people in traditional mission agency roles. We had developed some key relationships in the communist world, relationships that were now offering important advice for our future. We had grown well acquainted with the wide world of missions opportunity.

Finally focused, we were no longer merely wandering around the globe in search of open doors. We were now on a path clearly marked. Our objective was defined with certainty. Our course was set. **We were on the Road to Sarajevo!** Knowing where we were going had a corollary benefit as well. We now also knew where we were not going, or so we thought.

Future direction seemed clear enough at the time. We could now set our course but we could never have predicted that European communism would collapse under its own weight in the next six months. A storm was brewing on the horizon. By Christmas 1989, the "Evil Empire" of Russian domination over the Eastern bloc had disintegrated, and European communism was lying like a colossal corpse sprawled across the continent. By New Year's Eve, the global balance of power had shifted dramatically to the West. The Iron Curtain fell with fantastic speed, and nationalism filled the void left in the wake of declining Soviet influence. Behind the roar of celebration, no one heard the sounds of tank tracks, artillery shells and machine gun bursts which would become fully audible only as we rounded the first bend in our newly chosen roadway.

We were not prepared for the fury of nationalistic fervor released by the fall of Soviet communism. We were, however, at least aware of our being caught up in the momentum of the most cataclysmic political changes in the 20th century. The pace and the power of revolutionary forces had increased phenomenally in 1989. A solitary placard seen in a post-revolution rally in Prague captured the scene succinctly. As a commentary on the progressive momentum that marked communism's collapse in Europe, it read simply:

Poland: 10 years
Hungary: 10 months
East Germany: 10 weeks
Czechoslovakia: 10 days
Romania: 10 hours

The spirit of liberty was coming to life and exerting itself across the Eastern Bloc with lightning speed. Its presence and power were tangible, like the armored advance of Hitler's forces a generation earlier. These were heady days to begin working in Central Europe. If others experienced in diplomacy and affairs of state were unsure of the meaning of these momentous changes, far more uncertain were the leaders of our church.

We were unexpectedly faced with the reality of focused attention on a post-communist nation, and we found ourselves mostly wondering what to do next. It was time to take our first strategic steps on the road to Sarajevo. Unknown to us, the road would soon run red with blood as it passed through besieged cities, ethnically cleansed villages and refugee camps. We would never have dreamed we would share this road with the largest refugee population in Europe since World War II. We were moving by faith toward ministry on the road to Sarajevo with none of this in view.

Knowing the future may well have deterred us. We expected to fight spiritual battles, but we did not expect to face the threat of force in a brutal regional war. Like Israel at the time of the Exodus, God knew that if we were to face war immediately we might change our minds (Ex. 13:17-18). It was His providence that allowed us to move forward in our naiveté, going without knowing as so many other believers have done before us. We looked to God prayerfully as we took those first steps toward Bosnia, trusting the Lord to direct our steps along the way. How faithful our Heavenly Father would prove to be as He answered those early prayers!

Open Warfare, Open Doors

"... He who is holy, who is true, who has the key of David, who opens and no one will shut, and who shuts and no one opens, says this: I know your deeds. Behold, I have put before you an open door which no one can shut, because you have a little power, and have kept My word, and have not denied My name."

Rev. 3:7-8

Dr. Milton Coke, founder and president of Global Partners for Development, was the most experienced missionary to Muslims that our leaders knew personally in 1990. We had supported his work in Bangladesh for years, and I especially appreciated his acerbic straightforwardness. Dr. Coke's missionary methods were incredibly controversial, but his results were also unprecedented. He was accustomed to working in cultures where Islam was fundamentalistic, ingrained and completely hostile to the gospel. Decades of wrestling with this "last of the giants," as George Otis is wont to call the Muslim faith, was reason enough for Dr. Coke's painfully direct and unflinching tone.

We invited him to come and encourage our mission leaders as we gathered in early January to develop our initial strategy for traveling on the road to Sarajevo, but he was in no mood to encourage us. He fully recognized the seriousness of the mission before us, and he could see that we did not. As we casually shared our choice of the Bosnian Muslims as an unreached people group target, he quickly challenged our commitment to this goal. His perspective punctured the balloon of our naiveté!

An Early Wake Up Call

Offering a brief history lesson as a backdrop for his challenge, Dr. Coke reminded us that Bosnia was a strange and complex amalgamation of ethnic and religious identities. There the Muslim faith, however nominal its adherents, had managed to influence the culture and the conscience of the many to maintain the largest Islamic population in all of Europe. Four decades of communist dominance notwithstanding, Tito's atheistic propaganda had never overcome the intensely religious heart of Bosnia. The Muslim faith was first planted in Bosnia in 1463 when the Ottoman Empire overthrew the nation's last king. Islamic seeds sown in this conquest soon produced growing mosques alongside Jewish synagogues, Orthodox Churches and Catholic cathedrals. Islam's roots sank deeply during the ensuing centuries eventually producing a 40 percent Muslim plurality. Without a clear majority, however, Islam merely survived as one more player in this mixture of monotheistic faiths. Muslim religious symbols were allowed to decorate, though never to dominate, the nation.

Thus, by 1990, minority expressions of Judaism, Catholicism and Serbian Eastern Orthodoxy had shared limited space in the religious and political landscape of Bosnia-Herzegovina. The net effect of their presence had been to create a kind of cultural universalism where these "competing religious ideologies" peacefully coexisted in relative harmony and respect, linking faith not to eternal destiny but to ethnic identity. All roads in modern-day Bosnia were thought to lead to eternity with God. Croats could find their way to God as good Catholics. Serbs could order their way as directed by Orthodox priests. Jews could safely adhere to the laws of Moses following the God of Abraham. And Muslims could follow Mohammed. Most of Bosnia's Muslims were merely nominal followers of Allah, but they were Muslims nonetheless. Thus, the inseparable connection had been made between ethnic identity and religious affiliation in Bosnia. Such ethnic/religious convergence would guarantee that the road to Sarajevo would not lead to an easy mission field.

We were aware of Patrick Johnstone's conclusion that Bosnia's Muslims were the least evangelized people in all of Europe.[1] Milton Coke reminded us that this lack of response to the gospel should be seen as a native and communal resistance to the message of salvation by grace through faith in Christ. Another writer would later capture Bosnia's complexity in even more pointed terms. "Here, the battle between communism and capitalism is merely one dimension of struggle that (also) pits Catholicism against Orthodoxy, Rome against Constantinople, the legacy of Hapsburg Austria-Hungary against that of Ottoman Turkey — in other words, West against East."[2] Even before nationalism and ancient ethnic hostilities fueled the war in Bosnia adding still more complexity to the challenges of mission work there, this republic already represented the ultimate in historical, cultural and religious complexity.

Milton Coke was poised to ram his missiological sword home in the heart of the matter for us. "What in the world makes you folks believe a 250-member congregation located half a world away in Atlanta, Georgia, can make a difference in reaching a nation that has steadfastly rejected the gospel for the last 500 years?!!!" No match for Dr. Coke's logical and well-informed question, we responded with a one-word reply — FAITH! We simply had faith that God had led us to this commitment and would sustain us in it. That faith would be our only justification and our constant motivation for continuing down the road to Sarajevo in the years of wartime ministry that would follow.

We believed that God wanted these Bosnians to have access to the gospel and that He would see to it that they would hear. We were assured by faith that even our little church in Georgia could play a part.

As Rev. 3:10 declares,

> He who is holy, who is true, who holds the key of David, who opens and no one will shut and shuts so no one will open says this, "I know your deeds." Behold, I have put before you an open door which no one can shut, because you have a little power, and have kept my word and have not denied my name....

We saw an open door. We wanted to walk through it in spite of being ill equipped and under-resourced. Dr. Coke shook his head in response to our naiveté. He then gave us the benefit of his vast experience helping us prepare for our next steps on the road to Sarajevo. Since that day he has been an encouragement to us in this work and has consistently marveled at the outpouring of God's grace along the way.

Visiting Sarajevo

Four of our leaders visited Sarajevo for the first time in the summer of 1990. Our purpose was to gather information on the religious history of Sarajevo to better inform our intercessors as they led our congregation in prayer over this strategic city. We were still only "painting by the numbers" as we tried to position ourselves for the long-term work that lay ahead. Missiologists promoting the adoption of "unreached people groups" had formulated a strategy for the adoption process. Their recommended five-step process included, in sequence:

1. Selecting a people group for adoption
2. Organizing prayer for the people group selected
3. Conducting research
4. Networking
5. Church planting

After this research trip was concluded, a one-page prayer guide was prepared to summarize the findings of that first exploratory visit to Sarajevo. This simple form would be the primary resource tool to guide our intercession for Bosnia's Muslims over the next two years. Little did I realize when I left Sarajevo with my three companions that it would be five years before I would see this beautiful city again. Even less could I have imagined the devastation and destruction that would be unleashed on the city before my return.

In any case, conducting research and organizing prayer was the focus of our efforts in the summer of 1990. Our presence in Yugoslavia for this purpose also presented early opportunities for networking. We met several national pastors in Croatia and Bosnia — men who would later be long-term friends and co-workers in our mission effort. We also visited Peter Kuzmic at his seminary in Osijek. The trip allowed us to deepen our friendship with him while broadening our exposure to the students and faculty at Evangelical Theological Seminary (ETS). This was a step of major strategic importance in the long run.

Laying Foundations for Long-Term Relationships

Dr. Kuzmic invited me to return to ETS in January 1991, to teach as a visiting professor. This opportunity permitted additional networking efforts among students and church leaders alike. At the time I would never have dreamed that one of the sisters in that first class would later marry a key leader from NCC! Neither would I have suspected that Peter McKenzie, a British missionary of nearly 20 years experience in Croatia would later become a close friend and a fellow soldier in the Lord's Special Forces during the war in Bosnia. Peter served as a guide in 1991, leading me into Romania where I also taught in an extension seminary class he directed in Timisora.

These two early trips to Yugoslavia were filled with divine contacts, though I could little recognize them at the time. It seemed to me that they were merely prudent initial steps on the road to Sarajevo. During the January 1991 teaching visit to Osijek, I was struck by the increased tension in the city. Daily, as I drove from the hotel to the seminary complex, I passed a Yugoslav army barracks surrounded by Croatian civilian militiamen — the equivalent of our local police.

Apparently the Yugoslav authorities in Belgrade had demanded that Croatian citizens surrender all privately held small arms. I tried to imagine how the Georgia Chapter of the National Rifle Association might respond to such a federal order in the United States. The issue was equally absurd in Osijek. To protect Croatian interests in the event that the Serbian-controlled army decided to force the issue, the local police had "captured" the army in its barracks and was detaining them indefinitely. The scene was curious to me and seemed comical to the local pastors, professors and students. The city's militiamen were not very imposing as they guarded the enlisted men's barracks, keeping soldiers confined in an area secluded from their superior officers. However unintimidating and casual these civilian police appeared, they were nonetheless effective in holding the Yugoslav army in Croatia hostage for a time.

The BBC broadcasts we heard on short wave radio reported these events with a bit more serious concern than was apparent to an on-site observer. Listening to the radio commentary, one got the impression that the winds of war were already stirring in Croatia. My interest was aroused all the more by the incongruity of these conflicting perspectives. Trusting my Croatian friends' interpretations of events, I decided these circumstances were mainly an exercise in political posturing. I was relieved and returned to the states without a sense of foreboding as winter snows began to fall.

But with the spring flowers, genuine hostility also bloomed in Croatia. With the summer's rising temperatures, the political climate heated up and tensions escalated between the northern republics of Slovenia and Croatia and the Serb-dominated federation in Belgrade. It was as if non-aligned Yugoslavia had somehow been swept up in the same anti-communist spirit that was sweeping away Soviet satellite governments elsewhere behind the iron curtain. Since Tito had never allowed Yugoslavia to become a part of the Eastern Bloc, however, these revolutionary energies could not be vented toward the Kremlin as they were in other Central European states. Author Robert D. Kaplan summarized these events, "Because the pressure of discontent was being released horizontally, in the form of one (republic) against another, rather than vertically (against Moscow) ... the revolutionary path in Yugoslavia was (at) first more tortuous and, therefore more disguised.... That is why the outside world did not take notice until ... the fighting started ... Yugoslavia did not deteriorate suddenly, but gradually and methodically, step by step, through the 1980s, becoming poorer and meaner and more hate-filled year by year."[3] Somehow the world's most experienced politicians and diplomats missed the seriousness of the mounting political pressures in the Balkans. Consequently, we were completely surprised when the nation exploded in open warfare in the fall of 1991.

The war over Slovenia's succession from the Yugoslav Federation had ended in a matter of days and rather uneventfully. But in Croatia, the fighting dragged on for months into 1992. Serbian seizure of eastern territories in Baranja and the regions of western Slavonia were provocative measures. In the east, the Serbs overran and utterly decimated Vukuvar. But their advance was successfully halted at Osijek. We remained understandably attentive to these events watching the news reports on CNN in Atlanta. We were greatly concerned for the safety of our new friends and their families in this beleaguered city.

Peter Kuzmic reported on the siege of Osijek at the beginning of the war. "My estimate of the seemingly limitless supply of (Serbian) munitions had not been an exaggeration: in eight months an incredible 150,000 shells had rained down on the city, destroying some 24,000 homes and civic buildings — one out of every three. But the worst statistic was the one that prefigured Srebenica: 1,800 men had been taken captive, led away, and were never seen again."[4] Thousands were killed in the siege of Osijek. Tens of thousands fled the advancing Serb armies. The population of Croatia's fourth largest municipality dropped from 150,000 to 19,000 as the city was surrounded on three sides by Yugoslav National Army (JNA) forces. But in Osijek, a newly independent national government dug in and its hastily formed Territorial Defense Force managed to hold its ground.

Osijek survived for the balance of the war in this precarious posture, encircled by a sea of hostile troops. Threatening Serbian armies transformed the city into a peninsula of persistent resistance to Yugoslav aggression. Osijek's courageous citizens were afforded only a narrow western corridor connecting their city with the rest of Croatia and the outside world. The city was a symbol of this new nation's will to survive and its populace provided hope for the future of independent Croatians everywhere. In the interest of ensuring the safety of the ETS student body, the seminary moved its operations to Slovenia for the 1991-92 academic year. But the church family in Osijek could not be evacuated entirely. Even today, we have incredibly high regard for the brave Christian leaders, young and old alike, who chose to stay and shepherd God's people through the early horrors of war.

They are heroes of faith for us. The gigantic proportions of their heroism in the face of an unrelenting siege would soon be surpassed by the enormity of their hospitality to wartime refugees as Serbia turned its fury toward Bosnia. Eventually, nearly a third of Osijek residents would open their homes to share space with displaced families fleeing the JNA war machine. These haggard guests were grateful for the refuge from war. Their gracious hosts offered accommodations not for a day or a week, but in most cases, for several years. I was amazed and blessed to see how Croatia's generosity endured throughout the duration of the war.

The War Shifts to Bosnia

Despite the armed hostilities raging in the northern republics of what was now called "former Yugoslavia," Bosnia seemed to be safe throughout 1991. In fact, we printed the following report in our March 1992 mission conference brochure regarding the expected fate of Bosnia:

> While Croatia and Serbia are locked in civil war inter-rupted only by a shaky cease-fire, the United Nations is preparing to send nearly 15,000 troops to help maintain the peace. Sarajevo will host the UN garrison, a privilege which many believe will help guarantee that Bosnia will avoid civil war within its borders.***

We proved to be far from correct in our imperfect prediction of future events. Before the ink was dry on our brochure, Serbian forces shifted the focus of their aggression toward Bosnia. Though ethnic Serbs composed only 30 percent of the pre-war population of Bosnia-Herzegovina, Serbian factions backed by the Yugoslav army eventually occupied 70 percent of the republic's landmass. They did so under the guise of protecting Serbian interests in the region. Ethnic cleansing, war crimes, concentration camps and the largest refugee population in Europe since World War II were now the focus of the nightly news all around the world. In the face of this hotbed of hatred and exploding evil, we were disheartened to think that the war would effectively end our journey toward Sarajevo.

*** Twice in this single sentence I used the words "civil war" to describe the outbreak of war in Croatia and Bosnia. Such is not a suitable label for the conflict that began as a massive and premeditated land grab by communist leaders in Belgrade whose tight-fisted rule had been rejected by freedom-loving people in surrounding republics. I urge readers to take time to read a national's perspective on this matter prepared by Dr. Peter Kuzmic. His insights are clearly set forth in Appendix V.

Finding God's Open Door

In order to demonstrate our ongoing commitment to our Croatian friends and our goal to evangelize Bosnians in spite of the war, we concluded that a visit to Osijek was in order in the summer of 1992. By this time our sister church, East Gate Congregation, had prayerfully decided to turn its mission energies toward Bosnia as our partner on this field. While travel to Bosnia itself was a suicidal proposition at this time, it seemed plausible to plan a vision trip to Croatia to expose East Gate's pastor, Dan Burton, and his wife, Cheryl, to at least this part of former Yugoslavia. My wife, Ginger, also agreed to join us for her first trip to the region.

Memories of the new friends and cultural impressions made during my two previous visits to Osijek were still vivid in my mind as we approached the city and searched for geographical landmarks that I hoped would guide us to the ETS complex east of the town's center. As we drove in the bright August sunshine, the radiance of the day belied the residue of war apparent on all sides — burned and abandoned vehicles, bombed out houses, ill-fated factories reduced to rubble and idled by the devastation of war. These empty shells which had once fueled Croatia's economy stood now like a heap of skeletal remains showing no promise of coming to life again.

Roads and sidewalks were littered with craters created by the blasts of bombs, artillery shells and rifle grenades. Each point of impact looked as if some powerful hand had splashed explosives on the hard surfaces leaving shallow holes and a directional overspray of destruction to mark the occasion. Most walls were peppered and pockmarked to record the recent history of exploding shrapnel.

The evidence of the rain of bombs Peter Kuzmic had described over Osijek was readily apparent as we neared the city's central district. The brutality of direct hits or the concussion of near misses had long since blown most windows away. The broken glass was not yet replaced with soon to be familiar UNHCR plastic sheeting. As a result, virtually all living spaces, restaurants, shops and offices offered occupants an uninviting "open air" section. In some instances entire sides of apartment buildings were blown away, though the quarters were still occupied by their stubbornly courageous owners.

All attempts to reach the only high-rise hotel overlooking the River Drava proved fruitless. We were barred from the city's square not by debris but by determined soldiers. War-weary, armed and apparently dangerous (an impression intentionally conveyed), they spoke no English but communicated their intent with crystal clarity. Those unshaven soldiers in mismatched and rumpled uniforms succeeded in unnerving both of the wives traveling with us. Seeking to ease the tension of my traveling companions, I parked the car and walked without incident to find the central business district and Hotel Osijek, my best point of reference for refreshing the mental map that had grown obscure since my last visit. Along the river the savagery of the siege of Osijek seemed still more tangible — expressed in blown out bridges, boats sunken in their moorings, sandbags piled everywhere. I was dismayed when I first saw the grand hotel which had been the obvious easy target of Serbian gunmen dealing unending destruction, for sport more than for strategic effect. With just a glance, I got my bearings and concluded that the prognosis for the hotel's recovery was slim at best.

I chose not to report the deeper devastation at the center of town to my friends as we made our way to the seminary. How welcome was the sight of the school and its companion synagogue church marked distinctively by twin Byzantine steeples. We were grateful to find that virtually no damage had been inflicted on this kingdom property! I thought of Exodus 11:6-7:

> There shall be a great cry in all the land of Egypt, such as there has not been before and such as shall never be again.

> But against any of the sons of Israel a dog shall not even bark, whether against man or beast, that you may understand how the Lord makes a distinction between Egypt and Israel.

I rejoiced in silent prayer drawing on the confident declaration of II Peter 2:9, "the Lord knows how to rescue the godly."

Arriving at the seminary, we found all was now quiet because the students had been dismissed from Slovenia to go home until the fall classes began. The hour was late and meeting with friends would have to wait until the following day. We bedded down for what proved to be a fairly fretful night. Hot and sultry as that August evening was, the temperature did not disturb our sleep. Rather, we were kept awake by the repeated machine gun fire and falling mortar shells too close at hand for us to ignore. In the morning the sporadic small arms fire that had kept us ill at ease throughout the night, proved too common for local citizens even to notice. Our concerns were dismissed as laughable by those conditioned by constant shelling. Their standard explanation for the source of the random gunfire and occasional explosions in the night seemed laughable to them but offered little comfort to us. "Not to worry," they said, "those are just some drunks with guns!" Somehow that explanation just did nothing to ease our inexperienced nerves.

During this day we met with Damir Spoljaric, the assistant director of the seminary, and with Steve Paulus, an American missionary serving as Academic Dean at ETS. Damir was by now a dear friend. His good-natured charm and easy disposition was a great comfort to our wives, and I thanked God for his youthful maturity. He is truly an extraordinarily gifted man!

Steve Paulus was just returning with his family from the relative safety of the "seminary in exile" in Slovenia. He was unsure about resuming his family's residence in Osijek. Seeing this veteran of war demonstrate nerves made as edgy as our own somehow offered some small consolation, if not real comfort, in the situation. In any case, our visit was pleasant and endearing all around. Our decision to return to Osijek during the continued heat of the tentative cease-fire really did help demonstrate our firm commitment to stand with our Croatian brothers and sisters in the midst of their trial. I was glad we all had come.

Apart from the usual orientation and hospitable gestures gladly exchanged in the context of a Westerner's first visit to this new culture, I was looking to Damir to offer a more important opportunity for my fellow travelers and me. I wanted to visit a camp where Bosnian refugees were being quartered. Steve Paulus readily shared about the presence of refugees in large numbers in Slovenian camps and related some of his good memories of witnessing for Christ among the many displaced Muslims. Damir seemed to think that most Croatian refugee centers were located in the western part of the country, far from the front lines and therefore distant from Osijek. But as we talked, a colleague on the seminary staff shared about a news report he had heard the day before about a camp newly opened near Djakavo, a city some 25 miles away. Damir gladly offered to go with us to see if such a camp existed. We left Osijek that very afternoon.

Gasinci — God's Gateway to Bosnians

The drive to Djakavo was slowed by military traffic and checkpoint clearances required at regular intervals on major roads. We slowly made our way toward this beautiful Croatian village with its famous twin-spired Catholic cathedral. Turning north we made our way on a narrow farm road through what seemed an endless cornfield until we suddenly came to another military checkpoint. This one finally marked the entrance to Gasinci, a tent camp that was now home to some 3,500 displaced and desperate Bosnian refugees.

We parked outside the wire gate and walked toward the camp director's office. Before we had gone far, I felt like the Pied Piper of Hamelin. Dozens of children, recognizing us as Westerners, followed us playfully every step we took. Through broken English they sought candy, gum, cigarettes and most of all, simple conversation with someone not locked in their war-torn world. They joked and laughed at everything and at nothing. They were bright, bounding with energy, bursting with impatience and bored with their confined circumstances. We fell in love with these beautiful children, seeing in their faces hope for Bosnia's future.

Their transitional home was a sprawling collection of tents and cabins of all sizes and shapes. Lined along gravel pathways as far as the eye could see, these tiny living quarters were augmented with communal toilets, massive cafeterias and limited medical facilities. Every attempt had been exerted to make these temporary shelters feel like home. They were neat and clean inside and seemed almost to achieve an inviting if primitive comfort. Outside was equally clean and obviously cared for. Stove wood was stacked neatly, and there was no sign of litter at all. We were positively impressed at the Bosnians' ability to make the best of their bad situation, creating a home away from home in a Croatian cornfield. Their perseverance and courage moved us deeply.

Continuing our tour of the camp added darker colors to the canvas of our first impressions of Gasinci. There was a noticeable absence of older teenage boys and men under 60. All the able-bodied men one might have expected to be with these families in a time of such turmoil and trial, were nowhere to be found. Inquiries helped us realize that many were still fighting to defend their homes in Bosnia. Others were interred in concentration camps, or feared missing, or worst of all, known to be dead. The absence of husbands and brothers and sons was etched in the worried brows of women of all ages. The middle-aged and younger women were undeniably grieved and understandably grave, yet most managed a smile, conveyed warmth as we spoke through our translators and held firm to hope — for their children's sake if not their own. One could almost read their unspoken words in anguished and uncertain faces, "Could there be a normal life again when all this is over?"

Darker still were the faces of the elderly refugees and the sick. The loss they sustained in this war was deeper than anyone else's. For the young, energy still existed to fuel a new beginning. For the middle aged, maturity and marketable skills held some promise for rebuilding a life in Bosnia or in a new home in another country. But for the aged and the infirm, no such promises remained. They lacked the strength and the will to dream of the future. All they had lived to build now lay in ruins behind them. Life for these refugees was in the past. No new opportunities lay ahead. No countries wanted to open their doors to these "unproductive" folks. For them, Gasinci was no resettlement point holding out hope for a brighter tomorrow. It was instead the end of the line.

These elderly folk waited only to die. Their blank stares and empty expressions loomed from beneath the old women's traditional babushkas and from behind the old men's wrinkled stubble and weathered faces. The promises that had once fueled their passion for living had died in this war. Only pain and hopelessness were left, flowing from aching hearts and etched in faces full of despair. We cried as we looked on, only observing their pain, unable to touch the terrible sense of loss that consumed them.

Looking into their vacant eyes, I thought of Paul's words in I Cor. 15:19: "If we have only hoped in Christ in this life, we are of all men most to be pitied."

With this mass of first impressions, we were moved to stop and pray. "Could it be, Lord, that not allowing us to take the gospel to Bosnia in the midst of this war, You have chosen to bring Bosnians to hear the gospel in Gasinci? Could it be that You have used the horrors of this war among neighbors to break the fallow ground of these Muslim hearts? Are you using the tragedy of war to prepare them to receive the truth of Your word? Did You heap despair into their lives so You could deliver them in the end? Did You plan this war to open doors to their culture for Christ? Will You use us here, Lord, to lift up Your name and to minister Your hope and Your peace? Is this camp the next step on our road to Sarajevo? Is Gasinci Your open door for us?"

Only time would tell....

3

Dreaming in the Spirit

And it shall be in the last days, God says, that I will pour forth of My Spirit upon all mankind; and your sons and your daughters shall prophesy, and your young men shall see visions, and your old men shall dream dreams....

Acts 2:17

As we returned from our "vision trip" to Croatia we were overwhelmed with the potential for ministry that Gasinci represented. It was hard not to think of the possibilities such an open door could create for our churches in Atlanta.

Options for Ministry Abounded

The opportunities Gasinci presented brought lots of previously unthinkable ideas to mind. A multitude of options dominated our discussion during the flight home. We might actually be able to live in the camp with the refugees! We might be able to find English speaking students at ETS who would be willing to work with us in sharing the gospel with these Muslims. We might be able to add a little light to the dim existence faced day in and day out by the hundreds of children in the camp. We might be able to share the *JESUS* film in this context.

This evangelistic tool had been used all over the world to win people to faith in Jesus. Offering an accurate portrayal of Luke's gospel, the *JESUS* film gave a visual and verbal representation of the earthly ministry of Jesus and the message of salvation. Because a long-term Campus Crusade for Christ staff member was in our church, we knew that the film had already been dubbed into Serbo-Croatian, the national language of former Yugoslavia. Use of the *JESUS* film could be incredibly effective with the kind of "captive audience" now living in this camp. Using this special tool might greatly enhance evangelistic witness.

Even if we could gain access to the *JESUS* film, however, we wondered who would be there to show it? How would we get someone to serve our interests in this Croatian camp on such short notice and in the midst of an ongoing war? The words from Isaiah 6:8 reverberated in my mind, "Whom shall we send, and who will go for us?" Surely some of the mission minded members of our church would be led of God's Spirit to respond as Isaiah had, saying, "Here am I, Lord, send me."

If we could recruit people to respond to the open doors in Gasinci, I wondered how we could afford to send them. After all, we would have to cover round-trip airfare to Europe, the costs of food and personal needs. And we would need to be able to get people out of Gasinci in a hurry if the war moved northward! Full-scale battles were still being fought daily in Slavonski Brod only 25 miles south of the camp. An evacuation vehicle would be basic equipment for a mission team in this dangerous environment. We certainly had no money to meet that kind of expense!

The financial needs we could already see were staggering. Though our small church had very little available cash resources to draw on, we tried to assess the possibilities for raising funds to help equip this camp for the winter cold that soon would come to Croatia. Eighty electric heaters and a large supply of wood, coal and fuel oil would be needed in the next few months before the October freezes began. Our fiscally trained minds despaired even as our faith held on to the certainty that God could do this in spite of our limited supply. We cried out to God for help!

Could God Be in All This?

My head was spinning for the first half of the transatlantic flight back to America. Somewhere over the ocean I decided that too many unanswerable questions were crowding into my mind and I needed to take a break from the whirlwind of options stirring my imagination. As I picked up the paper, I was still reflecting on whether God was really in this discovery of the refugee camp in Gasinci.

Opening the current issue of *USA Today*, a front-page headline quickly caught my attention. The article under the headline reported a hot and ongoing business story that had surfaced while we were in Central Europe and out of touch with news from home. It told of fast and furious moves in the airline industry. Pan American Airways had filed bankruptcy and Atlanta-based Delta Airlines was acquiring the rights to their overseas air routes. This almost certainly would mean lower international fares in our local market — good news for a church getting more deeply involved in Europe every day!

I thought little more about either the prospect of reduced ticket pricing or increased opportunities for ministry to Bosnians as my mind finally got the break it needed and I fell asleep. We arrived uneventfully at home, grateful for the blessing of safe travel and God's protection from the dangers of war in Croatia.

The next day I opened the *Atlanta Journal* to catch up on the local news. Again, to my surprise, an airline headline caught my eye. This article reiterated what I had read the day before about the deal between Pan Am and Delta regarding overseas routings. But this story added a huge additional revelation. Delta was announcing an airfare price war that was designed to win transatlantic passengers from Sebena and KLM, two European-based carriers operating daily non-stop flights from Atlanta. Delta was offering a new $500 round-trip fare to Budapest. This represented a 60 percent reduction from the most favorably discounted fares then available on other airlines. My head began spinning again. Even a small church like ours could afford international travel at these rates! I checked the article again to confirm the story and to determine the limited six- month window of opportunity these reduced fares offered us if we wanted to send short-term workers to the camp in Gasinci. From mid-October 1992, through April 1993, we could fly cheaply to Budapest, just a few hundred miles north of Osijek. I began to believe that God might be shaping all these circumstances after all!

Getting Our Elders on Board

Dan Burton and I met the next morning with NCC's elders to share the emerging vision we had for ministry in Gasinci. Recognizing that re-entry is often an issue when people return to their churches from the excitement of cross-cultural ministry, we tried to make our joint report a calm one. But our enthusiasm was obvious to everyone. Fortunately, the unusual opportunity in Gasinci was obvious as well.

We reached a quick consensus that great possibilities for ministry to Bosnians existed there, but we also agreed that we needed to explore the viability of pursuing them — first with each other, then with trusted advisers who had credible missions experience. We prayerfully set about the process of determining how we might seize this opportunity.

A Plan Emerges

There were many details to be ironed out and even more questions that yet needed to be answered, but brainstorming with our elders had produced a skeletal plan for a six-month project in Gasinci. Our tentative steps toward the refugee center were scheduled to fit into Delta's window of opportunity for reasonably priced air transportation. In brief, we envisioned the following:

From mid-August to mid-October we were to recruit a small base team whose task it would be to live in the camp, maintain a constant presence for our church and facilitate the biweekly rotation of small teams which would be routed through Budapest.

During this same time frame, we needed to raise funds to purchase two vehicles, a small car which could accommodate the base team members and a van large enough to serve as an evacuation vehicle for teams of 8-10 people.

We needed a credible team leader to oversee the project. This person would lead the base team for the entire six-month period. We wanted at least two more people to serve with the team leader for the duration of the project.

We needed to consult with others about the wisdom of this sketchy plan. We agreed that we would accept general consensus about the plan as a green light from the Lord. We chose two points of reference in this regard. Ronnie Stevens was an obvious choice due to his long-term relationship with NCC. He was a Dallas Seminary graduate, an experienced pastor and an American missionary with extensive experience in Europe. Having served for years as pastor of the International Chapel in Munich, he was at the time serving as senior pastor of the Moscow Bible Church. Peter Kuzmic was a second obvious choice as the single most significant leader representing the Evangelical Church of Croatia. He had already served as the key national "mentor" for our developing vision for Bosnia. We were believing God to use these two men to confirm our direction or to call us back to reality.

We needed to raise funds for humanitarian relief supplies and to provide medium-term housing for our teams should accommodations in Gasinci prove to be unavailable. A promotional video was thought to be critical to the fund-raising effort.

If all else fell into place, we needed to begin immediately to recruit dozens of workers to serve on the short-term teams which would rotate in and out of Gasinci at two-week intervals. Our proposed schedule provided for twelve teams over the six-month window of opportunity. We began praying that of the 70-80 short-term workers, God might call 10 percent to remain long-term as a church planting team for Bosnia.

Finally, if we sensed God giving us a green light, it would be necessary for me to return with the base team leader at the earliest possible convenience to explore our options and set up the logistical details in Croatia.

This vision had come together so rapidly that even I could barely believe what we were proposing. The scope of our plan was overwhelming to our leaders, but it somehow also seemed plausible. The worst part of the whole list for me was the requirement to return to Europe with immediacy. While I felt up to the assignment, I expected resistance from my wife, Ginger, who generally preferred that I try to limit my out-of-town travel for the sake of balancing our priorities at home. I knew the elders were looking to Ronnie Stevens and Peter Kuzmic to confirm God's direction. But for me, the first real test was passing the plan by Ginger!

All Systems Are Go!

When I got home that evening I shared the result of the elder's meeting with my wife. To my great surprise, without hesitation and with unreserved enthusiasm, Ginger affirmed that I must make the return trip to Croatia. She had seen the Muslims in Gasinci. She had let her imagination run wild with the Burtons and me as we traveled together and dreamed about the vast ministry possibilities at the camp. She knew the Lord was moving! I shouldn't have been surprised at her clarity of vision and her willingness to take risks for the sake of the Kingdom. After all, she had sacrificed all her early aspirations for financial security to follow her accountant husband from the marketplace to the world of vocational ministry. We had shared so much in our 20 years together. God had always proven faithful and she felt no fear now. She was fully prepared to follow me even into the Bosnian war. Her affirmative support was all the encouragement I needed. Now I was more certain than ever that God was orchestrating these events!

Dan and I next called Ronnie Stevens in Moscow. As I reviewed the events of the last week and the outline of our plan for Gasinci, Ronnie immediately encouraged us to go for it! His words were incredibly reassuring and he made our plan seem less burdensome by not making a big deal of it. His brief remarks are still sharply etched in my memory. He said, "More opportunities to advance the gospel around the world have been lost in our lifetime due to caution than for any other reason. America's missionaries are often hindered because they move too carefully and too slowly. I don't think you guys have much to lose. More than that, I think you can do it. And I think you should do it!" What exhilaration Dan and I shared as we completed the call and sat in my office amazed over the momentum which seemed to be building in the heavenlies for this project.

Our last point of confirmation rested with Peter Kuzmic whom we contacted at Gordon Conwell Theological Seminary where he was ministering as a visiting professor. We needed to get his sense of the wisdom of pursuing the kind of ministry we were formulating. As I finished sharing the outline of our plan with Peter I remember concluding, "Well, Peter, are we dreaming strange dreams?" Without the slightest hesitation, he responded with his charming European accent, "No, my brother, you are dreaming in the Spirit! Bring your people to Croatia!"

Solomon says that a three-stranded cord is not easily broken. I felt that our vision for this project had gained strength with the ready affirmation I had received from Ginger, Ronnie and Peter. Now more than ever the elders and I felt released to keep on "dreaming in the Spirit."

All that remained for us to do at this point was to see whom God might call to direct our base team in Gasinci. This burden was the Lord's to carry for we felt His clear direction to a particular leader already deeply involved at NCC. It was time to see if that leader felt led to go to Croatia for the Lord, for the sake of the

Kingdom, for the benefit we wanted to extend to the Bosnians and for our church. Would this man join us as we continued to dream in the Spirit? We soon would know.

Ordinary People

*For God, who said, "light shall shine out of darkness,"
is the One who has shone in our hearts to give the light
of the knowledge of the glory of God in the face of
Christ. But we have this treasure in earthen vessels, that
the surpassing greatness of the power may be of God and
not from ourselves.*

II Cor. 4:6-7

From among our 250 church members, the elders had no doubt as to their first choice for a man to serve as leader of our base team in Gasinci. David Lively was a single, 35-year-old Trinity Evangelical Divinity School graduate who had previously served as a pioneer church planter in the United States. He had enjoyed his pastoral ministry and shared our passion for missions. Earlier overseas experiences had allowed him to travel on occasion to India and to Eastern Europe. But a sense that God had changes ahead for him caused him to leave his pastoral post. He had accepted secular employment for a season and had been in fellowship at Northside for a number of months.

Long-standing relationships within our small fellowship had allowed David to quietly flourish in our church and to quickly find his way into leadership. David had presided over the birth of a new singles ministry at NCC. His maturity and capacity were obvious, his example appreciated, his character above reproach. Soon, he was invited to join our Shepherding Team as one of our key leaders. We knew he was still interested in vocational ministry as he looked to the future, and we hoped this mission opportunity would capture his imagination.

David was also the son of a plumbing contractor. So, it was no surprise that he was able to earn his living in this field, serving an engineering firm as a plumbing draftsman. He was living with his folks at the time. With no debt, no restrictive lifestyle commitments, no pending romantic interests and no long-term obligations left unfulfilled, David seemed to be the perfect candidate to direct our work in Gasinci.

Clumsy Recruiting

I had no opportunity to speak to David personally prior to the Sunday Services following our return from Croatia. But by the time the weekend rolled around I had been released by the elders to approach David about this possible role for him. During the service, the elders shared the outline of our near-term plans for Gasinci so that our church body could begin praying for the effort and seeking the Lord about their own possible involvement. David heard the sketchy details along with everyone else in the congregation that morning. I don't know if he had imagined as he listened, that he might be painted into the center of this fuzzy picture.

After the service I saw David getting into his car. Raising my voice to project across the parking lot, I called out eagerly to get his attention, "David! Hey, David!" Without thinking of the usual protocol for this sort of thing, I continued to shout to him from a distance. "David, how about praying to see if God would release you to lead this ministry in Gasinci until next spring? Would you do that?"

He unhesitatingly responded with a one-word answer, "Sure!" Then got in his car to drive off and join the other singles for lunch. In retrospect, this exchange seems abrupt and almost cavalier.

Neither of us intended it to be. Surely neither of us could have imagined how pivotal that playful interaction would later become.

A Follow-Up Call

On Monday I checked into scheduled flights to Europe for later in the week. With the necessary information in hand, I called David at work early Tuesday morning. Making no effort to identify myself I jumped right to the point as he answered the phone. He must have been caught completely off-guard as I blurted out the words, "David, do you want to leave for Croatia on Thursday or Friday?"

After only the briefest pause, David laughed and responded, "Good morning, John! Hey, you weren't kidding on Sunday were you?"

"No," I said. "There are available flights on both Thursday and Friday. We really do need to get back to Croatia to make sure this project is feasible. Has the Lord released you to go?"

Laughing again, David said, "Yeah! Let's do it! Why don't we leave on Thursday." So we did just that. Little did David know then that his six-month commitment would grow to six years at the writing of this book. Little did he anticipate that he would become perhaps the best-known western missionary in all of Croatia and Bosnia. Little did he realize that he would play a primary role in helping to establish the first few churches in post-war Bosnia.

God had much in store for this priceless brother whom a writer reporting from Sarajevo years later would single out for attention. He described him as "a tall, thin, angular American ... shy and self-effacing, except when it came to encouraging the young converts with whom he was working.... This (encouragement he offered) in their own language, carrying on the tradition of all missionaries: time with the people, eat what they eat, respect their ways, learn their language, earning their trust so that they care to ask why you have come."[1] This tribute was offered by an independent writer who sought to compose a "short list" of notable peace-makers who had served heroically, yet unnoticed, during the war. His accolade would come much later in our story when we were no longer on the road but actually resident in Sarajevo. David was now only taking his first steps on that long and arduous journey. Suffice it to say, our early confidence in David Lively was well placed. He would prove to be God's man, divinely appointed for such a time as this!

The Plan Comes Together

David and I left the following Thursday for our eight-day whirlwind trip to Croatia. This incredible adventure only deepened our conviction that God was opening wide the door of access to Bosnian refugees.

The leaders at ETS were eager to get their English-speaking students involved as translators. The availability of these interpreters solved our biggest problem — the language barrier between us and the Bosnians. Damir Spoljaric at the seminary and Pavao Mogus, pastor of the Evangelical Church in Osijek, pulled out all the stops to try to make our plan work. They were clearly fellow soldiers willingly joining us in this spiritual battle from the very beginning! How grateful we were for their valuable help.

Being assured of available translators, we next dealt with the need for transportation. Pastor Mogus' personal car had been destroyed during the siege of Osijek in 1991. We determined that we would buy a passenger car for the base team that could be given to him at the end of our six-month project. He asked us to look for a Fiat with a diesel engine and we bought a car to fill his order. We also were able to rent a used van from Peter McKenzie, our missionary friend in Zagreb. We paid a few hundred dollars for seven months use of the "McKenzie Combi" which looked to be on its last legs but served us faithfully in transporting teams to and from Budapest. In the end we bought the vehicle and literally ran the poor van to death!

Missionary contacts in Germany agreed to do our car shopping for us, looking for the used Fiat passenger car. Even as they began to search for us, we had no idea how we would pay for this vehicle.

We simply kept moving forward hoping God's provision would be waiting just around the corner.

Recognizing that the base team's life in the Gasinci fishbowl would be wearing, we also desired to find a small apartment to serve as a retreat for them on occasion. The Evangelical Church in Djakavo had space for such a purpose, a modest upstairs apartment with two rooms and a bath, but the bath and kitchen were not yet installed. We agreed to pay for this work to be done in return for having access to the apartment for the duration of the project. Many would later thank God for this quiet resting place! I left $2,000 to permit the work to be begun without delay.

Finally, we investigated possible access to the refugee center. The Catholic camp director proved amazingly cooperative with us. He eagerly invited us to bring our teams to Gasinci, offering the same meager accommodations to us that the refugees were sharing.

At first this meant living in small canvas tents until it was too cold to do so. Later, as winter set in, we had our own "kucica" or little house to share. This rough-hewn plywood structure measured 15' x 25' and had a shed roof, a small wood stove and two rooms — each with one window. The smaller room used as a bedroom for women, took up one-third of the space. The larger served as a kitchen, a meeting area and a bedroom for men. With creative use of space, we were able to sleep up to twenty people in this modest home away from home. Those who would later come to Gasinci found their sense of community deepened considerably as they lived quite literally on top of one another in triple decker bunks!

We wondered who might complete our base team as David and I returned home exhausted but excited about all that God had done to pave the road ahead for us. David flew home ahead of me on a free ticket provided by his sister, an American Airlines flight attendant. I waited in Frankfurt for my Lufthansa flight and for a divine appointment that would mark the initial release of a steady stream of "manna from heaven." As I prayed thinking not at all of manna, I asked God to give us men and women to serve in Gasinci.

I was blessed with an immediate answer as the Lord brought the next base team member to my mind.

A Woman of Excellence

Fiorella Weaver had become a new believer just before our church began in 1984. She was led to Christ by a neighbor and guided by a mutual friend to the evening home Bible study that would eventually become NCC. Ours was the first Protestant fellowship this Italian Catholic had ever experienced, and from the beginning her heart was knit to ours in the kind of powerful spiritual union that only God makes possible.

Nurturing Fio through her early development as a Christian was a joy for my wife and me. She was a willing servant, a faithful friend, an affirming church member and ultimately a devoted disciple of Christ. Eager to learn and grow, she attended every meeting our church offered to stimulate her faith. Over her first six years of life in the Lord, she completed the women's Bible Study Fellowship course and became a facilitating leader, training other women in the Scriptures. She also became a dedicated prayer warrior.

Fio had been born in Italy and was a language teacher by profession. She was fluent in English, French, Spanish, Italian and Latin. Following her father's career as an Italian diplomat, she had lived all over the world including a brief period as part of Italy's delegation to Zagreb, Croatia.

She had later been married to a career army officer and gained U.S. citizenship. Fio was not apt to be left behind by a husband serving overseas. Consequently, she had lived in Panama, Germany and Korea with her officer husband, Bill. In the late 60s she even followed Bill to Vietnam choosing to live in Saigon so that she would be close at her husband's side. She was in Saigon in 1968 during the Tet Offensive. Even the rigors and risks of war were nothing new to her!

In the summer of 1992, Fio's life was in transition. Bill had died of cancer the year before. His death left this 50-year-old widowed grandmother with three adult children all of whom lived away from home. Fighting loneliness, Fio had filled her days in recent months building a mountain dream house in North Georgia. She was without a teaching contract for the first time in decades as the fall school year approached. To Fio, it seemed an appropriate time to take a break and enjoy the mountain homestead she called "One Accord."

More Clumsy Recruiting

I was eager to return home and talk to her. Though I took the day after my return to Atlanta to recover from the jet lag and fatigue of travel, it did not prove long before I had the opportunity to have that conversation with Fio. The day I first returned to the office, I was totally surprised to find her sitting on the stairs leading to our auditorium. Since she now lived more than an hour's drive from NCC, we seldom saw this dear sister during the week. I hugged her as we greeted and asked her to step into my office so we could talk.

She was already aware of the plans announced to the church two Sundays before, so I quickly filled her in on the result of my trip with David. She had been praying with our intercessors early that morning (the reason for her presence that day) and was excited to hear of prayers answered by my report. Finishing my briefing, I next posed the million-dollar question to Fio, "Would you be available to serve with David on the base team in Gasinci?"

Like Sarah of old (Gen. 18:9-12) and all too many women through the ages, Fio knew what an immediate response to a challenge of faith was supposed to be. *She laughed!* At first I think Fio believed I was kidding with her. As I pressed my appeal more earnestly, however, she became sober and reflective. Her countenance was filled simultaneously with a curious mixture of interest and impossibility. Wisely, she asked for time to pray about God's direction. I was glad to have her seek the Lord on the matter, and I didn't have to wait long for her answer to come!

The next day, Fio called and wanted to share the full story of how her sense of direction had come about before she told me what decision she had made. I was eager to hear from her.

Discerning the Call of God

That Monday as I rested from my trip, she had been sitting outside her mountain home admiring the woodlands of North Georgia. Settled in, financially secure and free from the demands of a job, Fio expected to feel deep contentment as she rested quietly in the summer sunshine. Instead, she felt restless and agitated. As she reflected on Scripture and prayed, she wept longingly and cried out to God, "Oh Lord, don't you have anything for me to do? Surely you still have some purpose for my life — some contribution for me to make for your Kingdom!" But God had been silent that day. Thankfully, in my fatigue, I had been silent too!

The next morning, before I rose to prepare for the day, Fio had decided to come to our offices to join the early morning intercessors. Leaving her home at 4:30 a.m., she had been praying for hours before I arrived to give my "recruiting speech."

There had come a time of quietness before the Lord as she and the other intercessors prayed over a variety of concerns. The group waited patiently and the Lord prompted one of the sisters to rise and pray over Fio. She had conveyed nothing about the previous day's wrestling with God, and her heart was amazed as this spontaneous prayer fell from her sensitive sister's lips. "I don't know why you have burdened my heart for Fio this morning, Lord. But I want to be obedient to the leading of your Spirit. Lord, I believe you have a word for Fio this morning. I believe you want her to know that you have a purpose for her life. You have a work for her to do. I don't know what the work is, Lord, but you do. Please, God, reassure her heart and reveal your plan to her." Fio had cried as her sister prayed.

When I arrived later in the morning, all this was still fresh on her mind and heart. When I called her into my office to ask her about the next seven months, it seemed she was hearing not from me, but from the Lord Himself. Fio's excitement and expectation were boundless at this point. Of course she would go to Croatia with David!

Recruiting Reinforcements

On Sunday, we announced to the church family the decision that David and Fio had made to go to Croatia. We asked others to pray for God's direction in this regard as well. We still believed one or two more people needed to join the base team in Gasinci. The next to step forward in answer to this call was a thirty-something legal secretary who had been at NCC for nearly two years. Vivacious, full of life and energy, Becky Coldwell was a born people-gatherer. She was a lovely sister in the Lord and a vessel through whom Jesus often demonstrated His love toward others.

Spiritually mature and well grounded in the word of God, Becky had been involved in vocational Christian service before. She had worked in a disciple-making ministry called Worldwide Discipleship headquartered in Atlanta. I am not sure her prior service had ever taken her outside the United States, but now her discipleship ministry really was taking on a global dimension. Her personality, enthusiasm and ability to stimulate the joy of the Lord in others made Becky a valuable addition to the team.

Finally, Stephen Ruff, an 18-year-old high school graduate, asked if he could be a part of this effort. The son of an elder, Stephen had no immediate plans for college or career pursuits. He was uncertain about how useful he would be for the team, but he was eager to lend his hands to help. Stephen's physical strength, his youthful perspective and his willingness to serve were welcome assets as he completed the original base team. He proved to be the vanguard preceding dozens of other teenagers into this outreach effort with Bosnian refugees.

Earthen Vessels

Who would have dreamed that our first team would have been made up of such ordinary people? Certainly, few mission agencies would consider this rag-tag band to be God's "dream team" to serve in Gasinci: a plumber, a widow, a legal secretary and a student — a pretty ordinary group! But we knew the lives of these folks well. We knew their heart for God, their character, their capacity, their giftings. We knew they would be faithful to serve. We believed in them!

More importantly, we believed in God's ability to manifest his power through them. Somehow, somewhere in the development of modern missions theory, we have so professionalized the ministry of evangelism and missions that we have relegated these redemptive roles to the realm of a privileged few. Most mission leaders are convinced that specialized training and well-developed cross-cultural skills are necessary to be successful in missions. Maintaining such high standards, we may have, in effect, over-professionalized the work of world evangelization. Ralph Winter, for example, has warned the missions community against the dangers of the kind of "re-amateurization" of missions our early work in Gasinci illustrates.[2]

But think of what the 1st century founders of the church were like. They were not professionals. They were ordinary people. Their qualifications flowed not from credentials but from character, not from completed course work, but from spiritual capacity and Christ-likeness. Luke makes that point dramatically in Acts 4:13:

> Now as they observed the confidence of Peter and John, and understood that they were uneducated and untrained men, they were marveling, and began to recognize them as having been with Jesus.

God has always used ordinary people to perform extraordinary tasks for His glory. Recall Paul's words in II Cor. 4:6-7:

For God, who said, "light shall shine out of darkness," is the One who has shone in our hearts to give the light of the knowledge of the glory of God in the face of Christ. But we have this treasure in earthen vessels, that the surpassing greatness of the power may be of God and not from ourselves.

The great apostle to the Gentiles is not subtle in pressing the point. For in his first epistle to Corinth he had already urged these fledgling believers not to fall into the trap of trusting in human strength or worldly wisdom in doing God's will on earth. Encouraging the Corinthians to take delight in their humble beginnings, Paul writes in I Cor. 1:26-30:

For consider your calling, brethren, that there were not many wise according to the flesh, not many mighty, not many noble; but God has chosen the foolish things of the world to shame the wise, and God has chosen the weak things of the world to shame the things which are strong, and the base things of the world and the despised, God has chosen, the things that are not, that He might nullify the things that are, that no man should boast before God.

As our "dream team" of ordinary people took the field in Gasinci, they moved forward in faith with their confidence in God not in their giftedness. They believed that the Lord could use common folk like themselves and a few small churches like ours to accomplish His purposes in the midst of impossible circumstances. They have become heroes of faith for us. For in time, hundreds would follow in their footsteps to serve the beleaguered refugees from Bosnia in Jesus' name.

And to this day God continues to use ordinary people to do extraordinary things for His glory in Bosnia. We are now more convinced than ever that mission is the purview of ordinary people, not the privileged domain of highly skilled professionals. In the Scriptures God chose to make fig pickers into prophets, prisoners into prime ministers, little Jewish girls into queens, shepherd boys into giant killers and kings, and common fishermen into founders of His church.

Why should we be surprised if he makes prize missionaries out of plumbers, teachers, secretaries and students? The simple truth is that God can use anyone He chooses to fulfill His purposes. Let the record be clear as we near the end of this millennium; today is still the day for ordinary people to serve God in extraordinary ways! Paraphrasing John Adams' reflection on the capacity of common men to rise to the occasion, let this be our prayer:

> By my physical constitution I may be an ordinary man.... Yet may the good Lord use some great events, some cutting expressions, some mean hypocrisies, to provoke my faith in His power that I might see Him throw this assemblage of sloth, sleep and littleness into action bold as a lion for His glory.[3]

This is exactly what David and his team of ordinary people did as they walked into the refugee center in Gasinci.

Manna From Heaven

Yet He commanded the clouds above, and opened the doors of heaven; and He rained down manna upon them to eat, and gave them food from heaven.
Psalm 78:23-24

Any small church leader directed to consider the possibilities of trusting God for major ministry in missions will quickly face the formidable obstacle of finances. Where does a small fellowship find the funds required to pay for travel, food, lodging, vehicles, resources and logistical support on a scale sufficient to touch an entire country or an unreached culture for Christ? My answer is a simple one, "I don't know!"

But God does! Of all the miraculous interventions we have experienced during our brief history in Bosnia, God's special means of providing financial resources are perhaps the most incredible to me. It did not take long for this to become an issue for us. Our little church could barely afford my airline ticket for the return trip to Croatia with David Lively in the summer of 1992. Nor could we afford the $2,000 advance already committed to complete the Djakavo apartment during that early reconnaissance trip. Beyond these first small investments, we still needed vehicles, humanitarian aid supplies, literature and Bibles. How were we to afford all this stuff? I am ashamed to say that God's answers to our needs began to come before we had even begun to pray about them. We should not be surprised at this though, for in Matthew 6:8 Jesus teaches us an incredible secret about prayer: "Your Father knows what you need, before you ask Him."

A Divine Appointment in Frankfurt

In the previous chapter, I mentioned being delayed at the airport in Frankfurt, Germany after David Lively's departure for his return flight to the states. I waited in the terminal for my own scheduled departure two hours later. My mind was primarily occupied with my thoughts of fatigue, my desire to get back home and my concern over finding more people to join the base team under David's leadership. I joined other passengers when the time for my flight approached. We were herded like cattle aboard a bus that would carry us to the remote loading area outside the terminal building.

The bus was over-crowded on this hot humid day. I was tired enough to be completely oblivious to those around me. Suddenly, one of the faceless, nameless bodies nearby reached in my direction and asked, "Say, aren't you John Rowell? Don't you pastor Northside Community Church in Atlanta?" Surprised out of my stupor, I tried to recognize this stranger, but a quick review of my mental card catalogue of names and faces found no record of this fellow. He quickly introduced himself and his wife.

They looked beyond my blank stare, and reminded me of a recent visit to Northside with friends who were members of the church. To my relief, they reassured me that we had never met; they simply had been in church and had heard me preach in the service. Obviously less tired than I, they energetically recounted the European vacation they were just concluding. Then, almost as a courtesy I think, they inquired about my reason for being in Frankfurt.

I gave a summary of our plans for ministry to Bosnian refugees in Gasinci as best I could in the remaining minutes of our bus ride to the airplane. Little interested in my topic, they acknowledged my story and exited the bus to board the plane. As I followed them onto the tarmac, I was approached by still another stranger.

"Excuse me," he said, "I couldn't help overhearing your story about Bosnia. What will a short-term trip like that cost anyway?" I had no idea as yet about the estimated expense involved for short-term team members and told the stranger so. I quickly offered a ball park number of $1,000 for a two-week trip. Still offering no name to go with his obvious interest, the stranger ascended the steps of the airplane just ahead of me. He wheeled around at the top to offer a business card without shaking hands or introducing himself. With the air of a man who is accustomed to giving others instructions he said, "I can't get involved personally in projects like this; I just don't have the time. But I would like to help somehow as others take part. My name is David Rocker. Give me a call at my office and let's talk some more about this."

He turned left up the aisle to take his seat in the first class cabin of the L-1011, a territory as foreign to me as Bosnia itself. I turned right to the familiar confines of the coach compartment and took my customary seat next to a fellow traveler who, like me, would probably have preferred more space than the airline provided between us. I looked at the card in my hand and wondered as I shifted to find a comfortable position in my cramped seat, why had God allowed David Rocker to cross my path that day. Only God knew. I soon fell asleep.

"To Be" or "Not to Be?"...

Back at work the next week, David Lively and I set about the preparations that had to be made within the few weeks that remained before the base team would leave for Europe. The first order of business was to try our hand at filmmaking. We combined poorly shot footage from Gasinci with halting "talking head" explanations by David and me, to communicate the need and opportunities before us in such a way that other churches and individuals might be moved to join us in launching this project. We were truly awful spokesmen for the cause, but since "one picture is worth a thousand words,"[1] we thought the video we hastily produced would be valuable to us.

Our filming effort was indeed helpful in recruiting additional support for Gasinci. Not nearly so much so, however, as the *JESUS* film dubbed in Croatian would prove to be! We had very specific ideas about how effective that evangelistic tool could be if used in the camp. Preliminary efforts to gain access to the film, however, made it seem like this helpful option was "not to be."

For good reason, the *JESUS* film Project staff had a policy that prevented this sort of "personal distribution" of the video in a new language if it had not yet been premiered formally in theaters. Initial mass exposure in each language group was a foundational strategy in using the film worldwide, and we could hardly quarrel with the rationale of these creative leaders. Still, we hoped that these brothers in Christ might see the uniqueness of this wartime application for witnessing to Bosnian refugees. We appealed for special consideration. Graciously, the *JESUS* film Project leaders agreed to prayerfully review whether in this unusual and limited context, use of the video ought "to be."

A return call the next day gave us word that a special exception was to be made and the film could be used in Gasinci. We were ecstatic! But our overflowing joy turned from gushes of excitement to a dry well as our hearts sank upon hearing the "price of admission" to show the film. Customarily, we were told, the ministry that initiates use of the film in a new language contributes $5,000 to help cover the dubbing costs involved. There was no way we could come up with that kind of money when all these other demands were facing us. So, we asked these dear brothers to pray once again for special consideration. In light of our limitations, we asked them to release the video without a fee.

Ephesians 3:20-21 expresses a great expectation that Christians should have when praying for God to move in a given situation:

Now to Him who is able to do exceeding abundantly beyond all that we ask or think, according to the power that works within us; to Him be glory in the Church and in Christ Jesus to all generations forever and ever. Amen.

We were asking for an Eph. 3:20 answer in this circumstance, and God gave us one. In what I understand to have been an unprecedented decision by the *JESUS* film Project staff, they decided to release the video for our use without a dubbing fee. Moreover, they were going to send us a gift of cash to cover the cost of buying the equipment necessary to show the film in Gasinci. We were deliriously thankful for the kingdom-minded and generous spirit these brothers exhibited toward us. We remain grateful to this day for this extraordinary kindness on their part.

Completing the "Frankfurt Connection"

Limited finances, however, remained one of our most serious problems. Just days before the base team was scheduled to fly to Germany to pay for our now located automobile, we realized that our fundraising efforts had fallen short of the money needed for these large purchases. As I reviewed possible sources for additional cash, I decided it was time to take David Rocker up on his offer to discuss our plans for Gasinci in greater depth. Calling to make an appointment, I could tell that he was a very busy man. Nonetheless, he wanted to honor his invitation and we scheduled lunch together.

Armed with our amateur video, I entered the 15 story office tower and rode to the top floor offices where David Rocker's firm conducted business. My palms were sweating as I entered the posh and professional environment common to his mortgage-banking world. I was still rehearsing the planned presentation I would never make when David dutifully met me in the reception area. He shared apologetically that it was necessary to cancel our lunch plans. Demands on his time were simply too great.

He hurriedly ushered me into the office's conference room and, trying to be patient, agreed to watch my seven-minute video. My sense of bankruptcy was dramatized by this unfamiliar and professional setting where men and women daily devoted themselves to the details of high finance. I was painfully aware of our pressing need and of how poorly this homemade video communicated our message. Only a few minutes into the taped presentation, David stopped me. "Listen," he said, "I promised to help you do this, and I want to keep my word. I just have very little time right now." As he spoke, he took a checkbook from his breast pocket and began to write. Without looking at me, he called for a secretary to bring in his business checkbook, which she did before he even finished writing the first check.

I sat in awkward silence as he now wrote a second check and folded it into the first. Sliding both across the table toward me as we stood, Mr. Rocker shook my hand. I put the two checks into my shirt pocket without looking at them as he led me out of the conference room. Apologizing again for canceling lunch, he cordially showed me through the reception area to the elevators. Saying goodbye, David Rocker was gone. I had been in the office building for less than ten minutes.

Still shaking my head, I found myself trying to figure out what had gone wrong. Why had I not been allowed to make my pitch? Why had our second meeting ended as abruptly as the first in Frankfurt? Why had he invited me to come to his office in the first place? Dejected, I walked out of the elevator and into the lobby. Only then did I reach into my pocket for the two checks. I thought I might as well see what he had given us and praise the Lord for this stranger's kindness. After all, something is better than nothing.

Opening the folded checks and fanning them so that I could see the amounts of each, I nearly fainted. Together they totaled $10,000! I had never seen David Rocker before our divine appointment in Frankfurt, and I have not seen him again since that day in his office.

But his spontaneous response to God's prompting served to fully fund the remaining cash needed to buy our evacuation vehicles for Gasinci. Phil. 4:19 was made powerfully relevant to me in this set of circumstances:

> And my God shall supply all your needs according to His riches in glory in Christ Jesus.

Déjà Vu

The third — and by far the most spectacular provision from God — came as unexpectedly as the gifts from the *JESUS* film Project and David Rocker. Only three months into our Gasinci ministry, manna again fell from heaven just before the end of the calendar year. Through the fall of 1992 we were faithfully sending teams to Gasinci every two weeks. In the meantime, our fellowship was also growing rapidly. By winter of 1992 we were completely full in our worship meetings. The number of children involved in our Sunday school rooms made them even more uncomfortably crowded than our auditorium. We were literally bursting at the seams.

In church growth terms it is a cardinal sin to permit a meeting room to become 100 percent full. Even before such saturation occurs, a church ceases to grow because newcomers feel there is no room left for them. The traditional maxim is, "when a room is 80 percent full, it is full." Well, we were more than full but had little time to think about our overcrowding problem at home. Cramped quarters in Atlanta were the least of our worries. We were too busy with our Bosnian ministry to be burdened by such a minor logistical issue. We certainly were not praying for this annoying circumstantial problem to be solved. But God knew our need, and He was again taking steps to deal with it. In fact, He had begun to do so before the crowded conditions began to occur.

In May 1992, I had been contacted by Paul Crafton, the chairman of the Board of Trustees for Riverside Bible Church. NCC had no special relationship with this independent fellowship of believers though our leaders knew some of their members casually. Our churches had little in common philosophically except that both were known to be especially committed to world missions.

Mr. Crafton was following up on a conversation from a year earlier in 1991. At that time Edgar Pinson, Riverside's previous trustee chairman, had contacted me expressing an interest in a possible church merger. Our leaders had declined that proposal for reasons too complex and too far off the subject to reiterate in this context. Suffice it to say that Riverside was in decline and had been for some time. A merger with NCC did not seem like a viable solution to their problems nor did we believe a merger was in our immediate best interest.

In this May 1992 phone call, Mr. Crafton wanted to revisit the issue of the challenge facing Riverside Bible Church. This time however, we spoke not about a potential merger but about whether we would be interested in receiving the Riverside facilities as an outright gift. Our elders were astounded by the generosity of the Riverside Bible Church family and were understandably open to the possibility at that time. Satisfied that we were seriously interested in the idea and facing a considerable amount of congregational "processing" with those under his own care, Mr. Crafton thanked me and ended our brief conversation.

I was not to hear from Riverside's board again until late July 1992. At that time they asked for a written explanation that would help them understand how we would use their facility should it be made available to us. I had prepared the necessary document on behalf of our church just prior to traveling to Croatia with my wife and the Burtons in August. Frankly, none of our elders had given the matter much thought since that time. Mobilizing to meet the opportunities in Gasinci had required our focused attention since late August.

Then, on the first Sunday evening in December 1992, I heard from Paul Crafton again. As usual he was warm, soft-spoken and businesslike. The purpose of this call was to inform me that Riverside's remaining members had voted that evening to give their property to NCC. A contract had already been prepared by their attorney, executed by their officers, and I could expect it to be on my desk by Tuesday morning. Mr. Crafton's call ended with very little additional interaction.

I was stunned. NCC's facility at the time consisted of 2.8 acres of land in a neighborhood off the beaten track. We had limited office and Sunday school space and no room for expansion. Our auditorium held 240 people at most. We had a total of $550,000 invested in the property.

Riverside's property — now ours — was just five years old. The auditorium seated 450 people with relatively spacious Sunday school accommodations. A separate office building offered ample room for growth. These facilities were located on a residential/commercial roadway in an upper class neighborhood within a mile of two major freeways. The buildings and 7.5 acres of developable land were valued at nearly 2.5 million dollars. All this was being given to our church for no apparent reason, at a time when we could not have afforded to buy even the playground equipment that came with the property. The gift came complete with furnishings, pianos, and office equipment — all debt free. We were staggered at God's generosity toward us expressed through the Riverside Bible Church family! The wonder of the gift was a déjà vu experience. Once again, God had seen our need and met it before we asked or even recognized that it existed. What a glorious God we serve!

The Rule Rather Than the Exception

These three detailed stories offer a view of God's miraculous provision that could easily seem unrealistic to the casual reader. While it is impossible to teach others how to reproduce this kind of dramatic result, I want to be clear that experiences like these have been the rule rather than the exception for our church since we decided to undertake our journey on the road to Sarajevo. As we have been faithful to serve as a conduit releasing material blessing into Bosnia, God has simply used us for His purposes. Perhaps we are simply experiencing the full impact of the Kingdom principles Jesus taught in Luke 6:38:

> Give and it will be given unto you; good measure, pressed down, shaken together, running over, they will pour into your lap. For by your standard of measure it will be measured to you in return.

This experience of God's repeated miraculous provision — even before we discover a need — has been a normal occurrence for our church. At the risk of running ahead of myself in the chronology of our story, allow me to illustrate with three additional examples from more recent years that may prove more easily reproducible by other ministries.

Continued Emphasis on Faith Promise Giving

In Chapter 1, "The Road to Sarajevo," I introduced the concept of Faith Promise Giving and its dramatic impact on the level of financial provision even a small church can accumulate. In that earlier discussion, I used the example of the results we saw in our first four years using this method of adding to and eventually replacing our regular budget for mission support commitments. Faith promise giving allowed us to effectively increase our total mission budget by nearly 400 percent in those first four years. The combination of mission budget allocations and faith promise receipts over these years can be summarized as follows:

	1987	1988	1989	1990
Missions Budget Allocation	$12,000	$12,000	$12,000	$11,321
Faith Promise Pledge Receipts	$8,000	$12,426	$25,715	$31,121
Totals	$20,000	$24,426	$37,715	$42,442

Since 1989 when our attendance totaled approximately 250 people, we have planted three other local churches in Atlanta. One is a Persian church made up of Iranian immigrants and the other two are more typical American churches. Eight adults and their children were mobilized as a church planting team aiming at the Persian community in our city. An entire start-up congregation was released to establish the two American churches. To start these congregations, we released more than 200 of our most committed people. Among them were many of those who offered financial support most faithfully for all our ministries, including missions.

The increased facility capacity that came with the Riverside Bible Church property has allowed us to grow to approximately 450 people in total attendance. This represents a net gain of some 65 percent in the size of our congregation in spite of our sending 200 members away in our church multiplication efforts. Over that same period, by involving new families and individuals in our church and by encouraging them to participate in our faith promise effort, our total missions giving has increased at an even greater rate. The specific results comparing missions funding in 1989 to totals in 1997 can be summarized as follows:

	1989	1997
Missions Budget Allocations	$12,000	$ 25,072
Faith Promise Pledge Receipts	$12,426	$101,656
Total	$24,426	$126,728

While our attendance grew by 65 percent over this period, our missions giving from these two sources increased by more than 419 percent — more than six times faster. God has provided remarkably because of disproportionate growth in our missions giving. We firmly believe this result can be achieved wherever the faith promise approach is consistently utilized.[2] But other reproducible steps we have taken have yielded even greater financial results for our missions ministry.

Ministry Resource Network

It became apparent as the work in former Yugoslavia progressed, that long-term commitments to Bosnia would be made by some of our members. We knew that our church could not provide for 100 percent of the support needs of a large ongoing mission team. We therefore committed to 20-25 percent of the total support required for each long-term team member. The balance of the support need had to be raised by individual team members elsewhere. Much of the additional funding our long-term workers required came from individuals and families in our church who made commitments to support missionaries in Bosnia with personal contribution **over and above** their tithes and faith promise pledges to our church. You can begin to see how generously our members have learned to give in this process!

In any case, we knew that some portion of the support long-term team members required would be given by individuals and churches outside our own local assembly. We started a separate 501 (c) (3) corporate entity alongside the church to facilitate those gifts. Calling this de facto mission agency, Ministry Resource Network, Inc. (MRN), we effectively made it far easier (in a psychological sense) for members of other assemblies, and even other churches, to give to this effort. Whereas few local churches (especially those outside our denomination) would be inclined to give to NCC directly, they feel perfectly comfortable giving to MRN as a separate mission organization.

What has been the result of MRN's support raising efforts to date? The following numbers give some comparative insight. (Please note that the numbers for 1993 are the result of efforts for only part of the year since we started the organization in the late spring.)

	1993	1994	1995	1996	1997
Total MRN Receipts	$110,208	$196,310	$291,503	$389,896	$377,604

Comparing 1997 missions-giving from budget allocations and faith promise pledge receipts, to 1997 income channeled through MRN, it is apparent how significant the impact of this extra-church corporate umbrella has been. In 1997 alone, MRN accounted for receipts nearly three times larger than our church-based missions giving. This multiplier would have been even higher if we had not "spun off" a ministry which began under our church's auspices as yet another, separate corporate entity. That new organization, Family Resource Network, would have added another $250,667 to the total funds passing through our hands in 1997, an increase of 51 percent over the prior year. From our perspective, these funds channeled through MRN represent more manna from heaven. But the key point for the reader to grasp is that this kind of vehicle is within easy reach of any local church willing to organize formally to facilitate mobilization for missions and local outreach. Even small congregations can do this! Combining missions funding, MRN receipts and local benevolences, our church is giving approximately $700,000 per year to other organizations or individuals. This represented nearly 60 percent of our total annual income in 1997! Having been so richly blessed by God financially, it is a delight to be able to bless others, giving away more than we keep each year!

Generous Partners Born From Networking

One final example of God's special provision came as a result of relationships built over years of networking. This effort will again demonstrate God's ability to be our provider. It is interesting to note that the English word "provide" comes from Latin roots. It stems from the prefix "pro" meaning before and the root "vide" meaning to see. Therefore, when we declare that God is our "provider" we are saying that He is the one who sees before the need arises — and moves to meet it. As He had done with our need for a building, so He would do with regard to needs for humanitarian relief in Bosnia.

At the height of the conflict in Bosnia, just before the war took a military turn in favor of the Bosnian-Croat Federation in the summer of 1995, I was speaking on the subject of church-based missions at an Advancing Churches in Missions Commitment (ACMC) conference in Chicago. As I shared some of the stories that are found in this present work, a representative approached me from World Relief. Connie Fairchild was a development officer for this organization with which we had worked over the years in sponsoring refugees to the United States. We had "partnered" with World Relief in aiding Romanians, Russians, and most recently Bosnians, in their transition to American culture.

She proposed that NCC and World Relief consider working together to provide humanitarian aid for Bosnia. There certainly was a great need for this kind of help, and by 1995 we had long been involved in helping to distribute aid in conjunction with church planting efforts in Bosnia. But we had also determined early in our wartime ministry that providing aid for millions of needy people was far beyond the capacity of a small church effort like ours. We were clearly not in the "aid business" and for good reasons we had left that work to mega-churches in the West and to specialized agencies like World Relief.

Connie accepted my explanation for declining her suggestion. But she also invited me to call later if I changed my mind. I would never have expected the events that would transpire over the weekend to bring us together again as partners for relief by the next Monday.

On Saturday morning, American press sources were reporting the fall of two UN "safe areas" in eastern Bosnia. The supposedly protected cities of Srebinica and Zepa, were left unprotected by the UN forces and were overrun by ethnic Serb armies. After securing the cities, the Serbs savagely executed thousands of Bosnian men. Other Muslim citizens by the tens of thousands fled for their lives, taking refuge over the weekend in a hastily prepared refugee center at the Tuzla airport. One of the churches we were helping to develop in Bosnia was in Tuzla. That church found itself overwhelmed as its small membership tried to respond to incredibly pressing humanitarian needs.

When I came to the church on Sunday morning, a fax message from Tuzla was awaiting me. Our friends in Bosnia were urgently appealing for help. Suddenly a genuine desire to be directly involved in humanitarian aid had come to the forefront of our thinking. Because of the sheer magnitude of need facing the local church and government authorities in Tuzla, our elders decided to contact Connie Fairchild first thing on Monday morning. Because she and her colleagues had experience that we lacked, we deferred totally to their sense of what might constitute an appropriate response.

World Relief suggested that together with their help, we should direct $20,000 toward the need in Tuzla. When we offered as a local church to contribute that much ourselves, World Relief unhesitatingly agreed to match our donation! Our denomination's aid agency, the Evangelical Free Church Mission Compassion Ministry, immediately added $5,000 more to this total. (Eventually, our denomination would add tens of thousands of additional relief funds to our ongoing effort in meeting the staggering needs of Bosnia's people). Hastily transferring funds to the proper accounts and scheduling air travel, leaders from our church hand-carried $45,000 to the Tuzla church before the week was out. For us, for the Tuzla church, and for the needy refugees gathered at the airport, this money was nothing short of more manna from heaven. We believe this aid helped many Muslims see God's love as supplies were distributed in the name of Jesus through the efforts of Christian workers from the church in Tuzla.

Not the End of the Story

God has truly performed miracle after miracle inspiring our awe and wonder as He has provided for our ministry in Bosnia. It is His faithfulness in supplying our needs that I want to emphasize here. These testimonies speak more about God using other people than they do about NCC. They affirm the obedience and generosity of men like David Rocker, the *JESUS* film Project leaders, and organizations like the Evangelical Free Church Mission Compassion Ministry and World Relief. They also illustrate the principle that God can link resources with kingdom needs through anyone He chooses.

Accounts like these are not unique to our church. Similar delightful experiences are typical wherever churches, agencies and individuals are trusting God for more provision than the natural eye can see. But such delights come only to those who believe that it is not presumption to trust God for provision.

I hope our experiences will encourage you to begin writing your own story of faith in God's ability to provide in Ephesians 3:20 fashion. After all, blessing others through His body has been God's expressed intention since the days of Abraham. And supplying manna from heaven has been our Father's heart since Moses led Israel into the wilderness. We should not be surprised to find that God wants to use us in similar ways today. Why not pray for God to make you, your family, your church or your favorite mission or service agency a channel through which His grace can be made manifest to others? If you will do your part, God will meet you along the way. He can be trusted to give what you need in order for His will to be done. Certainly we have seen Him demonstrate a modern day ability to provide manna from heaven. We believe that there is plenty of manna to go around. There always has been!

6

Tag-Team Evangelism

So then neither the one who plants nor the one who waters is anything, but God who causes the growth. Now he who plants and he who waters are one; but each will receive his own reward according to his own labor. For we are God's fellow-workers....
I Cor. 3:7-9

David Lively and the Gasinci base team were on station in Croatia ready to receive our first short-term team by mid-October 1992. At home in Atlanta, we were like school children waiting for the recess bell to ring. Every effort was being made to stay on task, to attend to business as usual and to maintain an air of normalcy, but these were not normal days. Our entire church could sense that God was doing an extraordinary thing in our midst. Recruiting for the twelve short-term teams was going well, and the first two were already full. Even staffing these teams had proven to involve a move of God's Spirit.

Intercessors First!

By now, our church family had been praying for Bosnia and Sarajevo for nearly two full years. None had so faithfully prayed as the group of early morning intercessors that met daily in our offices. These dear and dedicated folks gathered most weekdays at 5:30 a.m. to pray for a myriad of needs.

As the story of Fio Weaver's involvement in Gasinci demonstrates, they not only prayed heartily, but they listened to God as well. Knowing how sensitive these people were to God's Spirit, I was not surprised that they were keen to keep the base team and the entire Gasinci project before the Lord. This group included some of the older and more mature of the believers among us. They had always demonstrated the ability to persevere in matters of prayer. But I was surprised when they asked to speak to me about the first team going to Gasinci.

These folks came humbly with a sense that they had heard a clear word from the Lord. It seemed to them that God was indicating His certain direction that some of these intercessors should be on the first team going to the camp. More pointedly, they sensed the Spirit was indicating that they were to go on the first team for the express purpose of breaking up the fallow ground in Gasinci through prayer. If they were allowed to go as our initial short-term team, they believed God had clearly shown them that they would see no fruit in evangelism. But if they did not go first and do this work, they believed God had been equally clear that no one who followed the first team would see evangelistic fruit either. Intercession was to be the key to fruitful evangelism.

How powerfully their appeal hit our elders. These were not overeager and idealistic youngsters who wanted to be first in line. These were the gray heads among us who consistently gave to everyone in prayer, never asking anything for themselves. They didn't really feel up to the rigors of the trip, and would have deferred, were it not for the Lord directing them to go. So the first team was filled with "ringers" — not a random cross section of our congregation. We sent our star players in first. These seasoned prayer warriors took the battle over Gasinci to the heavenlies and spent their two weeks in intercession, in praise and in preparing the way for reinforcements yet to come.

So they went and shared the plight of the refugees, and endured constant sub-freezing temperatures while living in light canvas tents. They were never warm. They served mostly without interpreters, and they prayed from daylight to dark — sometimes 18 hours a day. They pioneered the *JESUS* film, learning the hard way how to control the crowds. They nearly caused a riot in the process! They also devised a map to help those who remained in Atlanta get the lay of the land in Gasinci.

Their map-making effort delighted us all as they christened streets in this Croatian camp with names from downtown Atlanta. The main drag was Peachtree Street with West Peachtree and Spring Street running parallel on each side. These three streets divided the camp longitudinally in thirds. North Avenue was the central street running perpendicular to Peachtree. With this creative approach to orientation, everyone who was familiar with downtown Atlanta felt more familiar with Gasinci. The first team's report to the church family excited everyone.

These dear praying saints had enjoyed the time of their lives in perhaps the worst conditions any of them had ever experienced. They wept with grief over the thought that perhaps they would never again have the privilege of two full weeks filled with night and day intercession. They had blazed the trail effectively and lived to tell the tale. Their report humored us, cheered us and inspired us. And in the end they challenged us as they intentionally dropped a gauntlet that shamed the more timid among us. "At our age," they said, "this was not an easy trip to make. But we would do it again tomorrow if opportunity allowed. We can't go back tomorrow, but you younger folks can. If we can endure these conditions so can you! You need to sign up for your tour of duty in Gasinci today! Now is the time to press the spiritual battle over Bosnia."

If recruiting had not staffed our teams fully to that point, the report of this first group ensured that future teams would not go unmanned. From that day, we never had a team that did not have members signed up in advance to go to Gasinci. The power of prayer had prevailed again. I praise God for our intercessors!

Passing in the Night

The dynamics of these rotating teams were amazing. The cycle went something like this. An inbound group left Atlanta on Friday evening, arriving in Budapest mid-afternoon on Saturday. By the time this group cleared customs and made the long five-hour drive to Gasinci (including an hour or two for the border crossing into Croatia), it was midnight or later before they got to the camp. By this time, most were hungry and bone weary, having gone 30 hours with little or no sleep. Body clocks were out of kilter and jet lag weighed heavily on everyone. Reveille would come late on Sunday morning to announce the start of their first day in Croatia. A light schedule allowed all the "rookies" a leisurely day to grope their way to moderate familiarity with their new surroundings. Then, Sunday evening brought a visit to church services in Osijek (always a highlight) and a first introduction to the student translators from ETS. Monday morning introduced the routine schedule of quiet times, orientation for the day and release to organized ministry efforts.

After eleven days of a vigorous ministry schedule, the outbound team would depart from Gasinci on their second Thursday in Croatia for the long return trip to Budapest. Leaving was always a tearful, drawn-out affair as newfound friends were forced to part. Arriving in Budapest on Thursday night allowed two nights and one full day to rest, recuperate and tour one of the most beautiful cities in the world. Then, on Saturday morning, the outbound team would leave Europe before the next team arrived on the same afternoon. Thus, each inbound team flew by the outbound team without the benefit of hearing the most current news from Gasinci.

Like ships passing in the night, the passengers flying in opposite directions might as well have been in totally different worlds. This lack of communication proved to be a huge blessing to the third team serving our refugees.

The 10 Percent That Never Got the Word

In any army, good communication is a vital priority. Even in the lower echelons, small unit commanders must be sure that everyone in their command "gets the word" when a new order or a change of command is being passed down the line. Communication almost always breaks down somewhere. In the Marine Corps, we used to have a saying, "Don't forget that 10 percent of the troops never get the word."

When team two returned from Gasinci they brought back "a word" that was understandable enough, but one which I wished they had not passed on so broadly to the entire church family. This group had enjoyed a tremendous experience in Gasinci benefitting from greatly increased accessibility to ETS translators. As a result, they developed closer relationships with more seminary students and far deeper relationships with the Bosnians in Gasinci than our first team had. Though they saw no evangelistic fruit, they did return with stories of families which seemed open to the gospel. Genuine efforts to communicate the gospel had been made and awareness of Christ had been deepened in the lives of identifiable Muslims with whom future teams could follow up.

Peter Kuzmic had addressed "team two" and their interpreters at a special dinner just prior to their departure for the states. He spoke in an effort to relieve any disappointment they might have felt over seeing no conversion fruit during their two-week tour of duty. As Milton Coke had done at the very beginning of this process, Dr. Kuzmic explained the centuries old resistance of Bosnia's Muslims to the gospel. His realism was justified as he reassured our team that we had no reason to expect evangelistic fruit so early in this new outreach effort. The sun had already set in

Croatia as this report was being reiterated in Northside's Sunday morning services. Our whole church family had received this "reassuring" perspective from team two's leader. All those who had already been in country, and all those who were yet to go to Gasinci, had heard the report as well. Everyone that is, except those on team three who were in the evening services in Osijek as we were meeting for morning services in Atlanta. Ninety percent of those destined to serve in our "army" in Gasinci had received a clear restatement of Dr. Kuzmic's briefing explaining why we should have limited expectations for early conversions from our efforts. But 10 percent, those on team three, never got the word. That 10 percent were on the field, approaching their mission full of faith and holding high expectations of fruit for their efforts.

From the Church Scattered

Progress reports from the field were routine in those days. We could send faxes from the Bible School in Osijek, and every couple of days David would write us a note or check to see if we had sent something to him or to other members serving on the teams in Gasinci. We developed a traditional communication technique, writing to the "Church Gathered" from the "Church Scattered" or vise versa. Often important events occurred while our brothers and sisters were far from home. The following are examples from my files. They are actually drawn from the third team that went to Gasinci:

> Dearest Bill,
> We had a very peaceful day today. One of the best in ages. I think it has to do with prayer. Please keep praying for us — for me! The children want a time every day for us to think of each other. How's about 6:00 p.m. for you. Isn't that 12:00 noon for us? Confirm. We'll be thinking especially about you then. Happy Birthday, darling. We sang to you today. We'll celebrate with you on your return. Have you looked into tentmaking

chances? Go for it while you can. Your mom called to check on you. Please pray for them. Write soon. I love you so!

Cheryl

Four days later, on a less peaceful day in Cheryl's life, she had to have a secretary in our office relay a telephone message via fax. It was less personal than direct contact, but the communication involved an urgent message for Bill and Cheryl had run out of available time. The message read as follows:

Dear Bill,

This is Lisa Williamson writing for Cheryl. She called and left a message to be faxed to you right away.

God is *so* good and things are going well at home in Atlanta. Everyone here is well.

Remember to look into tentmaking opportunities.

Dan Burton wants you to be prepared to share during the first hour on Sunday. (Tell Martin to be ready, too.) He is going to give you the entire service! So get together and plan!

Your grandmother Edna has passed away. Cheryl wanted to ask you to pray for your parents. She thinks this may be a key time for them.

I am so sorry to hear about your grandmother. May the Lord comfort you during this time! Cheryl sends her love. She misses you!

Lisa Williamson

This little note touches my heart deeply because a similar experience lay ahead for me. Two years later, while I was in Croatia teaching at ETS and visiting Gasinci, my own dear grandmother died at age 94. She and I had been planning her funeral together for two decades. It was an honor to have her ask me to preach in her memorial service, and I so wanted to be there! My twin brother served in my absence. Missions ministry does have non-material costs. Often those in Gasinci, especially the base team members who were in Croatia for an extended period, missed important events in the life of their churches and their families. One more example can be offered by sharing an excerpt from a fax I sent to this third team in November 1992:

> ... The Lawlers and the Betsills both had babies this week. Please pray especially for the Lawlers. Their fifth child, Isaiah, was born on Monday with mild symptoms of Down's Syndrome. His condition will need to be confirmed by genetic tests. The final results won't be back until next week but there is little doubt about the diagnosis. Johnny and Diana are doing great — evidencing much peace of heart and mind even as tears of joy not sorrow are shed. They think this could offer a spiritual breakthrough for Johnny's brother. The Betsill's little girl arrived on Tuesday but she has no name yet.

You can well imagine how much anticipated such letters were on both sides of the Atlantic. The most thrilling fax we ever received came on Monday, November 11, the first full day of ministry effort at the beginning of team three's tour of duty in Gasinci. This team's members all came from East Gate Congregation. Martin Morgan, an evangelist with Campus Crusade for Christ, led them. Martin is one of the most energetic, enthusiastic men I know. He has a winning personality and a warm smile that reflects his tender heart. Having "missed the word" with the rest of his team, Martin fully expected their efforts to yield evangelistic fruit. At about 5:00 p.m. on that Monday (11:00 p.m. Croatia time), the fax machine in our Atlanta offices began to sputter in recognition of an incoming call. I was standing next to the fax machine as paper began to roll out of the bin. The message read as follows:

November 11, 1992

From: The Church Scattered
To: The Church Gathered
Subject: Our First Convert in Gasinci!

Just wanted to report that today we saw the first
Bosnian Convert in Gasinci get born again. He is a young
16-year-old boy named Ilija. Praise the Lord with us and
keep praying!

Martin Morgan

Tears come to my eyes even as I write this report. I remember
the emotions of that moment as I stood weeping, and the short but
momentous message came from the Church Scattered. I was never
so glad to have had 10 percent of our troops not get the word! We
did not respond to let them know what Dr. Kuzmic had said
regarding what our reasonable expectations for winning converts
among the Muslims in Gasinci should be! Left unfettered by the
second team's report, the third team continued to share evangelisti-
cally expecting God to bless their efforts. Ilija proved to be only the
first fruits of this team's labor of love. By Wednesday of their first
week, a Bible study was meeting daily with eight new believers from
Bosnia. By Sunday, 23 new converts met in Bungalow One (which
also served as our movie theater) to share in the first Bosnian church
services in Gasinci. Here, in just our second month of ministry
among the refugees, a spiritual logjam broke. Before the next six
months passed we would see more Muslims come to faith in Jesus
in this one camp than Christian workers had seen in all of Bosnia
over the past fifty years. We praised God for the Church Scattered!

Evangelistic Methods That Work

Dr. Peter Wagner, noted missiologist and heir to the late
Donald MacGavran's leadership over the Church Growth Movement, has articulated seven vital signs of a healthy church. The need
for a local church to employ "evangelistic methods that work" is
among them.[1] He does not prescribe a universal outreach methodology but rather encourages churches to pursue those approaches that
work in their context. We found several effective means of winning
folks to faith in Christ as we labored among refugees in Gasinci.

I have already written about our use of the *JESUS* film. There was usually a standing-room-only crowd on hand when we showed this video in Bungalow One. Contact cards were used to encourage viewers to let us drop by their bungalows to visit and talk more about what they had seen. If those visits did not yield immediate fruit, they usually helped us begin ongoing friendships that could move toward a longer-term effort in **relationship evangelism.**

From time to time, we tried to do something practical to bless the entire camp. During the winter we occasionally bought enough firewood to provide some for everyone in the camp. At other times we would buy fruit for the entire camp — especially citrus fruits which were rarely seen on the camp kitchen table.

We kept a store of reading glasses of varying magnification strengths on hand in an effort to help the elderly refugees. We also tried to serve as a resource for procuring needed prescription medication which was virtually impossible to obtain in wartime Croatia.

In effect, every two weeks we had an opportunity to resupply Gasinci with needed but hard to get items. These efforts allowed us to combine **humanitarian relief** on a small scale with **lifestyle evangelism** as we tried to witness with our works of grace as well as with words of truth. A number of elderly refugees accepted Christ as a result.

Some of the Bosnians had been prepared to receive the gospel before they came to Gasinci. Through **dreams and visions** and visitations of Jesus "in the Spirit" some hearts were made ready to be born again, waiting for a contact with our team like ripe fruit waiting to drop from a tree. Such are common occurrences in recent years as Christians report on efforts to share the gospel throughout the Muslim world. We used to pray for such divine interventions regularly. Doing so on one occasion with Edin, a new 9 year-old Bosnian convert, led to the salvation of others in his "kucica" or little house. Edin was unusually bright, spoke reasonably good English and enjoyed visiting with our teams though our field tent accommodations were considerably colder than the former barracks building his family had been assigned. On one occasion, after hearing us pray for God to inspire dreams and visions among Muslims in Gasinci, this boy said, "In my bungalow there is a woman who had such a dream — maybe we should talk to her!" We were never surprised by such unexpected open doors.

Visiting Edin's small quarters our workers encountered a typical scene. Thrust together by the ill winds of war, eighteen people from several unrelated families now shared a 15' x 20' refuge from the storm. Each family uncomfortably occupied a corner of their common household. Sedeta, a twenty-something housewife had fled Bosnia with her husband who was medically exempted from service in the army. Several from our team entered the bungalow and, with Edin's help, told of their interest in her dreams. She hesitated to share her story with us as a number of her "roommates" drew nearer to satisfy their curiosity over our special interest in Sedeta's story. They had heard her express wonder before over the night vision that now intrigued us.

Overcoming her timidity, she haltingly agreed to recount her tale. In her dream, she was in her village walking past the Orthodox Cathedral that had been a friendly and familiar fixture in her childhood. This building also played a central role in the faith of Serbian playmates in those youthful years. As she walked past the chapel in her dream, however, the security this scene would once have provoked gave way to a sense of deathly dread. Ethnic cleansing had forced her flight from her childhood home and had turned life-long Serb neighbors into lethal enemies. In the dream, Sedeta quickened her steps and hid her face in the hood of her long coat hoping to pass the cathedral without incident.

But she had not escaped notice! Suddenly a horse came galloping from the churchyard to block her progress along the path. The nervous hooves of the large brown horse filled her field of vision as she kept her eyes downcast. Paralyzed by the intrusion of this imposing animal and its silent rider she was too frightened to run and too confused to speak. Slowly she raised her eyes to see the imposing image of a bearded man with white flaming robes. His eyes were clear and his bearing was confident.

Without a word being exchanged between them, Sedeta formulated a series of conflicting impressions from this towering spectacle. The rider's countenance alone conveyed an unmistakable air of majesty mixed with mercy. She could sense his power and yet felt somehow secure from harm because of the peace his eyes communicated. His strong arm raised a sword that she knew was meant to guard rather than to wound. The image was still vivid in her mind as she described the panic of the moment melting into peace. This man, she knew, meant her no harm. He wanted to protect her. He wanted her to know that hope and not hostility was his offering from this lonely village church. She awoke surprised yet serene and now full of a different kind of fear than she had known in the war. No sense of panic remained in her heart. Now she was overcome with a sense of reverence and awe. Since that time she had continually wondered, "Who was this man of peace that had visited her in the night?"

Our team delighted in sharing how Joshua, too, had been visited by a man with a sword, before Jericho was given into his hand. In Joshua 5:13-15 that "man of peace" was the captain of the host of the Lord who had come to call Moses' replacement to reverential fear. That event was used to reveal to Joshua that he had come to holy ground, to a place where he could meet with God. So too, had Sedeta's visitor intended to point her heart to a holy place in the midst of war, a place where she could meet the Lord.

With the group gathered around the center of this refugee bungalow, Sedeta, her friends and family first heard the good news about Jesus Christ. Having had her heart prepared for the word of God by her dream, Sedeta now eagerly opened her heart to the Prince of Peace. She prayed to receive Jesus as her savior with her countrymen looking on.

This new sister in Christ soon left Gasinci with other refugees seeking new beginnings elsewhere in Europe. We could not keep up with every convert who was moved out of our reach during these dark days of war. We rested though, in the promise of Philippians 1:6, "For I am confident of this very thing, that He who began a good work in you will perfect it until the day of Christ Jesus."

Sedeta's personal encounter with God had begun before we had the privilege of sharing the gospel with her in Gasinci. We were confident that her journey with Jesus would continue as she made her way onward in the company of her husband and under the protection of her newfound Lord. Like Philip with the Ethiopian eunuch in Acts 8, we had been privileged to lead this precious woman to a saving relationship with Jesus Christ. He now had plans for her that did not include us. We praised God greatly for His answers to our prayers as we said good-bye to Sedeta.

We were also able to do "**cold turkey**" evangelism with the invaluable help of students from ETS. The presence of Americans in Gasinci was an ongoing curiosity to the Bosnians. As we met new friends on the play fields, while walking on Peachtree Street, and in the restrooms (how much we all hated those "squatty potties"), they invariably would ask why we were there. "This horrible war has forced me from my home. I came here hoping to stay alive in this war, waiting to find a better place to begin again. I have no choice but to live in Gasinci. But why would an American come here?" What a great opening that question proved to be as we sought to share the love of Christ, our own love, and the message of the gospel! We were thankful for a wide variety of methods by which we could share the gospel with refugees. But two other methods of evangelism proved especially unique to this setting. Both were remarkably effective!

Tag-Team Evangelism

The limited two-week time frame our teams had to work within often allowed short term workers to develop relationships that brought Bosnians close to accepting the gospel but not to a firm commitment of faith. Departure days were for this reason often dreaded. Leaving Gasinci under those circumstances made going home especially painful for many. But we soon discovered that the departure of one team did not have to end focused evangelistic efforts directed toward specific individuals or families.

If team three, for example, saw Admir come close to salvation, team four would not necessarily be aware or find opportunity to follow up on him since they didn't hear team three's report. But when team five and subsequent teams came to Gasinci, they would come with letters and gifts to Admir from the members of team three who had begun witnessing to him. Often, the credibility and friendship earned by one team inured to the benefit of the teams that followed bringing more news and gifts from American friends who had already gone back home. Hearing fresh reports every two weeks allowed those of us in Atlanta to keep up with the "continuing saga of Admir's search for faith." Sometimes it was the third or fourth or fifth team in a sequence that would get to harvest the fruit previous teams had planted and watered. We learned the joys of laboring in a spirit of unity with cooperation, implementing this tag team approach to soul winning. As Paul describes in I Cor 3:7-9, we were truly one and all "God's fellow workers in the gospel." Some were planting, some were watering and others had the joy of harvesting. But everyone acknowledged that God was the One who caused the growth. The second evangelistic method unique to Gasinci offers a humorous demonstration of God's dedication to seeing lost people come to faith.

Accidental Evangelism

On one occasion in December of 1992, two team members from Atlanta were trying to fulfill their "tag team" responsibilities by delivering mail and gifts to Bungalow 33. These men were helped along the way by a Slovenian student from ETS. The student, Klemen, was himself only six months old in the Lord, but his English was outstanding. Their search was made more difficult as these three groped their way in the darkness of night hindered by a heavy snowfall. Under the circumstances, they were simply unable to locate Bungalow 33.

Impatient and eager to put their hand to the "evangelistic plow," the two Americans became frustrated with their winter night's wandering. Klemen suggested that they seek God's help in finding the elusive bungalow. So they stopped and prayed in the midst of the falling snow. The door of the closest bungalow opened as they prayed. In the light splashing from the open building, they could see the number "32" next to the doorway.

The Americans immediately thought the old woman in the doorway might help them locate the next building in numerical sequence. They urged Klemen to ask her if she knew where Bungalow 33 was to be found. In his Slovenian dialect, Klemen obediently inquired, and as the woman responded, a look of amazement came over his face as she spoke in her slightly different Bosnian dialect. "Gentleman," the student said with excitement, "this woman said, 'I don't know God!'"

Committed evangelists that our team members were, the Americans urged Klemen to tell the woman that they had come to Gasinci just to tell her about God. Dutifully, Klemen used his Slovenian dialect to translate this message. Much to everyone's surprise, the woman reared back with a giant horselaugh revealing a mouth with many missing teeth and lungs filled with smoke from the unfiltered cigarette in her hand. Laughing and sputtering, she recovered from her fit of laughter and spoke again, more slowly this time in her Bosnian dialect. Klemen, understanding better now the intent of her words, erupted into laughter of his own and then spoke to the Americans to let them in on the joke. "Gentlemen," he said, "I made a mistake. This woman did not say, 'I don't know God.' She said, 'God, I don't know (where bungalow 33 is).'" Now everyone was laughing! And in the merriment of the moment, Kadira extended the ever-hospitable Bosnian courtesy of inviting the men in for Turkish coffee.

Our team members accepted the invitation. Over the course of several hours of conversation, they were able to share more with this family about Jesus. Kadira was a lifelong Muslim from Sarajevo. Her middle-aged daughter, Asima, was an atheist, married to a communist who was still fighting in Bosnia. Asima's two sons, Damir, age 15, and Dario, age 10, were with them in Gasinci. Speaking of the spiritual purpose for their being in Croatia, the Americans explained their desire to help Bosnians learn more about God's love and the possibility of having a personal relationship with Him through Jesus Christ.

Asima mused about her desire to know if God really existed. She described her anguished heart worrying night and day about her husband. Was he safe? Was he even alive? For months since coming to the camp they had received no word from him. She also told of watching her eldest son, Damir, trying to pray for his father just the night before. He had come in late after everyone was asleep. Thinking he was alone in the darkness, he knelt and put his face on the floor as Muslims are taught to do. Then, as if not satisfied, he raised his head from the floor, and still kneeling, he crossed himself and folded his hands as Catholics are taught to do. In desperation, he had begun to beat on his chest and cry! The truth was, Damir **did not know God** and neither did Asima.

Our team members, with Klemen's able assistance, shared the way of salvation with this family. That night Asima and Damir prayed to receive Jesus as their Lord and Savior. They also prayed for Asima's husband, asking God to move him to contact his family. In direct answer to that prayer, Asima was called to the camp commander's office the very next day. She had received a phone call from Sarajevo — it was her husband! He was safe!

Amazed at the answer to prayer, Dario also gave his life to the Lord. But Kadira, the committed Muslim matriarch, would not budge as she considered the claims of Christ. Not, that is, until the time came for her new and now dear American friends to leave Gasinci. As the van was loading with its downhearted passengers trying to cope with the mixed emotions of wanting to stay but needing to go home, Kadira came running toward them frantically waving her hands.

She was out of breath but eager to speak her piece. So much had changed in her family over these two weeks. They were all reading their Bibles and praying. New songs of praise to God were being sung in her home. Prayers were being answered. Most of all, Asima who had been bound in desperation and worry for months since they had left Sarajevo, was somehow now experiencing perfect peace and joy. God was alive in her household. His presence was tangible in the heart of her daughter and her grandsons. Could she too pray to have this Jesus save her? What a thrilling end this was for the Christmas team's visit to Gasinci!

These three generations of Bosnians are just one example of dozens who came to Christ through what we came to call "**accidental evangelism**." Asima was to become a vocal and committed leader among the converts in Gasinci. She was never too timid to speak in defense of our work or to insist on our rights to remain in the camp sharing the claims of Christ with other refugees. She served on the camp counsel as a representative for the refugee population. In effect, she became a modern day Lydia for us, a woman of excellence in the Lord. The next spring, Asima and Dario were the first Muslims willing to follow Christ in water baptism, the boldest public testimony a new convert could offer regarding their identity in Christ. For much of the war years, this family resided in Northern England maintaining their commitment to the Lord. In June 1998, they returned to Sarajevo where they have joined us in efforts to plant a new church.

7

Paris, Beirut and Antioch

And when the news about them reached the ears of the church ... they sent Barnabus off to Antioch....

Acts 11:22

It was not the best of times; it was the worst of times. It was not the age of wisdom; it was the age of foolishness. It was not the epoch of belief; it was the epoch of incredulity. It was not the season of light; it was the season of darkness. It was not the spring of hope; it was the winter of despair. It was December of 1992, and Asima and her family were celebrating the birth of the Lord Jesus Christ in Gasinci, Croatia. This was their first Christmas away from their beloved Bosnia and their first Christmas as born-again believers.

They were in a place of relative safety. The United Nations and the Croatian government were providing their most basic personal needs. Further to the south, where their wartime nightmare had begun, things were neither so calm nor so secure. Sarajevo was under siege. Ethnic cleansing continued unchecked in spite of the good intentions of UNPROFOR troops sprinkled like salt across Bosnia's battered landscape. Reports of mass rape, concentration camps, war crimes and genocide had begun to flood the media outlets of the world. Diplomatic leaders around the globe seemed at a loss for solutions to the conflict. It appeared that the combined military powers of the earth could not force a sustained cease-fire between ethnic Serbs and the Muslim-Croatian Federation that opposed them.

While Cyrus Vance and Lord David Owen directed policy debates in Geneva, people were dying all across Bosnia, if not ravaged by the wounds of war then savaged by the winds of winter. The world-class snowfalls that had brought the world to Sarajevo for the 1984 Winter Olympics were now the indiscriminate enemies of soldiers and civilians on both sides of this conflict. No one outside Bosnia knew what to do. No one inside Bosnia knew where to turn. The icy cold breath of winter was adding its toll to the body count in Bosnia.

Under these horrific conditions, governments could excuse inaction and delay. But the people of God could not so easily stand by and watch, content merely to wait and see who would intervene. The words of Proverbs 24:11-12 spoke too clearly to the duty of Christians to respond:

> Deliver those who are being taken away to death,
> And those who are staggering to slaughter,
> Oh hold them back.
> If you say, "See, we did not know this,"
> Does He not consider it who weighs the hearts?
> And does He not know it who keeps your soul?
> And will He not render to man according to His work?

So it was that the mandate of Scripture and motives of Christian love compelled believers in England to respond to the situation in Bosnia. Representatives from Spring Harvest, a British-based Christian teaching and conference ministry had come to Bosnia in the winter of 1992 to investigate possibilities for their direct involvement in the war relief effort. Spring Harvest holds its conference in various UK cities every spring, calling as many as 80,000 young Christians each year to a deeper commitment to Christ. The team visiting Bosnia was searching for a project toward which these young people could direct their prayers and their gifts.

A Vision Takes Shape

The Spring Harvest delegation was led by Paul Brooks. He and three other British leaders met with Croatian Protestant leaders in late 1992 to discuss possibilities for Spring Harvest's commitment. During four days of deliberations they became acquainted with two key pastors from the Baptist Union. Stevo Dereta, an ethnic Serb, was married to a Croatian national and ministered in the Baptist church in Rijeka, on the Adriatic coast. Peter MacKenzie was a British missionary who had served in former Yugoslavia for seventeen years. He was also married to a Croatian national and resided in Zagreb. Peter served as a pastor of the largest Baptist church in Croatia. His teaching ministry allowed him to reach routinely across denominational boundaries that normally separated Baptists, Pentecostals and other minority Protestant communities. His missionary zeal extended his influence beyond his own church. Peter had guided me into Romania two years earlier. Now, with Stevo, he would give direction to his fellow countrymen.

These pastors proved invaluable to the Spring Harvest leaders. They both were directly involved with the Baptist Union's humanitarian relief organization Moj Bliznji (My Neighbor). Peter also had ties to the Evangelical Church's Pentecostal aid ministry, Agape. These two relief agencies immediately provided vehicles through which British Christians could deliver both money and material supplies to needy people in the name of Jesus. They were already established and functioning. Their credibility and capacity to perform effectively had been demonstrated by their substantial involvement with World Vision, Samaritan's Purse and other internationally renowned Christian aid organizations.

In October 1992, just a few weeks prior to the meeting with Spring Harvest leaders, Stevo and Peter had braved the dangers of war to evacuate the last pastor and his family from Sarajevo. With the removal of that Baptist pastor from the capital city there remained no known churches in all of Bosnia. The church had in effect become another casualty of the war. The church was dead in

Bosnia, though some of its members lived on in exile or in hiding. Stevo and Peter's rescue mission to Sarajevo had taken them through other cities which, though less known to the world, were suffering on a scale that surpassed the massive pain of Bosnia's capital. Mostar had weighed particularly heavy on their hearts. Now they had a chance to encourage help from the West as Paul Brooks and his colleagues expressed interest in this city in Bosnia-Herzegovina.

The Paris of the Balkans

Prior to the war, Mostar was a city of 120,000 people that enjoyed a reputation for exquisite beauty. Nestled among the modern development of businesses and high-rise apartments was a beautiful old city center. This citadel of gentle stone and eager hospitality was an architectural treasure chest. Hundreds of personal residences, open air restaurants and artisan's shops preserved the unmistakable influence of the Ottoman Empire. Many of these ancient structures seemed hewn from the steep sides of the Neretva River canyon that divided the city. With windows and patios overlooking the emerald green river below, this section of the city was a tourist's delight. The aroma of Turkish coffee filled the air. Tables filled with roasted meats and vegetables invited hungry travelers to rest and eat. The bargaining tradesmen in their private shops lured lovers of hand-crafted art to a limitless supply of paintings, woodwork and intricate pewter and copper souvenirs.

The city was peaceful and prosperous, unencumbered by Tito's unusual brand of communism. Immune as well, it seemed, from the history of earlier Balkan wars, Mostar had been a place of tolerance, trust and ethnic harmony, a pleasant stopover for Catholic pilgrims flocking by the millions to nearby Mejorgoria. What Mostar provided in terms of sights to see and amenities for travelers, it equaled in picturesque appeal. Neatly formed to fill a valley surrounded by mountains on all sides, the city had a delicate beauty that was apparent to all who visited. The Neretva River lay deep in its gorge crossed by seven bridges. The most famous, the Stari Most (Old Bridge), had given the city its name.

This bridge had survived four centuries of international wars, hostile invasions and intermittent earthquakes. It had also supported the footfalls of multiplied millions of tourists. The single span arch that set the bridge apart from others crossing the Neretva was made of stone held together at its original construction in 1566 by mortar made from eggs and goats' hair. The Stari Most was so uniquely beautiful that no visitor could ignore its central place among the city's architectural attractions. Its presence was as recognizable and as important to this "Paris of the Balkans" as the Eiffel Tower or the Statue of Liberty are to their cities. Mostar had been known as the city of a million postcards and the Stari Most bridge graced many of them. Now the bridge was gone, as were the Ottoman splendor and certainly the peace.

The Beirut of Bosnia

Historians will no doubt attach great significance to the destruction of the Stari Most bridge. It was the last of Mostar's seven bridges to fall. Its destruction was not an indiscriminate act of war. Neither was it a strategic target for the Serb forces occupying the high ground around Mostar. The Stari Most bridge was destroyed to make a point. The famous arched bridge was blown up to dramatize the separation between the ethnic Croats on the west bank of the Neretva and the Muslims on the east side. It had fallen not under enemy artillery fire or aerial attack but from the cannon and mortar assault of residents within the city. Once joined in a strategic alliance to defend Mostar from Serbian aggression, the Croats and Muslims had somehow turned their guns on one another. The mayhem of death under the relentless hail of mortar shells from the Serb-held high ground had barely subsided when neighbor turned against neighbor in the killing fields of the valley floor. It was as if the ethnic hatred of Serb soldiers outside the city had spread like a virus to infect the hearts of allies trying to hold the city from within.

Close friends became bitter enemies, venting their hatred at close range across the narrow river gorge and at times hand to hand. Six months of such provocation from all sides eventually led to a dramatic display of the depths of ethnic animosity — the destruction of the Stari Most bridge.

By this time, the old town had been completely destroyed. Nearby office buildings and the most modern high-rise residential structures were reduced to twisted skeletons of melted metal girders. The citizens of Mostar had effectively made the city a victim of their unmitigated malice. They murdered their city with their own hands. Unable to annihilate each other completely, they hurled furious insults at one another across the river gorge. The Croats offered the ultimate affront by destroying this irreplaceable symbolic link between the east and west banks of the Neretva. The ancient bridge between Mostar's two cultures, between its two world-views, between its two faiths was no more. Croats and Muslims thus declared in deed what could not be stated adequately in words. They preferred to decimate even their dearest treasures rather than share them with each other again.

As stones from the Stari Most fell into the Neretva and began to wash downstream, it seemed that any hope of restored peace collapsed with the bridge. Fighting within the city between Croat and Muslim residents proved hotter and more costly in lives than conflict with Serbs all throughout the war. This vitriolic violence spilled out like lava from an erupting volcano and flowed wherever it found a path.

UN peacekeepers, foreign diplomats and eventually NATO troops themselves would come under attack by Mostar's townsmen. In August 1993, hundreds of angry residents even mobbed humanitarian workers bringing a UN convoy relief supplies into the city. Mostar had become the Beirut of the Balkans. Even to this day, ethnic cleansing continues and the tension is palpable though peace has been a technical reality for over a year. IFOR and SFOR troops have been impotent as they watch violations of the Dayton Accord continue. Croats on the west side of the city continue daily to force Muslims from their homes and businesses into decimated hovels in the Islamic enclave on the east bank. Nowhere in Bosnia was hatred held with any greater intensity than in Mostar during the war. Nowhere does it hang on more stubbornly The animosity that still prevails in Mostar had been tangible to Stevo and Peter as they passed through the city on their mission of mercy in October 1992.

Who Will Go for Us?

When these two pastors returned from Sarajevo they grieved as they thought of their role in removing the last church leader from Bosnian soil. In the face of this kind of ingrained ethnic hatred they both knew that only God could salvage a civilized way of life from the ruins of the war. They were also completely convinced that only the church of Jesus Christ could be an effective broker of the supernatural forgiveness required to restore order. As Stevo said, "People must find a new power (for their lives), the power to forgive. Reconciliation won't work as long as it remains a theory. People need to see it, to give it arms and legs. We believe that this time is like a crucible for the church: when we must choose to play our part or not."[1]

As Protestants, these two pastors and the Christian communities they represented were uniquely suited to lead the way. "Protestants had always been a tiny majority in Yugoslavia, and the Baptists were a smaller group still. Their great strength was that they stood apart by definition from the three monolithic faiths of the region: Roman Catholicism, Islam and Orthodoxy. With no vested interests in the success of any one of the main religious power groups, [Protestant leaders were] free to respond to human need openly and without prejudice. Their churches had never been aligned to any one nationality, and usually reflected a complex pattern of membership with many mixed marriages."[2]

Soon after returning to Northern Croatia, Stevo and Peter began to accumulate relief supplies for beleaguered Bosnians. They secured western European funding for a ten-ton delivery truck and needed only to find a trustworthy man to serve as a driver. But who would go to Bosnia for them? Peter contacted a single man for help, an experienced driver and well-known Christian among the Protestants in Zagreb.

Years before, Nikola Skrinjaric had been divorced while still dabbling in the occult. He had gained a reputation as a spiritualist effecting supernatural healings and performing water divination for a fee. With his own "clinic," the practice of new age diagnostics and healing arts had become a considerable source of income for him. Nonetheless, an inner emptiness had prompted Nikola to keep searching for truth until he heard the gospel at an evangelistic meeting run by a Catholic priest in Zagreb. There, as he heard the words of Jesus from John 14:26, Nikola responded by praying that God would forgive his sins and grant him the grace of salvation by faith in Christ. His prayer to God was put simply, "From now on, you will be *my* way, *my* truth and *my* life."[3]

Nikola had been a believer for seven years before he was recruited to drive relief supplies into the war in Bosnia. He was reluctant when first asked to assume this responsibility. Eventually, though, he was compelled by God's Spirit to surrender his life and his driver's license to the service of the kingdom. In December 1992, Nikola made his first delivery to Mostar, transporting a consignment of heating stoves to the freezing citizens of the city. The long distance trip was made more arduous by frequent military checkpoint crossings, sniper fire and the threat of mortar attacks. The dangers he faced became more intense as he neared the city. The closer he got to his destination, the more mortar shells and intermittent gunfire seemed to be directed at his truck. But God protected Nikola, and he arrived in Mostar appropriately enough on Christmas day. The risks he took proved worthwhile when he saw firsthand the great needs of the people in the city. Nikola spent six days in Mostar on that first trip. During that visit he found his perspective radically changed by his face-to-face exposure to the people's desperate need.

Nikola was especially grieved to see that there was no church in Mostar to serve those suffering from the misery of war. He was convinced that alongside the provision of humanitarian aid, there had to be some form of gathering that could express the life of Christ within a community of believers. Nikola was not confused about his role in bringing relief to the city. But he strangely felt his priority shifting from distributing aid to sharing the gospel. He determined that his first commitment should be to evangelism. He felt invigorated by the hope of building, person by person, the living church of Jesus in Mostar.

Driving in on Christmas day, Nikola had approached the city in fear and trembling. As he left on New Years Day, his heart felt strangely full of hope and love. He came as a short-term truck driver bringing practical relief. He returned home driven to respond to the long-term spiritual needs of the people he had met. He arrived as an aid worker, but discovered in his practical service to the city that the need for spiritual relief exceeded the need for humanitarian relief. When he was nearing Mostar, Nikola had thought only of danger and the potential for loss. Now he reflected on his Christian duty and the potential for the joy of Christ coming to the city.

As he made his way back, God's Spirit increasingly convinced Nikola that he should return to Mostar soon. But he would not go back as a visiting relief truck driver. He felt clearly led of the Lord to relocate to the city, to dig into the lives of lost people there, to make a difference for Christ in the midst of all the hatred. Nikola wanted to see the light of Jesus shining in the midst of darkness in the Beirut of Bosnia. He looked forward to his return to Mostar, but he would not return alone.

A Suitable Helper

Stevo and Peter would never have anticipated such a radical decision on Nikola's part stemming from a single trip into Bosnia. Their surprise was completely over-shadowed however, by that of Sandra Baljkas, Nikola's fiancée. She had blessed his service in

Bosnia knowing that it flowed more from the depths of conviction than from daredevil courage. God was clearly drawing Nikola to serve as His "delivery man" to Bosnia's war-weary people. He was called, she believed, to spread goodwill and the gospel during occasional short-term relief forays into the war. She had never anticipated his being called there as God's primary ambassador of peace!

But such was the news upon Nikola's return. Sandra was somehow serene and unshaken as Nikola opened his heart to share his burden. She had been raised in a traditional Catholic family and, like Nikola, had come to saving faith in Christ in a Catholic evangelistic meeting in Zagreb. The charismatic influence of the presiding priest had led to Sandra's conversion from a "family religion" to a genuine personal faith in Jesus. Her experience in being filled with the Spirit of God had deepened her spiritual desire and her intimacy with the Father. God's love born in her heart had prompted an overflow of compassion for others from the time of her conversion.

Her earliest spiritual impressions were focused on reports of Mother Theresa and her Sisters of Charity. Looking to their model of self-denial and service, Sandra had often considered such a choice for herself during her fellowship in the Catholic Church. She had worked occasionally with nuns in the order as they served the poor in Zagreb. After her conversion, she had prayed steadily for God to fulfill her sense of call to sacrificial service of those in need. Her sense was that becoming a born again believer had only deepened her desire to minister to the least of these (Matt. 25:45). She believed wholeheartedly that, in God's time, she would find a place "somewhere out there, somewhere where God wants me, and where the needs are greatest."[4]

Eleven years Nikola's junior, a two-year courtship had convinced Sandra that God was leading them toward marriage. Nikola was now asking her to confirm his sense of call to ministry by agreeing to begin their life together in Mostar. Would she be willing to follow him into the pressure cooker of war-torn Bosnia? Though she had never anticipated such service was in their future, Nikola's leading seemed to perfectly coincide with the long-term longing of her own heart. If the Lord wanted to call her husband-to-be as His ambassador of love to Mostar, then Mostar was the right place for her as well. Nikola's clear direction somehow confirmed and reinforced Sandra's own. The two, therefore, presented themselves to Stevo and Peter, volunteering for relief ministry and church planting in Mostar.

Spring Harvest Provides the Springboard and a Church Is Born

With Nikola and Sandra's permission, Stevo now encouraged the Spring Harvest delegation to consider supporting them as they made their way toward a new life together in Mostar. These brothers agreed, and since early 1993 British believers have provided a reliable base of financial support for the Skrinjaric family.

Stevo and Peter had removed Bosnia's last pastor from Sarajevo in the fall of 1992. They were confident that rescuing this man and his family was the right thing to do. Still, they shared a deep conviction about the need to re-establish the church in this beleaguered nation. The winter was passing. Spring Harvest was coming to Bosnia, and with it the church would be reborn with their help. Everyone was mightily blessed to have a part in this turn of events.

Nikola returned to continue the relief-work in Mostar in early 1993. He and Sandra were to be married in March but the pressing needs in Bosnia could not wait. In those first few months of ministry Nikola's vision for combining relief work with relational evangelism proved remarkably fruitful. Initial meetings were informal and unpretentious as would be expected when a pastor shares not just the Word of God with his people but the work of his hands as well. Nikola labored alongside his new converts by day rebuilding homes and businesses. By night he began building into their spiritual lives as well. Investing himself without restraint, Nikola realized the dream he envisioned when he first drove out of the city on New Year's Day. Loss was giving way to renewed hope. Clouds of grief were parting and the sunshine of joy began to appear. One man could really make a difference.

One of the early joys to be restored by the Mostar fellowship grew out of Nikola and Sandra's decision to marry in the city that would be their home. Peter MacKenzie joined Sandra for this her first visit to war-torn Bosnia. He had been so integrally involved with the beginnings of the work in Mostar; it was fitting that Peter would serve the new pastor and his wife by performing their marriage ceremony. New converts joined with grateful recipients of relief supplies to expand the numbers of witnesses of this wedding to a happy company of fifty people. This was the first they had seen since the war had begun two years before. Few had ever witnessed a Christian wedding and half were drawn by sheer curiosity. Even strangers wanted to see who in their right minds would choose Mostar as a wedding site.

The witness of Christ's love manifest in this simple marriage ceremony made a deep impression on the church members and the community at large. As they exchanged their vows, the couple made commitments that would forever change their lives. Their promises were reflective of the conversion commitments their neighbors in Mostar had only recently made. The love of God, the protection of mutual submission, and unity born of faith in Christ were taking root in the Mostar Church. This wedding put these spiritual realities on open display. Unsaved acquaintances watched with interest and observed a growing and tangible oneness demonstrated among church members. That depth of love quickly became a "novi most," a new bridge, between the ethnic enemies in Mostar.

Reconciliation achieved in the name of Christ caught the attention of many in the community. The dynamic of newfound faith combined with the dangers of war to bond new believers from Muslim, Croat and Serb backgrounds together. In the unity of newly uttered marriage vows and fresh discoveries of life in Christ, the church was reborn in Bosnia. These first new converts power-fully demonstrated the transformation and healing which Christ can bring to life. They walked in the truth and offered by example their affirmation of Paul's teaching from Ephesians 2:15, Jesus is our peace! When He rules in a heart He puts enmity to death and we learn afresh how to love our enemies. The church seemed to grow spontaneously as the love of Jesus invaded the Neretva River valley. In the presence of such profound darkness shrouding all of Bosnia, the bright light of God's love could not be contained within the city limits of Mostar. It soon glowed like a beacon set on a hill. Others far away were drawn to its brilliant rays of hope and healing.

The Antioch Church

Over the next two years into fall 1994, the Mostar Church continued to expand, its membership eventually exceeding 150 souls. This made the first church born in the midst of Bosnia's war the youngest and one of the largest Protestant fellowships in all of former Yugoslavia. After the first year of ministry, Nikola began to extend his efforts to bring relief and evangelistic work to the Muslim enclave on the east side of the river. He divided his pastoral energies and available time between the east and west sectors of Mostar. The church on the west side of the Neretva grew steadily while humanitarian aid distribution demanded attention in both sectors of the city. It was soon apparent that Nikola could not keep up the responsibilities of the burgeoning church and the relief work alone.

Long-term friends from Zagreb came to help. Karmelo and Ivon Kresonja braved the last days of war by moving into Mostar in early 1994. They quickly emerged as capable leaders, assuming primary pastoral oversight of the West Mostar Church. Nikola was developing a still more expanded vision for multiplying churches. He had successfully completed his own ordination under the Pentecostal Evangelical Church of Croatia, establishing at the same time, a denominational branch serving all of Bosnia-Herzegovina.

Klaus Domke had also come from Germany to reinforce the team responsible for distributing humanitarian aid in Mostar. He would eventually marry a Croat sister from his new church home. Initially, though, he provided substantial assistance with humanitarian aid under Nikola's direction. As Nikola, Klaus and Karmelo were learning to work as a team, a call for urgent help came their way in October 1994.

Come to Tuzla and Help Us!

Seventy-five kilometers northeast of Sarajevo, the Muslim city of Tuzla lay only a short distance from the front lines and the permanent borders of Serbian controlled territory. A steady stream of Muslim refugees flowed from that occupied area throughout the war. Tuzla was effectively cut off from the rest of the world and the situation was critical. Its people were isolated and with the huge influx of refugees, they were starving. Death awaited many if emergency measures were not soon taken to provide practical help.

Nikola and Karmelo felt compelled to attempt bringing relief to this city but needed first to get the lay of the land. They responded immediately, making a perilous journey on treacherous roads that were almost impassable in the winter weather. Once in Tuzla, these brothers discovered workers available to help distribute relief. Local authorities eagerly committed to provide a warehouse, office facilities and even an apartment for humanitarian aid leaders. By telephone they relayed their findings to England, looking to Spring Harvest once again for additional help. This time, however, they were not appealing for support for Mostar. They were crying out on behalf of the tortured people of Tuzla.

In the face of overwhelming need, the newest church in the Balkans was now devising a strategy to give sacrificially in its own support of ministry opportunities beyond its own context. Within weeks, Klaus was dispatched to Tuzla to open a relief office there. But his first priority was evangelistic work and church planting.

His British partners noted Nikola's perspective at the time. Their recollections reflect the apostolic nature of his gifts and his vision. Spring Harvest's leaders reported that Nikola's clear priority was to seize the strategic opportunities that the crisis in Tuzla presented for advancing the church in Bosnia. Evangelism was the primary motivation for going there. Nikola knew that spiritual hunger would be found where physical hunger was so great. The heart of the Lord Jesus was reflected in Nikola's compassion in the face of such dramatic circumstances. His response was both spiritual and practical. "Church or no church, we have a duty to tell the world what is happening in Tuzla, and to do everything we can to keep people from dying this winter."[5] This was an incredibly mature response to an incredibly great burden by a leader with not yet two years of ministry experience to his credit! God's special anointing on Nikola's life was apparent to all around him. He was God's perfect man to stand in the gap for Bosnia.

Mostar had been renowned before the war as the Paris of the Balkans. In the brutality of war it had grown to more closely resemble Beirut. With the establishment of the church under Nikola's capable leadership, it was now emerging as the Antioch of this new republic. From Mostar, as from Antioch in the first century, missionaries were first being intentionally mobilized to start churches in other cities. This work would continue in the months ahead. As of this writing, the "Antioch church" in Mostar has assumed the responsibility for providing pastoral leaders, for nurturing new churches and for supplying a continual stream of humanitarian aid in east Mostar, Tuzla, Sarajevo, Bihac and Jajce. Additional mission stations have begun work in several other communities.

The Mostar church is young and small and relatively deprived of resources in its post-war setting. Yet it is growing rapidly and reproducing. Under Nikola's leadership, the church is making a disproportionate impact on the whole nation of Bosnia and he is becoming an important national leader. Like the Macedonian believers of II Cor. 8:3-4, Mostar's Christians are giving according to their ability, and beyond their ability of their own accord. They are delighting in the favor of participating in the support of the saints in other cities.

Our Invitation to Antioch

By the summer of 1993, our base team had been forced out of Gasinci by the Croatian authorities. We maintained a nearby presence in Djakavo trying to minister to converts as best we could. Short-term teams still visited the camp but could no longer reside there. The pace and the scope of our work with refugees had slowed substantially.

This was not all bad because we were developing a longer-term strategy to field a team of language-proficient missionaries who would be ready to re-enter Bosnia when peace was finally restored. David Lively had agreed to lead that effort and in 1994 was trying to complete his language studies. Fio Weaver, Becky Coldwell and Stephen Ruff had returned to the states having completed their base-team service commitment.

Now, Janice Freytag, a veteran of our short-term team ministry among refugees, was residing in Djakavo. She was also preparing for long-term service in Bosnia. Kevin Conway, another Northside member whose call to long-term ministry was confirmed while sharing Christ in Gasinci, was involved in formal language study at the University in Zagreb. Joined there by his Croatian wife, Rahela, these four composed the nucleus of our emerging team of missionaries poised for ministry in post-war Bosnia.

During the year from summer 1993 to summer 1994, we were hearing more and more about Nikola Skrinjaric and the Mostar church. Nikola had heard of our commitment to Bosnia as well. All of us were eager to meet. Urged by Peter Kuzmic and his colleagues in Osijek to visit the church personally, several leaders from NCC planned to join David Lively and me for a trip to Mostar in November 1994. On the day of our scheduled departure from Atlanta, however, my mother passed away. Responsibilities with my family prevented my going along with the team under those circumstances. But we felt it was important for the others to proceed as planned.

While my friends flew off to rendezvous with David for the trip to Mostar, I traveled to Alabama to help arrange my mother's funeral services. It was a blessing to share in preaching her funeral along with my twin brother. As mentioned earlier, I had missed my grandmother's funeral during a previous trip to Croatia in 1993. Though I felt disappointed over missing the trip to Mostar, I was overwhelmingly grateful that I was still in the states when news of my mother's death came. I would not have wanted to find myself overseas again at such an important time for my family.

The day of my mother's funeral, a large number of friends and family gathered to celebrate her life. In the midst of the grieving one would expect on such an occasion, there was also an outpouring of gratitude expressed to God for a life well spent. The memories people shared about the impact of her gentleness and care for others blessed my heart. So did the presence of many from my church who had made the three-hour drive from Atlanta to pay their last respects and to support my family and me.

It had been three days since I had spoken with my office in Atlanta. In the flood of emotions that one experiences when a parent dies, I had completely lost focus on the team traveling to Mostar. On the way to the grave-side service however, the chairman of our elder board brought the trip vividly back to mind. He delivered a fax message expressing the team's condolences and their prayer support. The team's brief update included with this thoughtful message held a special surprise for me. The elders who were representing us in Mostar were reporting an incredible sense of God's hand at work in the ministry of this new church.

The note ended with an urgent appeal. "The move of God among believers here is obvious John, and we are sensing that NCC is meant to be a part of it. We know that your family is still in the grieving process and that the timing is inopportune at best. Nonetheless, we believe that you need to be here with the rest of us as we consider the implications of working alongside Nikola Skrinjaric and his team. If it is possible for you to make the trip later this week, we will drive to Zagreb and back to Mostar to permit you joining us here. That's a twenty-hour round trip for us, so you can bet we think it is important. Let us know if it is possible for you to come."

Interestingly, this note was no intrusion at all in this most solemn moment for my family. The thrust of the message was one combining sympathy for my family with serious concern for the ongoing commitment of our church in Bosnia. I remembered Acts 11:22-25 as I made my way from the car to the grave side where I would offer a final prayer over my mother's earthly remains. In that passage, Luke records the experience of Barnabus when he was first dispatched by the apostles to visit the Antioch Church. As he witnessed the grace of God at work in Antioch, he rejoiced, encouraged the new church in the things of the Lord and immediately thought of the priority need to get Saul to come from Tarsus to join him. That same urgency was the motivation for this message from Mostar. It was also the impetus for my priority response.

My mother was buried on Sunday, November 6, 1994. Just one week later on November 13, I had the privilege of preaching in the Mostar church. Klaus Domke was present to give a report of the progress of his work in Tuzla. I shared the story of the message received at my mother's grave side in Alabama and preached about the Antioch church. In truth, the west Mostar congregation had become a modern mission church with a similar heart and vision to this great pioneer church in the book of Acts. The west Mostar church was the Antioch of Bosnia! It was a deep privilege to affirm them in their important role.

Doing What God Is Blessing

The work of Henry Blackaby on behalf of the Southern Baptist Convention has significantly touched the entire body of Christ. Especially in his book, *Experiencing God*, Blackaby has captured the hearts of believers longing for greater intimacy with the Father and a greater sense of impact for the kingdom of God. One of the most simple and profound insights he shares in this important work is our need to watch and see where God is working so that we might join

Him.[6] Following the example of Jesus, Blackaby is urging Christians to be alert to the Spirit's direction through the revelation of what the Father is doing. From John 5:17-20, the following formula summarizing Jesus' ministry model is offered by Blackaby:

- The Father has been working right up to now
- Now God has me working
- I do nothing on my own initiative
- I watch to see what the Father is doing
- I do what I see the Father is already doing
- You see, the Father loves me
- He shows me everything that He, Himself, is doing

We had already learned Blackaby's secret that God is always at work around us, and we tried always to be alert to His will as it became known on our road to Sarajevo. That attentive spirit served us well as we gathered in Bosnia to dialogue with Nikola. During this November 1994 visit to Mostar, we were able to clearly see the Father working. Accepting Nikola's invitation, we were led of God to become partners with him and the other Evangelical Church leaders in Bosnia. Our road to Sarajevo was taking a new turn and bringing us within 100 miles of our destination! By January 1995, David relocated from Osijek to Mostar taking on the responsibility of training emerging leaders in the church.

The details of the months that followed would fill another book and are beyond the scope of this work. Suffice it to say that we have enjoyed an incredibly fruitful pioneering partnership with these Croatian "missionaries" in Bosnia. We have worked alongside these national leaders, taking our cues from them as to how to advance our joint interests in Bosnia. We share a mutual commitment to eventually see a saturation church planting movement established across the country. We have helped along the way, as we were able, encouraging and facilitating Bosnia's infant churches in their efforts in humanitarian relief and church planting. We have also assisted in raising capital investment funds and in founding the first Bible school in Bosnia, located in Muslim East Mostar.

David and Nikola first visited Sarajevo together in the spring of 1995. This was the first time David had ever been there, and it was the first time one of our church leaders finally reached the end of the road we had chosen in 1990. During this visit, David and Nikola discovered a small group of believers who had endured the siege of Sarajevo together for four years. David's e-mail to us following that visit best tells the story:

4/26/95

To the Church Gathered:

Just a quick note to say we have arrived safe and sound back from Sarajevo. It was three days I will not soon forget. That tunnel (which runs from the base of Mt. Igman under the airport into a block of flats in the Muslim sector of Sarajevo) is something straight out of the "The Great Escape". It's about two and a half feet wide and five feet high. Frequently it's about two inches deep in water. Try walking a half-mile bent over with a pack on your back, and you have an idea what it was like!

There is currently "low-level fighting in Sarajevo" — occasional shells fall, and stray shots and sniper fire can be heard. Plenty of people are on the street because compared to the past situation it's much better right now. They know where to go and where not to go.

After we arrived at the home of Ankica, the only baptized believer remaining from the ministry of the Evangelical Church in Sarajevo before the war, Nikola organized a meeting of the eleven believers. At the meeting we distributed the load of audio and video teaching tapes he brought in through the tunnel. Then we talked about baptism and listened to a tape on that topic. Nikola announced that we would baptize everyone who wanted to be baptized the next day. Most of the people in the group had trusted Christ in 1991, through the ministry of the three pastors who had been in Sarajevo before the war. When the war started, all of the pastors left because they had small children. They felt that their families needed to get out of the city to safety. These new believers had never been baptized.

So on Tuesday in Dragan's bathtub we had eight baptisms! Everyone shared their testimonies and I got to share a word of encouragement from Romans six on baptism. It was a time of great rejoicing. Then we took the Lord's supper "American style" with a fruit drink because none of the stores in the area had wine! We encouraged the group to believe that they are a real church now, not just a group of believers. We prayed for 31-year-old Dragan formally designating him as their pastoral leader.

What a blessing it was to be with this little band that has remained faithful to their newfound Savior through the most difficult time! Despite having stood through all that, baptism was still a tough question for some of them from Muslim backgrounds. What a joy to watch them say yes again to Jesus! They have now rented a room to meet in and will start public services in the near future!

So, the church in Sarajevo was re-born and David was on hand to represent our church in the delivery process! What a thrill, for him and for us, to see our long-held dream become a reality. Subsequent trips to Sarajevo solidified David's relationship with the growing church there. At Nikola's request and with our enthusiastic blessing, David moved to Sarajevo in January 1996. NCC had by that time purchased a three-story residence near the center of town to serve as the church's first facility. We had finally reached the end of the road to Sarajevo.

The Road Goes Beyond Sarajevo

As I write in August 1998, I am amazed to reflect on all God has done in and through our church as a result of our vision for evangelizing the Muslims of Bosnia. Hundreds of thousands of dollars have been invested in buildings for several of the new churches emerging in the country. Our summer short-term teams have labored for the Lord this year in five different cities. David has just completed his first furlough after five years on the field in Croatia and Bosnia.

The Bible School that opened in November 1996 has doubled its cadre of students from 15 to 30 emerging leaders. Through this training center, new national leaders are being prepared for the churches Nikola and our missionaries dream of starting across the expanse of post-war Bosnia. David is co-director of that school. Our full-time team in Mostar has expanded to a complement of four Americans and three nationals from ETS in Osijek. A second long-term team is now functioning in Sarajevo and should eventually include eight to ten additional career missionaries from NCC.

As of August 1998, plans call for the team serving in Mostar to share responsibility for the Bible School and for the church planting effort among Muslims on the east side of the Neretva River. The Sarajevo team has been asked to plant a second Evangelical Church in the capital city. Our relational network is extending our influence far beyond these two key cities. Having reached the end of the road to Sarajevo, we now realize that the road branches from our target city to other communities all across the country.

Partnerships are forming. Innovative alliances between churches and mission agencies are bringing far more resources than we alone could ever provide to reach Bosnia's unreached people and to help rebuild their nation. (More information on those partnerships can be found in Part II of this book.)

These partnerships will, we hope, be able to assist the Evangelical Church of Bosnia-Herzegovina to establish new congregations in thirty-eight key population centers. These targeted cities represent communities of 50,000 or more people where there are still no known believers and no churches. When those churches are established, a giant step toward an indigenous movement to evangelize all of Bosnia will have been largely accomplished. I expect in my lifetime that the work of reaching the unreached Muslims of Bosnia will be completed. NCC will be ready, when that day comes, to take a new road to another unreached mission field. Everything in our experience on the road to Sarajevo makes us eager for yet another such journey!

Seeing With Spiritual Eyes

I hope that this account of the progress of our work with Bosnians will open each reader's eyes to the excitement of mission involvement at the end of the 20th century. I can hardly imagine a more thrilling time to be living and serving the cause of Christ in the world. The timeless stories of God's kingdom being advanced in the book of Acts are not ancient history: they are still being lived out and written today. The dynamic of divine intervention is not a thing of the past, it is a present reality. I hope you won't miss your chance to be a part of God's powerful intervention on behalf of His church in your generation. The unreached people of the earth will be reached! God's mandate for global evangelism guarantees that outcome. Don't wait until it is too late for you to play a part in the process. With spiritual eyes, you too can discern where God is working. You too can make preparations to join Him. Should you decide to do so, it is my expectation that you will never regret getting on board with God's mission agenda.

Some day, the events described in these chapters will be ancient history. Natural men will then see only what the news media and world governments have made the focus of their attention during this period — civil war, genocide, military atrocities unparalleled since World War II. Historians will also recognize new nations formed from the carved up carcass of former Yugoslavia. And many men will have been made famous. George Bush, Bill Clinton, Colin Powell and Cyrus Vance among others will be remembered for their part in this period of amazing transition. So will Lord David Owen, Buhtros Buhtros-Galli and Francois Mitterand. Izetbegovic, Milosovic and Tudjman will find a place in those accounts, as will war criminals like Miladic and Kradic.

But these people and the events they have superintended merely represent God's scaffolding for His building program in Bosnia. The real story from heaven's point of view will not be that which recalls military conquest, diplomatic accords and governments rising and falling. The real story in Bosnia from God's perspective, has revolved around love not hatred, compassion not cruelty, and spiritual births not physical deaths. For in the upheaval of ethnic strife and armed conflict, the church of Jesus Christ has gained a firm beachhead in Bosnia. Behind the scaffolding of human history, God is tracking the inexorable advance of His kingdom. It is this kingdom advance that has been the focus of God's spiritual development program throughout the ages. So, the story of God's Kingdom coming is the real story behind the war in Bosnia today.

Spiritual eyes will see behind the hatred and ethnic cleansing, to observe God's hand moving in a great intervention of love. The names He records will include national leaders like Peter Kuzmic, Stevo Dereta, Nikola Skrinjaric and Karmelo Kresonja. God will remember the likes of David Lively, Fio Weaver, Janice Freytag, and Peter MacKenzie. Courageous and committed couples like Kevin and Rahela Conway will find their names in God's list of key figures acting for the Kingdom during this war. These are the heroes of faith, the men and women who have left their homes to carry the love of God to anguished refugees fleeing the war in Bosnia. The great story in Bosnia is not the one written by international dignitaries noted for their brilliance and intrigue. Among such are many men thought to be great and powerful. The greater story in Bosnia has instead been written by ordinary people under divine appointment. Among these notable Christians, who have served as God's ambassadors to Bosnia, are men and women of whom the world is not worthy. They have gone largely unnoticed by the correspondents of war. Their names, however, are indelibly recorded in heaven. Among them, there are not many mighty. God has always preferred it so.

Part 2

Principles for Church-Based Missions

Introduction to Part 2

Enlarge the place of your tent; stretch out the curtains of your dwellings, spare not....

Isa. 54:2

Having described the unusual impact NCC is enjoying in Bosnia, I earnestly hope that readers will be moved to develop greater faith in the missions potential for their own local church in particular and for smaller churches in general. For too long, small assemblies, which make up the huge majority of churches globally, have been marginalized by the limited vision of denominational leaders, mission professionals and pastors alike.

For small churches to play a more meaningful role in the progress of world missions, we must rethink our structures, review our strategies and reconsider the strengths small congregations have to offer. I remind the reader of the point made in the introduction to this book; **it is not the size of our resource pool but the limits of our faith and our vision that determine our impact for the Kingdom of God.**

The chapters which follow are intended to offer a basis for re-examining the misguided thinking of missiologists and mega-church proponents which has, perhaps inadvertently, denied more than 80 percent of the churches in the world their rightful place in fulfilling the great commission. These chapters will encourage us to reevaluate our perspectives and the prevailing understandings of local church life that have caused the general appreciation for small church ministry potential to suffer so severely.

This kind of re-evaluation will not be easy. Hadden Robinson has noted that, "It is difficult to think. It is more difficult to think about thinking. It is most difficult to talk about thinking about thinking."[1] Even with Robinson's acknowledged challenge in mind, this is precisely what I want to do in Part II of this book. These remaining chapters are designed to have us "think about how we think" about church life and about missions.

I expect the casual reader to find the chapters that follow to be more challenging than the preceding ones which simply tell the unusual story of our mission effort in Bosnia. Many people have been inspired by the "Holy Ghost stories" that capture the history of our practice of missiology. The underlying principles that made those stories possible, however, make for more technical reading. They are nonetheless, vitally important to those who would risk adopting a similar model for their own mission involvement. My goal in this book is to be both inspiring and instructive. I want to urge my readers at this point to press on to the end. Especially for small church pastors and mission practitioners, the instructive material which follows is foundational for any serious attempt at unleashing the latent potential that local congregations hold for involvement in global evangelism.

Reading about what NCC has experienced will be of little value if it fails to inspire other churches to follow suit. And inspiration alone will fall short if I fail to provide practical ideas to show how others can lead their churches (especially small churches) into major missions ministry. The rest of this book will provide the philosophical framework and practical insights necessary to release the untapped resources churches hold for advancing the Kingdom of God around the world.

As you read, remember it is the limits of your faith and your vision that will determine your impact for God in this age. My prayer is that "rethinking the ways that we think" about church and about missions will expand the limits of our faith and our vision so that the commands of Isaiah 54:2 will be within reach of us all:

> Enlarge the place of your tent;
> Stretch out the curtains of your dwellings, spare not;
> Lengthen your cords, and strengthen your pegs.
> For you will spread abroad to the right and to the left.
> And your descendants will possess nations,
> And they will resettle the desolate cities.

$\mathcal{N}$ot $\mathcal{M}$any $\mathcal{M}$ighty

For consider your calling, brethren, that there were not many wise according to the flesh, not many mighty, not many noble....

I Cor. 1:26

It was Aristotle who wisely warned that, "All that glitters is not gold." This sage axiom applies in many situations, and I want to make sure we don't dismiss it from our thinking about the body of Christ. After all, the church that Jesus promised to build is constantly under threat of being compromised to the point of ineffectiveness. Satan has planned from the beginning to oppose and to destroy the church as a force for world evangelism. Quite apart from the supernatural sabotage worked by the powers of darkness, sinful men, however well intentioned they may be, have also been prone to defile the body of Christ in a myriad of ways. We must, therefore, be careful to maintain a wise and sober outlook as we evaluate the quality of our modern churches.

It is the concern of this chapter that churchmen, especially leaders in Western Christendom, have failed in their responsibility for developing healthy models of church life. Having diverted attention from the qualitative dimensions of church growth to focus primarily on the quantitative ones, many church leaders are mistaking at least some extraneous glitter for ecclesiastical gold. In effect, man's propensity to judge from outward appearance, a tendency that has a long and lamentable history within the family of God, may be negatively affecting our current judgment about the health of our churches. I believe it is time for us to refocus on the qualitative factors that God prizes in His body. If indeed we have missed something as the church developed in the west, refocusing on qualitative concerns could reveal the oversight. If our examination leads us to conclude that changes are in order, we must be willing to adjust, to alter our thinking about what makes for local church success and to bring forth fruit in keeping with that adjustment.

I believe that some of the characteristics we have come to associate with success may, upon more careful evaluation, represent symptoms of sickness. My concern is that undetected disease in the Western church could create a health crisis that will infect not only our own believing communities but also our church-planting efforts on the mission fields of the world.

Like the European explorers who were motivated as a service to God to discover and colonize the New World, we may find that the most honorable intentions may be completely overshadowed by the impact of unintended results. As colonization progressed in North and South America, thousands of native-American Indians died from diseases the white man introduced to their cultures. Could it be that in a similar way, though we intend to bring blessing as we introduce the gospel to the modern world's unreached peoples, we carry with us ecclesiological germs that will have a negative impact on those we hope to reach? No serious missiologist wants to infect unreached populations with an undetected disease, but if the "church-planting seeds" we are sowing are laden with infectious germs, sickness may result in our mission harvest anyway. This concern is at least worthy of our consideration as we investigate the impact our mind-set has on missionary church planting.

Is the Multiplication of Local Churches Important to Missions?

In this century's most revolutionary and comprehensive summary of mission theory, *Understanding Church Growth*, Dr. Donald MacGavran wrote the following about the need to focus our efforts in cross-cultural evangelism:

> In mission today many tasks must be carried on together; yet the multiplicity of good activities must contribute to, and not crowd out, maximum reconciliation of man to God in the Church of Jesus Christ. God desires that men be **saved** in this sense: that through faith they **live in Christ** and through obedience they are **baptized** in His name and live as **responsible members of His body**. God therefore commands those of His household to go and 'make disciples of all nations.' Fulfilling this command is the supreme purpose which should guide the entire mission, establish its priorities, and coordinate all its activities (emphasis added).[1]

Recognizing that the "multiplicity of good activities" pursued by missionaries includes efforts aimed at meeting desperate humanitarian needs, mobilizing resources for agricultural and economic development, and undertaking educational and vocational training to eradicate illiteracy and poverty, Dr. MacGavran's book insists that the major mission priority must not be turned solely to these laudable activities. He suggests that missions must always be aimed at winning lost souls to saving faith in Christ. Dr. MacGavran proposes that the single most important evidence of success in reaching the unsaved is seeing people converted and making visible commitments to discipleship. He declares that success in having new converts follow Jesus as Lord can be best observed and measured by their post-conversion commitment to what he terms **"responsible church membership."**

This view of the mission enterprise drives one to conclude that the goal of our cross-cultural efforts must not be merely to make a *difference* in an unreached culture by relieving human suffering, educating the illiterate or stimulating development. Neither is it enough simply to make certain that everyone has heard the gospel message or to elicit personal *decisions* for Christ. **Those who would establish the gospel in unreached cultures must be dedicated to making *disciples* for Christ: men and women willing to follow Jesus by obedience to His word lived out in the context of responsible church membership.**

Church Growth theory and modern missiology have embraced this premise which places a premium on evangelistic methodologies which incorporate formerly unreached and unchurched people into local communities of believers where they can live together in submission to the Lordship of Christ. Thus, establishing churches has become integral to every mission strategy that would purport to effectively take the gospel to thousands of unreached people groups in our world. Dr. MacGavran makes the point by saying unequivocally:

> ... for the welfare of the world, for the good of mankind — according to the Bible, one task is paramount. Today's supreme task is effective multiplication of churches in the receptive societies of earth.[2]

This "church growth" perspective regarding the central focus of missions has become broadly accepted by the world's leading experts in global evangelism. For example, Dr. Ralph Winter, founder and director of the U.S. Center for World Mission, has offered this corroborating testimony to Dr. MacGavran's theory:

> I used to be an expert in the gadgets and the gimmicks — the various means and types of ministries common to most missions. Recently it has become steadily clearer to me that the most important activity of all is the implanting of churches. **The care, feeding and reproduction of**

congregations is the central activity to which all the gimmicks and means (of mission) must be bent. (emphasis added).[3]

The Small Church, God's Key to World Evangelism

Accepting this view of the pressing priority facing those who would commit their lives to the unfinished task of global evangelism, one might rightly ask, "What sort of church will be most effective in enhancing the rapid multiplication of believing communities within formerly unchurched people groups?" Dr. MacGavran speaks directly in answer to this question when he notes that the most advantageous missions alternative is a model that succeeds by using a pattern of church growth which is *indefinitely reproducible*. He writes,

> In short, the congregation should be of such structure and pattern that **common people can operate it and multiply it indefinitely** among the masses. In North America, the indefinitely reproducible pattern **is not** the highly successful church, led by a very exceptional preacher, which erects a set of buildings covering a city block and counts its members in the thousands. That is one good pattern in certain situations, but it is impossible in most places (emphasis added).[4]

Dr. MacGavran's insights regarding the value of indefinitely reproducible models of church life that can be operated by ordinary people helped fuel some of the most significant advances in mission theory developed in the last two decades. Particularly relevant is the concept of "Saturation Church Planting" which is nearly universally accepted as the most viable approach to winning an entire nation for Christ. In this approach to evangelism and mission, the goal is not merely to proclaim the gospel to every individual but to plant churches in every community in an effort to serve new converts born into the kingdom and committed to a local fellowship.

Jim Montgomery's DAWN 2000 strategy is a good example. Under this "Discipling A Whole Nation" plan, it is suggested that if 7,000,000 new churches could be planted before the year 2000, the task of global evangelism could be essentially completed. Theoretically, these 7,000,000 churches would represent one church for every 1,000 people on planet earth, assuming that the global population will reach seven billion by the turn of the century.[5] Such plans to "saturate" a nation or a people group (or the entire world!) with churches as a means to completing the great commission now dominate strategic mission efforts in every part of the world.

Indonesian Chris Marintika offers another example. He is encouraging a saturation church planting effort for his own nation. He calls the strategy "Indonesia One, One, One." The goal is to encourage graduating seminary students to plant "one" church in each "one" village in "one" generation in Marintika's homeland.[6] This would produce 50-60,000 new churches by AD 2015 in the world's largest Muslim country — effectively reaching a population of 175 million!

The Alliance for Saturation Church Planting is urging similar strategies for the various Eastern and Central European nations recently liberated from Soviet domination. The AD 2000 and Beyond movement and its Joshua Project 2000 team advocate that saturation church planting goals be established among all 1,739 unreached people groups which remain "identified but unadopted" in their list of possible mission targets published in 1997.

Inherent in this centrally important modern missions concept is the notion that churches should seek to multiply in order to "saturate" (and thereby more effectively win) their communities and the world for Christ. It may seem obvious, but nonetheless I want to declare that the most efficient "saturation church planting" ministry is likely to be performed, in Dr. MacGavran's words, by *"indefinitely reproducible churches which can be operated by ordinary people."* That is to say, we need to realize that small churches may well hold the key to successful implementation of the saturation church planting strategy for world evangelization.

Interestingly enough, this theory, which prizes saturation church planting methodologies and local church multiplication as a means to the most rapid completion of the evangelistic mandate is being encouraged all over the world — except in the West. In the West, and particularly in America, church leaders hold stubbornly to the notion that local churches should grow bigger rather than multiply rapidly. This reality represents a major contradiction between the theory and the practice of church growth principles among Western church and missions leaders.

The Mega-Church, the Meta-Church and Missions

Dr. MacGavran's description of the "highly successful" American church is a reasonable portrait of what has come to be known in the West as the "mega-church." Characterized by prominent and expensive buildings, a highly educated and gifted multiple staff team (led by an unusually capable and articulate senior pastor) and a membership measured in the thousands, the mega-church has become *the* model for success in the minds of America's church leaders. This wide acceptance of the mega-church as a standard for success in building a local church ministry has naturally paved the way to a pervasive "bigger is better" mentality.

As numerical growth has been made synonymous with success, it is not surprising that the scope of the mega-church ministry would eventually be exceeded by an even larger model envisioned by church growth devotees. The "meta-church" model now offers the ultimate expression of the "bigger is better" mindset.

Eliminating sub-congregational structures (groups involving 35-120 people), leaders like Carl George (formerly of Charles E. Fuller Institute)[7] and Ralph Neighbour (Touch Outreach Ministries)[8] are promoting a concept that would combine small groups and celebration structures, theoretically, to make any church's growth potential unlimited. David Young-gi Cho's Yoido Full Gospel Church in Seoul, Korea, the world's largest single church with a membership exceeding 700,000, is the primary working model for these pundits of perpetual growth.

Promoting the meta-church concept, Carl George sees even this massive congregation as unnecessarily small. He offers an amazing prophecy as he urges leaders to prepare their congregations for a "meta-church future" where no church is too big and Cho's church is too small:

> I predict that many churches of the future will be larger than anything we've imagined. In fact, the next generation of churches will dwarf our current successes — including the world's largest, the great congregation in Seoul, which is rapidly pushing toward a three-quarters of a million figure![9]

Carl George's complicated view of the future is, in my judgment, unfounded in fact and holds potential for the kind of dream-turned-nightmare that viewers flocked to see in Stephen Spielberg's "Jurassic Park." Appropriately enough for this analogy, George adopts a "meta-ZOO" metaphor to discuss churches of varying sizes. In his meta-church menagerie, a house church is a mouse and a small church is a cat. There are also lap dogs (under 200), yard dogs (under 1,000), horses (under 5,000) and elephants (under 10,000). He dubs the meta-church, which by definition exceeds 10,000 people, the dinosaur of the ecclesiastical world. If the highly successful mega-church of Dr. MacGavran's day was clearly not a "highly reproducible model", it takes a dinosaur-sized leap of faith to see the meta-church model as being any more promising.

In any case, this kind of "bigger is better" mentality has become the prevailing perspective among Western Christian leaders and has completely dominated the application of church growth principles for the last two decades. Dr. Peter Wagner has encouraged this trend by promoting insights geared toward achieving sustained growth for local churches. In his popular "Breaking the 100...200 Barrier" seminar, Dr. Wagner has observed that the 100-200 barrier is a universal growth plateau that must be overcome by would-be "mega-church" or "meta-church" pastors in every culture on earth. His seminars teach techniques that have proven helpful in breaking through this barrier, which is the most common obstacle to success-ful quantitative church growth worldwide. Others like Dr. Bill M. Sullivan have written entire books on strategies that successfully catapult church attendance beyond the 200 mark.[10] Yet, in spite of more than two decades of constant emphasis and considerable influence from church growth thinkers, it remains a fact that fully 85 percent of all churches in America have never exceeded 200 in attendance.

Refocusing on Reality

By observation, it is easy to prove that the vast majority of churches in all evangelical denominations remain small. The average size for churches in the Southern Baptist Convention is 152. George Barna suggests the average size among all American churches is 111. In my own Evangelical Free Church of America denomination, the median size is approximately 100. Lyle Schaller, America's foremost church consultant, suggests that the typical American congregation involves less than 40 people.[11]

The statistical evidence supporting the notion that most churches are small is only strengthened when one looks beyond the US to observe the global scene. According to Ralph Neighbour's figures, 33 percent of the world's churches are comprised of 50 or fewer members. Another third of the world's churches accommo-date only 51-150 members, and just 33 percent ever exceed that number. Only 5 percent of the world's churches ever grow beyond 350 members.[12] Put another way, 66 percent of the world's churches are smaller than 150 members, and 94 percent are smaller than 350. **In the real world, smallness is an observable characteristic of the overwhelming majority of churches in every culture.**

God's Plan — Not Many Mighty

Making this observation, one might wonder if God has a purpose in generally allowing churches to remain small. Does church size have anything to do with, for example, effective efforts to win people to Christ? Surely Dr. MacGavran seemed to think so. His words noted earlier make it clear: **mega-churches and meta-churches may well not be the answer to penetrating the vast majority of remaining unreached people groups** which are the proper strategic target for mission attention at the end of the 20th century. It seems quite possible that rapid multiplication of smaller congregations could be an equally viable strategy and a more consistent application of church growth theory than a focus on planting typically non-reproducing mega-church and meta-church models. It is my conviction, therefore, that smaller churches committed to extension growth and bridging growth have powerful potential for adding to the mission force of the future. This is especially true if larger churches remain committed only to growing bigger.

In church growth theory, **extension growth** is the technical name given to growth strategies that attempt to allow a congregation to "grow outwardly" by starting new local assemblies in a neighboring area with a team or a nucleus drawn from the initiating church. **Bridging growth** refers to similar efforts to grow outwardly by creating new congregations. In bridging growth, however, the target communities for the new church plant represent "cross-cultural" ministry contexts. **Expansion growth** methodologies are aimed at evangelism which simply serves to make an existing church larger.

In spite of the preponderance of small churches globally, church growth theorists have historically majored on encouraging and measuring quantitative growth. Under that influence we have unintentionally succumbed to a worldly sort of "success syndrome" which too easily concludes that "bigger is better" in everything, including the church. We would do well to reflect again on Paul's words in I Cor. 1:26-29:

> For consider your calling, brethren, that there were not
> many wise according to the flesh, not many mighty, not
> many noble, but God has chosen the foolish things of the
> world to shame the wise, and God has chosen the weak
> things of the world to shame the things which are strong,
> and the base things of the world and the despised, God
> has chosen the things that are not, that He might nullify
> the things that are, that no man should boast before God.

In God's economy, He has never been constrained to work through the many rather than the few (I Sam. 14:6). So we should not be surprised to observe that among today's global array of churches, the vast majority is made up of small congregations. Perhaps it is God's plan to keep the majority of His churches small in order to keep more of his people humble and to confound the impressive institutions of the world. There simply is not much to boast about when we recognize that not many members of God's family are considered mighty in the eyes of the world.

Perhaps the average church would see its qualitative health decline if its mass expanded beyond the 200 barrier. If God has imposed a "divine limitation" of sorts on the numerical growth of more than 90 percent of the world's churches, perhaps He is concerned about His children's propensity for pride in the face of apparent prosperity. Seen in this light, unlimited growth might be more an evidence of **sickness** than an evidence of **success** for local churches. Expansion growth, preserved in a single body of believers, might be more a **barrier** than a **blessing** to church health in general and to world missions in particular. This notion deserves a closer look by those serious about taking the gospel to all the unreached peoples of the earth.

Seeing as God Sees

*Do not look at his appearance or the height of his stature
... for God sees not as men see....*

I Sam. 16:7

r. Ralph Winter seems to hold at least some concerns about the unqualified affirmation of churches of unlimited size. In his "Mission Frontiers" magazine, he once wrote about the shift in church values that has accompanied the global migration of the masses from rural to urban locals. One effect of this trend toward urbanization over the past 100 years has been growth in the popularity of larger churches. He acknowledges that, as larger churches have captured our attention, Western church leaders have become uncritically consumed with the "bigger-is-better" mind-set. Dr. Winter expressed his concern about this phenomenon in this way:

> ... the wealthiest, most vocal — the leading members — of the denominations today are denizens of the large urban congregations, and the Schuller syndrome has now heralded what may be the largest single trend in the history of American Christianity, the New Testament itself being revised to fit. Someone has put it, "The California version

now reads, 'Where two or three thousand are gathered together, there am I in the midst of them.'"

Is this the logical outcome of church growth thinking? It all depends. If expansion growth were the only valued measurement, we would have to say yes. But one of the serious unsolved problems which fairly shouts for the attention of everyone, including church growth thinkers, is the simple fact that anonymity may increase with the size of a congregation and perhaps even succeed in outbalancing the other benefits of large congregations. It's like saying, 'If three children in a family are nice, thirty would be better!' Internal ministry and accountability, formal or informal, tend seriously to suffer in the large church.[1]

It would be foolhardy even with this perspective in view, to conclude that large churches are sick or unsound simply because they have broken "the 200 barrier." It would be equally foolish to suggest that big churches are successful and healthy just because they have large constituencies. But there is good reason to bear in mind that qualitative elements of ministry suffer as extraordinary quantitative growth is achieved and maintained in a single congregation. Dr. Winter sees anonymity, limited discipleship and lack of accountability as growth-oriented weaknesses common to the mega-church context.

To this list we could add the reality that ever-increasing numbers also present formidable barriers to a genuine sense of belonging in the Christian community, to the availability of individual pastoral care and to our capacity to offer personal support for members in crisis. Larger churches also often struggle more than small ones with the dynamics of administering biblical discipline for rebellious parishioners. Because bigness can make it difficult for elders to be well acquainted with all those under their care, the process of church discipline (which is unpleasant in any setting) becomes especially impersonal and often unthinkable in large congregations. These kinds of qualitative factors suffer increasingly as churches grow beyond "the 200 barrier."

I don't want to be unduly negative about large churches as I omit from the discussion which follows some of the obvious merits of mega-church ministry. And I readily admit that small churches are not universally effective in the qualitative aspects of body life just because they are small. I simply want to make the point that ever-larger numbers do in fact make important facets of qualitative ministry difficult if not impossible to provide. This reality leads us to an important premise for the concerns I am highlighting in this chapter. *We need to acknowledge that unlimited numerical growth in a single congregation often has an observable and negative impact on the qualitative dimensions of church life.*

With this premise in mind, it may not be going too far to suggest that the American Christian community is not getting healthier as it focuses attention almost exclusively on quantitative measures of success. I believe that we err when we uncritically accept increasing church size as the singular sign of congregational vitality. Bigness alone is not inherently positive. I am personally convinced that the trend urging Western leaders to embrace unlimited expansion growth at the expense of local church multiplication is an unhealthy development. The following material will offer evidence to support my conviction by developing an analysis of the kind of thinking that leads to the "bigger-is-better" mentality. I believe I can demonstrate how enthusiasm for unlimited growth has adversely affected the health of the church in the West and in the rest of the world where Western influence is being felt.

Institutionalization of the Church

For purposes of discussion, I will call this problem in our mindset the *"institutionalization"* of the church. When I speak of institutionalization, I am referring to a deficient or even unbiblical philosophy of ministry that depersonalizes ministry by valuing increased numbers over intimate relationships, programs over people, and leadership by a professional clergy over the priesthood of believers. Institutionalization has a far-reaching negative influence on local churches. It affects the vision church leaders hold for the formation of intimate spiritual relationships within the body of Christ; for the capacity a church offers for developing leaders; for the priority given to mobilization of the laity; and for the limitations that membership size places on the potential a local assembly possesses to impact its community and the world. Institutionalization shapes our functional ecclesiology, our sense of why the church exists and why it functions the way it does. Institutional influences affect both large and small churches.

Institutionalized thinking emerged as a pervasive problem in the West when it became the prevailing view of influential leaders in large congregations. It is not a problem related directly to the size of a local congregation as much as one stemming from the surrender of qualitative concerns in church development in favor of a focus on quantitative emphases alone. The problem lies in the mindset of church leaders not in the size of the church membership they serve.

This bigger-is-better mindset and its attendant weaknesses have been perpetuated in recent decades by an avalanche of books, conferences and mass media exposure which have drawn attention to prominent mega-church leaders notable for their numerical successes. Such leaders have been promoted as a special source of inspiration and direction for pastors of smaller ministries to emulate. Rick Warren, Robert Schuller and Bill Hybels are just a few of the American mega-church pastors leading the current drive for ever-larger ministries. These men have pioneered some of the most numerically successful churches the world has ever known. By encouraging others to seek similar mega-church stature, they have helped to spread institutionalized thinking about church ministry in epidemic proportions.

These ministries, born in particular circumstances and under the unique personalities and giftedness of these uncommon men, have been offered as a standard to which all pastors should aspire. Their quantitative successes have been assumed to be within easy reach of any church leader willing to follow their models and methodologies. Hopeful pastors of smaller congregations eagerly apply the lessons learned from such mega-church mentors in a quest for achieving extraordinary growth themselves.

Thus institutionalized thinking has become the rage among leaders of small and large churches, denominational executives, mission professionals and seminary professors alike. The goal of achieving dramatic numerical growth is now the nearly universal priority of pastors in spite of mounting evidence that simply applying similar methods in dissimilar settings holds little promise of yielding mega-growth results. Overlooking the experience of thousands of church leaders who have failed in their pursuit of mega-church strategies, the mindset of many leaders remains stubbornly focused on quantitative measures of success. Perhaps inadvertently, we have "institutionalized" the bigger-is-better mentality by making mega-church growth synonymous with local church success. By observation, it seems that this kind of perspective grows more persistent as it takes root. It also appears to be highly communicable. Left unchallenged, institutional thinking impacts the mentality and the philosophy of ministry of all the peoples among which it is promoted, spreading like a virus among leaders who are unaware of its less favorable consequences.

The Root of the Problem

In directing my readers toward a careful examination of institutionalized thinking, I recognize that I run the risk of sounding overly negative about large churches. It needs to be re-emphasized that I am not criticizing large congregations per se. Dr. MacGavran said it well in the quotation attributed to him in the previous chapter. The mega-church is one good pattern for church life in certain situations. But in many cultural settings, the mega-church is an impossible congregational goal to pursue.

I am not questioning the legitimacy of large churches where God is pleased to see them developed. I am rather trying to raise concerns about the wisdom of widely accepting institutional perspectives that make bigness the singular goal for every church leader in every situation. If what I see as an unhealthy trend toward institutional ecclesiology persists, I fear the majority of churches in the world (the smaller ones in particular) will be deemed undesirable to serve. More importantly, smaller churches may be led to conclude that they have little to offer the Kingdom of God.

As institutionalization has spread in the West its influence has generally relegated smaller churches to obscurity, teaching their pastors that small ministries don't matter much. A sense of irrelevance in world missions is only one manifestation of this problem presently observable among small church leaders. Smaller congregations are also viewed as inconsequential in their potential for impacting their communities for Christ, for providing adequate services for their members, and for generating an exciting and growth-oriented environment for leadership development. These are in my opinion, stereotypical weaknesses institutional thinkers assume will be found in most small churches. But as is the case with most stereotypes, these limitations need not prevail in all small ministries. Because God is pleased to allow small churches to proliferate in every culture we need to be careful about minimizing the ministry potential of the majority of the churches in the world!

I believe we desperately need to find credible culturally relevant approaches to church growth that are more inherently reproducible by ordinary people than the mega-church has proven to be. But doing so will require that we overcome institutional inertia which works against that goal. If I seem to overstate my case as I try to reassert a perspective that finds a high value for smaller church models, I hope my hyperbole will not provoke a defensive response on the part of mega-church leaders whose views rule the day. I am seeking to generate honest concerns in the minds of those who share responsibility for teaching Christians what it means to experience healthy church life. I do not want to offend those who appreciate large church models and who find them suitable for their context.

I do want to suggest that such mega-models will not serve well in all settings.

I also want to make it clear that unbridled excitement over numerical growth can, in its own right, be an unhealthy mindset for modern ministers of the gospel. If such enthusiasm is not balanced by a corresponding concern for the qualitative factors of church growth the health of Christian communities everywhere will suffer. The truth is, when it comes to our desire to develop healthy local bodies, being enthused over increasing numbers alone can be like finding cause for rejoicing in the face of discovering cancer or obesity in a human body. Such conditions may offer evidence of unparalleled growth, but unprecedented growth of this kind is more harmful than helpful. It doesn't make sense to be enthusiastic over disease pathologies – not in the human body and not in the body of Christ. The challenge is to be certain that we can discern between an increasing mass of muscle tissue and a developing malignancy. Institutional thinking often obscures our vision in this very respect.

I believe that wrong thinking about quantitative growth consistently undermines the priority qualitative dimensions of church life should enjoy by changing our perspective about what makes for a biblically balanced, spiritually healthy experience within the Christian community. I also believe that the mentality associated with a passion for explosive growth is often accompanied by a corresponding lack of concern for qualitative factors. But let me say once again, the problem I am highlighting has surprisingly little to do with the actual size of a local church.

Rather, it has to do with our thinking about the nature of balanced church ministry and the potential we see for powerful impact vested in churches of all sizes. The problem is the propensity of institutionalization to result in the loss of mental and philosophical commitment to relational ministry and the dynamics of body life. These are essential elements of biblical Christianity. When we loose sight of the fundamentally relational nature of the body of Christ we can easily stop valuing the more organic or communal dimensions of Christian fellowship. As this happens institutionalized perspectives replace concerns for community and the high value the New Testament holds for the church serving its members as an extended spiritual family or a vibrant organism can be lost. This is the usual result of applying institutional thinking to church growth initiatives. Institutionalization may well allow some local assemblies to succeed in growing larger but they also often grow less healthy in the process. As Dr. Winter has suggested, increasing size is a dynamic that may well create such a state of anonymity that qualitative decline in the church may completely outbalance any perceived benefit flowing from bigness.

Again, it is important to emphasize that the root of the problem I am addressing lies in our mindset more than the actual size of the memberships we serve. Institutionalization is the culprit; large churches are not. Neither is church growth per se. Growth is a good thing for the body of Christ. The problem institutionalization poses stems from its influence on our sense of how we are to respond to continuous growth when God blesses us to experience it. Sustained growth in a single congregation always makes institutionalization harder to avoid. Avoiding the problem requires a focused effort either to subdivide expanding churches into meaningful communities or to multiply rather than pursuing an expansion growth strategy.

It is important to note that remaining small does not indicate that a church's leaders are not institutionally minded. That is, smallness by itself does not solve the problem. Some churches can be highly institutionally oriented and still remain small for reasons unrelated to this kind of thinking. They may, for example, lack the vision required to generate healthy growth. Or they may lack leadership necessary to maintain ministry momentum that produces a growth environment. They may also be growing in the hard ground of a highly resistant population. My point is that institutionalization affects large and small churches alike. Regardless of the size of our church, institutionalization can become our normative perspective. When such occurs, we begin to embrace and to propagate wrong thinking about church life. We accept perspectives that would have us trade depth for breadth and a high value for substance in relationships for a vision focused on increased size in our church rolls. Too many church leaders have lost touch with the weaknesses that such wrong thinking produces.

No one would argue against sustained growth as an appropriate goal for every church. But growth should be directed toward reproduction – a universal quality characterizing healthy living organisms. I am not opposing church growth strategies. I am asserting that unlimited size in a single congregation should not always be considered an evidence of success. I want to demonstrate that runaway growth should in some instances be recognized as a potential sign of sickness. I am arguing that multiplication in the face of sustained growth can be a healthier option than maintaining larger numbers in a single mega-church. We need to reproduce more Christian communities rather than seeking to build bigger ones in every setting.

It is my observation that most modern church leaders, in hopes of achieving numerical success, have come to favor "institutional" church dynamics at the expense of the dynamics of "community." Pursuing this trend, such leaders enter into a numbers game that demands the sacrifice of their commitment to relational ministry. When body life dynamics begin to suffer as a result of trying to minister to the masses, I believe churches of all sizes fall sick and begin to malfunction. Whenever this occurs, institutionalization has taken its toll again!

If institutionalization is contagious we need to recognize that this kind of thinking can be transferred from one culture to another just as a virus can be spread from person to person. This is my chief concern as I think of the global implications of institutionalization. If this kind of thinking about church is harmful, and I believe it is, we need to be appropriately cautious as we penetrate previously unreached people groups. If we are not careful, our missionaries can become the unsuspecting carriers of a contagion that could have adverse affects on the long-range potential of church multiplication all over the world.

Like the explorers who spread destructive diseases when they encountered native Indian populations in the New World, we can unwittingly infect those we most want to help. The good news is that we can prevent the unintentional spread of institutionalization because its primary symptoms are not difficult to discern. For the sake of the health of the church worldwide, they are worth recognizing. Learning to diagnose institutionalized thinking will help us rediscover the simple truth that our mindset matters as we extend our ministry influence globally.

The way we think about church life will inevitably shape the church experience of our converts in other cultures. I am arguing that some of our thinking should be corrected before it is cultivated like contaminated seed in the soil of unreached mission fields. I believe the church around the world will be more healthy and more effective in completing the Great Commission if it is less institutional. Let me clarify what is involved when institutionalized perspectives dominate our thinking.

Four Primary Symptoms of Institutionalization

1. There's a primary focus on quantitative growth as the measure of success in a local church ministry.

This symptom has been addressed adequately in the preceding material. It is therefore sufficient to note here that increased numbers invariably bring increased demands for qualitative ministry dynamics while forcing a simultaneous reduction in the capacity of a church to deliver them. The stress (or even the distress) of these conflicting consequences of sustained growth are felt well enough by large church leaders. Who in a growing ministry has not encountered the pressure of overwhelming demands for personal counseling, or one-on-one discipleship, or hospital visitation? Even on a more practical plain, growing ministries struggle with the recurring need for bigger facilities and increased parking. As large church leaders struggle to keep up with the demand for relational services they cannot reasonably meet, they often don't recognize other symptoms of sickness that come as a result of burgeoning numbers. Among the additional symptoms of institutionalization which result directly from numerical success are the following:

Depersonalized Fellowship: A loss of intimacy occurs as churches attract increasing numbers of people to their services while failing to provide adequate incorporation and assimilation vehicles to draw them into meaningful relationships with other believers. From my own consulting experience, I would note that typically less than 40 percent of an institutionalized church's membership is actively involved with their brothers and sisters beyond attendance in the Sunday morning worship service.

Readers can test this statistic in their own church by comparing the numbers of people involved in congregational groups (those involving 35-120 people) and cells (small groups with less than 15 members) with the total number attending worship services. This rough approach to evaluating the level of local church assimilation beyond worship will seldom yield a measure exceeding 40 percent of the church's membership. This is generally true whether the church is large or small. Depersonalized fellowship always contributes to under-assimilation and significantly reduces expectations for "life-to-life exchange" among church members.

Spectatorism: This symptom of member passivity chiefly affects laymen and is a natural outgrowth of the impersonal fellowship dynamics that characterize institutional churches. Rather than anticipating active participation in the church's ministry, most laymen come to institutional churches with a desire to "watch a sacred drama" performed by paid ministers and a well-prepared choir. As institutional leaders accommodate that desire, the average layman is actually taught to see himself as one member of a larger **audience** that gathers primarily for Sunday worship rather than as a soldier in God's **army** being trained to wage war against the forces of darkness in the world. By creating an environment where passivity is an acceptable option for complacent parishioners, institutionalized leaders reinforce an unhealthy and unbiblical spectator mentality among laymen.

"Staff Infection": This symptom surfaces chiefly among the clergy and is perhaps the most devastating consequence of emphasizing numerical growth at the expense of qualitative dimensions of church life. Since less than 10 percent of the world's churches achieve sufficient numerical growth to be "successful" in megachurch terms, the vast majority of pastors and ministerial staff members who think institutionally suffer from a constant sense of failure. As numerical growth is seen as the most significant measure of success, plateaued growth brings with it discouragement for the pastoral leader. Small church leaders who hold to institutional perspectives often feel this frustration in their ministries. Looking to the leaders of large churches for inspiration, they instead feel dwarfed by comparison to their more successful colleagues. They feel overworked, underpaid, under-resourced and under-appreciated. They lack fulfillment in their work and sometimes even desire to leave the pastorate altogether. Educational credentials too narrowly focused on theology can however, make changing careers seem impossible. Such pastors consequently feel trapped by their training for professional ministry. Confined by a narrow calling, they experience even deeper discouragement and often resentment. Small church pastors (whom we noted earlier serve in 80 percent of the churches in the United States and 94 percent around the world) are especially susceptible to this kind of "staff infection." This problem stems directly from institutionalized thinking and it is producing a low sense of ministerial self-esteem among small church leaders around the world.

Diminished Capacity: This symptom is observable when churches lack the ability to provide a context for relational involvement for the bulk of their members. Diminished capacity is often accompanied by a limited expectation of interdependent living. As a result, independence is over-emphasized and robs members of any opportunity to experience the support, encouragement, stimulation and nurture which God intended for believers sharing fellowship in Christ's body. Institutional churches simply lack congregational and small group structural development sufficient to accommodate personal ministry for expansive numbers of people. In effect, **leaders in such churches don't have the infrastructural capacity to care — even if they have the heart to do so.** Consequently, most members in institutional churches experience isolation, lack of accountability and retarded spiritual growth. The New Testament never suggests these are permissible characteristics of life in the family of God.[2]

2. The second major symptom of institutional thinking is the privatization of faith.

This symptom is related to the dynamics of depersonalized fellowship which I have already mentioned. Where relationships are seldom intimate and where independent living is valued over an interdependent lifestyle, there is almost no mechanism to permit institutional churches to hold their members accountable to carry their faith into their homes, their schools and the marketplace. In effect, individuals are allowed to compartmentalize their convictions so that only a part, often a very private part, of their lives is affected by their faith. Consequently, the average believer's walk with God falls short of complete surrender to the Lordship of Christ. Symptoms that accompany privatization of faith include:

Montessori Ministry Methods: This condition results when impersonal programming exposes members to biblical ethics and standards for righteous living, but leaves them to experiment freely in applying these principles without the benefit of experienced and mature leadership attention. Laymen are expected to learn by trial and error without the safeguards offered by the guidance of a shepherd, the help of personal discipleship, the benefits of mutual accountability and the boundaries set by the exercise of church discipline. Left to their own devices, many members fall unsuspectingly into serious sin and have little access to counsel or correction to remedy the situation. Lack of personal pastoral care allows a laissez-faire atmosphere to exist where members are left unattended to sustain wounds and scars that more faithful personal shepherding might well have prevented.

Theoretical Orthodoxy: This is a kind of spiritual pretense that places high value on espousing biblical principles without requiring consistent practice of those prized convictions. When theoretical orthodoxy shapes an environment, behavior need not be affected by belief so long as one is able to articulate a doctrinally sound explanation for one's personal convictions. Hypocrisy then replaces holy living, and our walk fails to match our talk. The average institutional pastor, for example, might hold deep convictions about the power and priority of prayer without making a significant place for prayer in his schedule. Or a pastor might believe in the sanctity of life without taking any concrete action to oppose abortion. In effect, such a pastor is theoretically orthodox but practically unmoved by the truth he espouses.

Muted Pain: This symptom is observable when wounded people are left to suffer through their difficulties in silence. Where privatization of faith removes the expectation that the ravages of sinful behavior will normally be brought to the light and healed, an assumption also prevails that it is illegitimate to voice serious personal needs for counsel, support or encouragement. In such an environment, grace gives way to gross neglect and hiddenness is more common than healing. Where institutionalization has taken root in a church, opportunity is seldom made available for members to verbalize their pain. Most often there is no forum to do so outside the clinical counselor's office, and often this kind of counselor is seen by referral as a "surrogate priest" who is not formally connected to the church. Following this methodology, institutional pastoral leaders demonstrate by their actions, if not by their words, their preference that those suffering from serious hurts remain mute rather than making their pain a problem in the church.

Even if a cry of anguish or despair is sounded, institutional churches are poorly prepared to respond at a personal level because their leaders' time is consumed primarily by program responsibilities. The absence of capacity to provide personal care makes referrals to paid professionals outside the body a necessity. Professional clinical care is, however, a poor substitute for the personal and practical support God intended hurting people to receive through the body of Christ.

Carl George, a well known church growth consultant, captures the institutional church's dilemma when he identifies those with troubled souls in the meta-church concept as "extra grace required people" — in his vernacular, EGR's. George suggests that, "Some of these hurting members are bottomless wells who can siphon off all the love, interest and energy an entire group can offer. If a church offers no technique or system for dealing with these people ... they will kill the group." [3]

But technique and technically qualified health care practitioners operating outside the local church cannot replace the high-touch dynamics the body of Christ was designed by God to deliver. The church is called to minister to wounded people, not to mute their cries of anguish or to simply manage their demands by referral to professionals. The last thing our Lord would encourage is for people suffering from heartache and sin to remain silent. His calling on pastors and elders is to equip the body so that it may meet the needs of people — not mute their pain. He sets himself against shepherds who neglect this responsibility (Ezekiel 34:10).

3. Programmatic ministry is the third primary symptom of institutionalization.

In most affected churches there is an increasingly observable shift away from staff emphasis on personal relationships and people-oriented ministry toward more efficient program-oriented leadership. In effect, institutionalized congregations view themselves as being in the "church business" rather than the "people business." For those who see themselves in the church business, there is constant pressure for the church to become a "full service" provider organized to meet the widest possible range of spiritual, physical and emotional demands made by the surrounding public. Responding to this pressure, institutional churches attempt to attract people by adding athletic programs, health club facilities, day care services and hot meals to the menu of ministries they make available. Some have even built bowling allies and food courts into their facilities as they build ever-bigger building complexes. Thus, very real expectations are placed on institutional pastors to make certain that their churches offer the attractive programming options to lure people from their respective communities. Two secondary symptoms result from these programmed approaches to ministry.

Consumerism prevails when members come to church not to contribute their part to the overall work of the assembly, but instead, to shop for services that meet their felt needs. As in the secular society, consumer-oriented members of institutional churches demonstrate a desire to buy cheaply (i.e. at low cost to themselves), and they maintain little "brand loyalty." Members manifesting this symptom are easily attracted to other local bodies offering "new and improved" program alternatives. Believers who have been influenced by institutional leaders keep their options open about church affiliation. Many even claim membership in several churches at once, attending services as the alternative "menus" strike their fancy.

George Barna offers a futuristic look at the implications of this symptom in his book, *The Frog in the Kettle*. He writes about the modern church member's tendency to opt for what he calls, "Multiple Church Homes:"

One of the trends that church leaders will find distressing is the redefinition of the concept of a church home. Traditionally, individuals have evaluated the churches in their area and chosen a single local church to be their religious center. In the coming decade, however, increasing numbers of people will instead select between two and five local churches and consider those to be their *group* of home churches. On any given weekend, they will determine which church to attend based on their most keenly felt needs, and the programs each of their favored churches has to offer. Their financial support will be splintered among each of those churches, and the aggregate amounts given are likely to be less than average since they will have decreased loyalty and softened their commitment to any single church. Today, approximately 10 percent of adults follow this multiple church home pattern. By 2000, as much as one-quarter of all adults involved with the Christian church may be involved in this approach.[4]

By emphasizing the role of superstar pastors and the wide-ranging programs offered by supermarket churches, we have taught laymen to believe that the best church is the one which meets their needs today. The local church has come to represent just another service-oriented shopping outlet to many believers, and is no longer seen as the meeting place for "my part" of the larger family of God. This kind of consumer orientation is contrary to the biblical concept of body life espoused by Paul in I Corinthians 12. It is also inherently unhealthy, offering another evidence of the negative influence of institutionalization.

Competition between churches also grows as programmatic church leaders see themselves struggling against each other to maintain and expand their "market share." Instead of seeing Christians from other churches as soldiers in the same army pressing a spiritual battle against a common enemy, institutionalized leaders see these brothers and sisters as their competitors. Consequently, other churches are often not trusted, new churches are unwelcome in already churched neighborhoods, and cooperative efforts to serve the larger community in Christ's name are almost unthinkable.

Two examples will help illustrate these institutional influences on local church ministry in our day. Near my house is a "full service" mega-church with several thousand members and a huge facility. It happens to be a moderate Southern Baptist congregation. I play racquetball at this church, which offers the community a state-of-the-art health club and fitness center. The sports complex houses an indoor Olympic pool, a gymnastics training center, an indoor quarter-mile track, racquetball courts, a free weight room, a separate Nautilus weight training center, treadmills, Stairmasters, exercycles, rowing machines, two indoor basketball courts and two softball fields. Other programs include day care assistance, pre-school opportunities, drama classes, art classes, diet classes, mime classes and a wide variety of services and social offerings for single adults. The slogan for the church is "ministering to the whole man," and they are obviously serious about pursuing that goal.

Within the last several years, another Baptist congregation, the largest in our city, made the decision to move to the northern suburbs of Atlanta in an effort to move closer to their increasingly suburban constituency. Finding adequate property to facilitate this northward migration for a church numbering over 10,000 was no simple matter. In the end, the congregation purchased property from a large secular company converting its headquarters into a new home for the church. The transition was made slowly, and the relocation plan was reputed to eventually require an investment in excess of $60 million including acquisition costs, new construction and renovation expenses. The new location for this migrating mega-church is within two miles of the large church where I play racquet-ball — the one with the "full-service" marketing plan. How do you think this long established ministry feels about the largest church in our city becoming a new next door neighbor?

On the surface at least, it appears that the sense of competition is palpable. The amount of direct mail advertising I have received from these Baptist churches (and other large Lutheran, Episcopal and Charismatic churches in the area) has noticeably increased. It is obvious that with a new "competitor" moving into the neighborhood, the existing institutional churches are getting nervous. They feel the pressure that comes with a felt need to maintain their market share.

On a much smaller scale, something similar occurred on my first visit to Sarajevo in 1990. As mentioned previously, there were three small congregations serving Sarajevo in 1990. One was an independent charismatic church with 19 people attending services. Another was a Pentecostal church affiliated with the Evangelical Church denomination. This was a new church-planting effort with only six people attending. The third was a Baptist church that had its own building. This congregation had existed for decades and still had less than 25 people attending its services. Together, less than 100 people were gathered in these churches which were trying to reach a city with a population exceeding 500,000.

We came to Sarajevo interested in church planting, so we tried to meet with the pastors of these three existing congregations. Much to our surprise, one of these leaders refused to see us. His response to our visit was clear. Sarajevo already had three churches, and that was enough. He had no desire to see another "competitor" come to town!

We grieved over the myopic perspective that would not allow this pastor to grasp the importance of multiplying efforts on behalf of Christ's Kingdom to preach the gospel in Sarajevo. Even as a small church pastor, his institutional view of ecclesiology led him to see us as competition for his work, not as reinforcements for the warfare he was facing. This kind of thinking hinders the advance of the gospel and the cause of Christ wherever it is found – and it is found all around the world. Yet, in many places where the church is being birthed among unreached peoples, institutionalized perspectives like this are being imported by church planting missionaries who don't realize they are sewing contaminated seed. The fruit of this error will only be recognized after the harvest comes. By then, it will be too late to easily remedy the situation.

Among mission leaders, there is no dispute that competitive thinking of this sort takes its toll. Most mission agencies, fearing reprisal from churches that supply both people and funding for their ministries, simply will not plant new congregations — not even on unreached fields. To keep the "resource pipeline" filled, and to suit local church leaders who see missionary church planting as a competitive enterprise, many para-church leaders have abandoned church planting in favor of other endeavors. In so doing, they have eliminated the single most strategic thing they can do to evangelize unreached cultures. Dr. Winter has spoken with concern to this issue:

> ... many of the mission agencies founded after World War II, out of extreme deference to existing church movements already established in foreign lands, have not even tried to set up churches, and have worked for many years merely as auxiliary agencies in various service capacities trying to help the churches that were already there.... (As a first priority) there needs to be deliberate, intentional effort to establish fellowships of believers (churches) no matter what else is being done ... we must believe sincerely that this....is one of the most important things that can be accomplished.[5] (Parenthetical comments added.)

Generally, institutional leaders will not support new church planting as long as they view evangelism, at home and abroad, as competition with other Christians. Extending the church through multiplication only makes sense when Christians of all stripes see their ministries as a part of the common warfare that must be waged globally against the powers of darkness to see souls won for the Kingdom of light. One well-known mission leader noted in my hearing that, with an ever-increasing proliferation of mission entities, it is inevitable that competition will increase among agencies vying for the church's disposable missions dollar. He said,

"Whenever two people do the same thing, there is a built-in basis for competition."

I would appeal for church leaders to radically re-evaluate such thinking. In truth, competition only results when two people do the same thing **for a different master.** Drawing from the world of business, a Coca-Cola distributor doesn't view it as competition when Kroger, A&P and Costco all sell the same Coke products. All these supermarket chain stores serve the same bottler's interests. It is only when the stores also sell Pepsi and Royal Crown products from the same shelves as Coke that competition results. In this sense, viewing the various denominations as competitors would seem to deny the biblical reality of the unity of the body of Christ. In truth, we all work for the same distributor. Perhaps we can put an end to this competitive mindset in the church by embracing Paul's words from Eph. 4:4-6 at a practical level: "There is one body and one Spirit, just as also you were called in one hope of your calling; one Lord, one faith, one baptism, one God and Father of all who is over all and through all and in all."

4. Professionalization of the ministry is the fourth and final primary symptom of institutionalization.

The need to enhance program quality in an effort to successfully compete with other growing churches also increases the pressure to recruit men and women who are "professionally trained" to do the work of ministry. "Professional training" is usually measured in terms of "institutional credentials" rather than spiritual ones. Rare is the church that will fill an open staff position by discerning the gifts, confirming the calling and observing in practice the proven worth of individuals already within the church who might be considered for the vacancy. Rather, we recruit men and women from outside our churches. Often these people are little known to us. We accept them because they attended the appropriate schools, earned the appropriate degrees and came with the appropriate references. This approach to staffing further weakens the relational dimensions of pastoral leadership. Ministry is therefore increasingly professionalized, and credentialing standards steadily narrow potential fields of service.

As institutionalization steadily moves us toward depersonalizing the work of ministry, even the role of the pastor has not escaped the impact. The traditional role of the pastoral generalist has given way to that of the preaching professional. Consequently, pastoral leadership has more and more to do with secluded time in the study or with program management, and less and less to do with personal ministry in the lives of people. When personal ministry expectations are still demanded of pastors, they are usually focused on the pastor's staff and a few key lay leaders. Pastors are just not able to extend themselves broadly to touch the lives of large numbers of people when programs demand so much time and prove so much more efficient in dealing with the masses. Pastors have therefore tended to narrow the scope of duties they feel available or equipped to perform. Professionalizing the ministry has so specialized credential requirements that even the most highly educated pastors are "trained" for an ever-narrower field of service.

Uneducated laymen fit rather poorly into such a highly professional, education-oriented, and institutionalized scenario. They are offered little opportunity for meaningful ministry though they were designed by God to serve as active members of the priesthood. In the rarefied air of the professional, laymen have little room to breathe, and our commitment to the concept of the priesthood of believers becomes another aspect of theoretical orthodoxy. That is, we hold to the doctrine of the priesthood of believers but allow prepared laymen lacking formal training few opportunities to serve meaningfully in ministry. As our demand for professionalism progresses, institutionalized leaders expect less and less from their "spectator membership," and laymen no longer believe they are intended to do the work of the church. Rather than training them for the work of ministry, we are in fact training laymen to passively accept the notion that they are patently unqualified for the task. This symptom manifests in two additional ways:

Atrophied membership: This condition occurs as the vast untapped spiritual potential of the body lies dormant, under-mobilized and functionally irrelevant to the church's ministry. The potential for redemptive contribution by laymen diminishes over time due to under-activity and overeating. Prolonged disuse of the members of the body in meaningful ministry can lead to permanent, irreversible paralysis in whole or in part. The essence of this problem is captured when church growth specialists observe the accepted maxim that, in most churches, 20 percent of the people do 80 percent of the work.

Richard Halverson, former chaplain of the U.S. Senate, illustrates the problem when he reports on his experience while serving as a pastor. In a circumstance where one of his key lay leaders had to resign from a volunteer church ministry assignment for personal reasons, Pastor Halverson was initially concerned about how such a critical person might be replaced. Careful reflection soon revealed how horribly under-mobilized the members of his church were. He writes of the experience, "As I pondered the loss of this fine young man ... I asked ... 'How many do we need to really do the work of the organization of this church?'... many of the men and women in the church had several jobs... They were very busy with the ecclesiastical establishment. But suppose that each could hold only one job, how many would it take to do the work of that large congregation? At the time, the membership was about 7,000. To my amazement I found that it would require only 365 to do the work that was required to maintain the program of the First Presbyterian Church of Hollywood ... This meant that most of the members of the church could never have a job in the institution. It followed ... that if the work of the church is what is done for the institution, very few, relatively speaking, will ever have an opportunity to do the work of the church."[6] In such a situation where most of the church is inactive, the strength of the local body declines and the "muscle tissue" atrophies.

Learning Disabilities: These disabilities are manifest as pastors abdicate their responsibility for equipping and mobilizing the members of the church for ministry. Narrowly focused and highly trained professional ministers are simply not prepared to train generalists among the laity to put their faith into practice. Moreover, though institutional leaders are charged by God with the primary duty to equip laymen for ministry (Eph. 4:11-16) program responsibilities keep them so busy they simply have little time to make the kind of personal investment which training others would require.

If laymen happen to develop a sincere desire to play a larger part in the work of ministry, they are commonly urged to pursue training in formal institutional settings. This tendency has allowed Bible college and seminary education to become the best hope for "equipping the saints" for the work of service. But even in these institutional settings, theoreticians rather than church practitioners most often instruct laymen.

It might be more accurate to call this symptom a "teaching disability" since it has more to do with clergy deficiencies in teaching and training than with the ability of laymen to learn. In any case, both personal discipleship of laymen and individualized training of emerging leaders were designed by the Lord of the church to occur primarily in the context of the local assembly. Such church-based alternatives to ministerial formation are being largely neglected. Where intensive church-based training is being practiced it is not being much appreciated. Institutionalized leaders are likely to choose instead to refer aspiring leaders to residential seminarians divorced from the church. This tendency is likely to keep on increasing the influence of institutionalization.

Community Ecclesiology as a Healthy Alternative

The prevalence of these symptoms and their side effects make it apparent that concerns about "institutionalization" should not be quickly dismissed. In fact, thinking pathologically about this problem, it is interesting to consider whether or not the condition is treatable. Certainly, one would hope that recognition and early detection of the symptoms could make successful treatment possible. But, effective treatment presupposes that the patient (the institutionalized leader) recognizes that unhealthy symptoms exist and that he or she desires to reverse those symptoms before they worsen. Institutional thinkers are not often willing even to admit the problem. So they live in denial, like an ostrich with its head in the sand, feeling secure and defending the status quo. This makes redemptive change difficult if not impossible to implement. If leaders want to face the problem, there are **alternatives** to these prevalent but unhealthy institutional perspectives.

A Change in Ecclesiology Must Precede a Change in Missiology

"Community Ecclesiology" offers an organic model for church life that builds its ministry around strong relationships and deep personal commitment rather than around programs. While the church gathered is important to this model, most meetings are intended to support and encourage members in their personal ministry within the church or in their individual arenas of influence outside the body. The regular meetings are less formal, less rigidly structured and highly responsive to crises faced by church members. Even the Sunday morning service can be radically changed by issues facing a single member. In this model, anything that impacts one member in a serious way affects the whole church family seriously.

In applying a community ecclesiology, small groups enhance the intimacy and cohesiveness of the membership as a whole. But by themselves, small groups are not a substitute for congregational structures (groups of 35 to 120), which are necessary to support community dynamics. Because much of the life of the church is identified with congregational sized groups, small churches are uniquely well suited to operate within a community-oriented philosophy of ministry. Generally, small churches will be more effective in this highly relational paradigm than large ones. When highly relational, community-oriented standards are used to establish goals and to measure success a small church has the potential to be healthier and more dynamic than a large one. This is good news for the 330,000 small churches in America!

Not necessarily centered in a building or identified with specific facilities, members gather in the community model for meetings that are relationally supportive and highly responsive to need. Members are active participants in the community's corporate meetings and most are well known to one another through frequent contact and interaction which goes beyond church-wide meetings. Instead of relying on programs to meet needs, people are encouraged to bear one another's burdens as they become known within the body. In this model of church life, a forum is routinely made available for members to make their serious burdens known to one another. Need meeting, burden bearing, truth telling and love giving are non-negotiable community dynamics.

Leaders in this model are identified in the course of ministry within the body, and they "emerge" by proving themselves to be servant hearted. Emergent leaders demonstrate their wisdom in the context of ministry. As they serve, they also exhibit both the gifts of the Spirit and the virtues of experience. Implementing community ecclesiology demands a shift in our convictions regarding leadership development. Godly character, a sense of calling, and consistent redemptive ministry within the community replace institutional credentials as prerequisites for serving in key leadership roles.

In the community model for local church life, leaders may develop their knowledge and ministry skills through progressive non-formal or informal training. They need not have obtained official institutional credentials for their efforts. Emergent leaders are men and women of proven worth who are qualified to give guidance to others because they have **earned** the right to lead, they have **learned** the skills necessary for their roles and their gifts have been clearly **discerned** in the context of their participation in the local assembly.[7] This model perpetuates the apostolic approach to leadership development and takes us back to biblical parameters for recognizing good and gifted people fit to assume responsible roles in the church. Paul's affirmation of Timothy in Philippians 2:19-23 is an excellent example of apostolic recognition for leadership developed in the context of the church.

"But I hope in the Lord Jesus to send Timothy to you shortly, so that I also may be encouraged when I learn of your condition. For I have no one else of kindred spirit who will genuinely be concerned for your welfare. For they all seek after their own interests, not those of Christ Jesus. But you know of his proven worth, that he served with me in the furtherance of the gospel like a child serving his father. Therefore I hope to send him immediately, as soon as I see how things go with me."

Community ecclesiology liberates church leaders from the competitive pressures engendered by an institutional perspective. Instead of viewing other churches as competitors, community-oriented leaders see other assemblies as additional households in the extended family of God or as additional fighting units in the same army serving the same king — even if under a different small unit commander. While tending their own flocks well — evangelizing, shepherding, training, mobilizing, multiplying—community leaders readily encourage ministers in other churches to do the same. In fact, community leaders view such positive support among diverse churches as being in the best interest of accomplishing the mission ordained for the larger body of Christ.

Let me illustrate this reality by going back to my earlier example concerning the large Southern Baptist congregation's relocation to North Atlanta. I have already explained how this move created a sense of competition among institutional churches in the area. Our own facility at Northside Community Church is also located in the shadows of this mega-church's new building complex. I don't, however, see this mega-ministry as a competitor. It is instead a much-needed reinforcing army adding substantial muscle to the Lord's host in our community. My surveys show that if every church in North Atlanta were filled to capacity twice each Sunday, half the population of our neighborhoods still would have nowhere to go to attend services. Even with the influx of Baptist believers by the thousands, we remain a substantially under-churched and still under-evangelized community. We can use all the help we can get to reach our lost neighbors!

Furthermore, it is no threat to have this church's famously gifted pastor, a world-renowned speaker, as our new neighbor. Members of my church overwhelmingly affirm his special abilities as a preacher of God's Word. Many in my congregation faithfully tune in to his TV and radio ministry and some no doubt regularly buy his books. But members of my church aren't considering a move to this mega-church. They already have a home at NCC.

By way of analogy, I could use my own family. My wife and I have four sons ranging in age from 18-23. They are avid baseball fans. If John Smoltz, last year's Cy Young Award winning pitcher for the Atlanta Braves, moved next door to our home, they would all be thrilled. They would want to talk to him, and to get autographs (maybe even to get tickets!). But they wouldn't vacate their bedrooms to move in with John Smoltz. They already have a family. So it is with members committed to a community approach to ecclesiology. As a stable family of believers, we are committed to each other and to our corporate goals. We welcome new neighbors into our area, but when a new neighbor does move in, our members don't consider moving out. New churches in the neighborhood are reinforcements for the King's army. They are not competitors, and they do not threaten our ongoing existence.

Redefining Success in Community Terms

Pursuing a community-oriented ecclesiology, the emphasis is no longer placed on being bigger or better than other local bodies. Rather, we are striving to be the best kingdom family we can be —

maximizing the quality of our ministry to others. Redefining success in community terms places emphasis on two key factors:

    (A) Personal care and spiritual development aimed at mobilizing all church members for meaningful ministry, and

    (B) increasing the potential for spiritual reproductivity.

In the Community Model, *maximum mobilization* of members and *maximum multiplication* of believing communities replaces maximum numerical growth as a measure of success. With these two goals in mind, most small churches can be quite effective in ministry. Few large churches can match a small church's capacity to care for everyone identified with their ministry. Redefining success in this way can relieve small church leaders from a felt need to compete at a program level with mega-churches. In effect, redefining success puts all churches on a level playing field when each one, regardless of size, has a role in defeating a common enemy. I look forward to the day when leaders in the church stop striving with each other and instead bless one another in our respective attempts to advance the kingdom.

Citing George Barna's work again, he suggests that redefining success in church ministry is one of the most significant needs facing churches in America at the end of the 20th century. He writes:

> As our culture and social environment change, we must also consider the opportunity to redefine how we determine the success of a church. Typically, we do so by counting. We count the number of people who attend on Sundays. We count how many people are in Sunday school classes. We count the number of members in the church. We count how many dollars have been contributed for ministry and maintenance. We emphasize quantity toward determining the success of a church. Perhaps the '90s will enable us to examine **quality** rather than quantity, as a better indicator of success and church growth.[8] (emphasis added)

But it is not enough for institutional leaders to simply shift their focus in part to qualitative growth factors. Responding to institutionalization will require more comprehensive transformation of our churches. In fact, trying to bring about institutional renewal in a larger church simply by integrating community dynamics into subgroups may only bring about greater distress. Howard Snyder has written much about the need for church renewal. He speaks to this concern concisely:

> Is there hope for churches whose spiritual spontaneity and community life are stifled by rigid institutional forms? This is a question of institutional renewal. In such churches individual spiritual renewal among the believers is not enough, and by itself may provoke divisions and factions, just as new wine bursts old wineskins. A general principle for highly institutionalized churches is that *institutional renewal must accompany personal renewal.* Where this is not possible, or where the official guardians of the institution will not permit it, the old institution may have to be abandoned and new structures formed. There are times when old wineskins must be replaced by new ones. This has occurred repeatedly in church history.[9]

Synder is recommending that new communities begin wherever institutional resistance would tend to retard the dynamics of relational ministry. He also suggests that "the guardians of the institution" may not be favorably disposed to admitting the dynamics of community into an existing programmatic context.

We should recognize that such resistance is born of very real concerns and should be anticipated. Shifting the institution's philosophical focus from programs with mass appeal to highly relational personal ministry can require massive change. Serious attempts at establishing community may call for a redesign of facilities, a replacement of staff, a reorientation of priorities, a realignment of schedules and a release of large numbers of members to multiplying ministry. In most cases, creating new wineskins will prove to be an easier option than this kind of comprehensive institutional renewal. As the saying goes, having babies is simply far easier than raising the dead!

Implementing community dynamics will certainly require more of laymen than the present approach to programmed ministry. In effect, the transition must move the local assembly from a "hired gun" approach to ministry, to a "posse" paradigm. Laymen will rightfully feel that they are assuming far more risks and far more responsibilities as they return to a model in which they are expected to actually *do the work of ministry.*

Committed institutional church members will shoulder the burden and experience the benefits of doing more themselves. Many will refuse to respond to the challenge. Some will resist the openness of others to doing so — especially if a majority move in the direction of a more community-oriented ministry. After all, the very nature of the church is at stake. As I mentioned earlier, the guardians of the institution will naturally be inclined to protect the status quo.

Anticipating such resistance to change, we must acknowledge that rethinking our measures for success will be easier than retooling to implement a different approach to ministry. Retooling will, however, pay great dividends at home and abroad. The next chapter will highlight some of the priority changes that need to be considered by small church leaders. In that chapter, we will see that the key to retooling will be found in our ability to refuse the natural and ingrained tendency to be enamored with numbers alone. God's Word is clear, outward appearance has never been the Lord's guideline. He sees not as we see. The question is, "are we willing to look at the world of the church through His eyes?"

Allowing David to Fight Goliath

You are not able to go out against this Philistine to fight him; for you are but a youth....

I Sam. 17:33

Paraphrasing the pessimism of I Sam. 17:33, we might imagine the King Sauls of our own time saying to the leaders of small churches, "You are not able to go into the mission field to fight the giant of Islam, for you are too small!" As one who has been arguing for the place of modern-day Davids on the battlefields where the giants of ignorance and idolatry dominate the unreached peoples of the earth, I can assert with some confidence that Saul's skepticism is alive and well in the church of Jesus Christ. Mission professionals, denominational leaders and traditional institutional pastors simply seem to forget that God still delights in showing Himself strong on behalf of the underdog. In this chapter, I want to argue again for the merits of small church ministry in general, and for small church mission potential in particular. I want to root my argument in the scriptures.

To release the latent resources, both human and financial, residing in the small churches of the world, we need to be willing to re-evaluate alternative approaches to battle and to retool our methodologies to fit our modern-day Davids as they take the field. Reflect for a moment on the familiar story of David's encounter with Goliath. Don't let your previous exposure to this text deprive you of a fresh look at what God is teaching us here. As David became aware of Goliath's challenge to the armies of Israel, the scripture records his response to the situation.

> David said to Saul, "Let no man's heart fail on account of him; your servant will go and fight with this Philistine." Then Saul said to David, "You are not able to go against this Philistine to fight with him; for you are but a youth while he has been a warrior from his youth." But David said to Saul, "Your servant was tending his father's sheep. When a lion or a bear came and took a lamb from the flock, I went after him and attacked him, and rescued it from his mouth; and when he rose up against me, I seized him by his beard and struck him and killed him. Your servant has killed both the lion and the bear; and this uncircumcised Philistine will be like one of them, since he has taunted the armies of the living God." And David said, "The Lord who delivered me from the paw of the lion and from the paw of the bear, he will deliver me from the hand of this Philistine." And Saul said to David, "Go, and may the Lord be with you." Then Saul clothed David with his garments and put a bronze helmet on his head, and he clothed him with armor. David girded his sword over his armor and tried to walk, for he had not tested them. So David said to Saul, "I cannot go with these, for I have not tested them." And David took them off. He took his stick in his hand and chose for himself five smooth stones from the brook, and put them in the shepherd's bag which he had, even in his pouch, and his sling was in his hand; and he approached the Philistine. Then the Philistine came on and approached David, with the shield-bearer in front of him. When the Philistine looked and saw David, he disdained him; for he was but a youth, and ruddy, with a handsome appearance. The Philistine said to David, "Am I a dog, that you come to

me with stick?" And the Philistine cursed David by his gods. The Philistine also said to David, "Come to me, and I will give your flesh to the birds of the sky and the beasts of the field." Then David said to the Philistine "You come to me with a sword, a spear, and a javelin, but I come to you in the name of the Lord of hosts, the God of the armies of Israel, whom you have taunted. This day the Lord will deliver you up into my hands, and I will strike you down and remove your head from you. And I will give the dead bodies of the army of the Philistines this day to the birds of the sky and the wild beasts of the earth, that all the earth may know that there is a God in Israel, and that all this assembly may know that the Lord does not deliver by sword or by spear; for the battle is the Lord's and He will give you into our hands." Then it happened when the Philistine rose and came and drew near to meet David, that David ran quickly toward the battle line to meet the Philistine. And David put his hand into his bag and took from it a stone and slung it, and struck the Philistine on his forehead, so that he fell on his face to the ground. Thus David prevailed over the Philistine with a sling and a stone, and he struck the Philistine and killed him; but there was no sword in David's hand. — I Sam. 17:32-51

Who Says We Are Not Able?

I want to direct your attention to just four of the many insights that can be gleaned from this account. They will hopefully help us get beyond the negative influence of 20th century naysayers who, like Saul, simply cannot see the wisdom of allowing modern-day Davids to fight contemporary Goliaths. In this passage:

Too many were too much focused on the fight: We often miss the important premise that prompted God to empower David to defeat Goliath. In verse 46, David declares that the giant from Gath would be delivered into his hands by God, that Goliath's head would roll and that the dead bodies of Philistine soldiers would be fed to the birds and the beasts for a specific purpose. In David's victory, the Lord Almighty was to be glorified in such a way that all the earth would know that there is a God in Israel. Moreover, all the soldiers from both armies in the field would recognize that the Lord does not deliver by sword or by spear. From the shepherd boy's victory over the grand Philistine warrior, mankind would be better able to see that "the battle is the Lord's."

In effect, God blessed David and Israel in order to call all the nations of the earth to attention. He wanted the whole world to see that the living God is sovereign in the earth and that He reigned over Israel! Unlike all the men involved, God was not worried about the battle at hand. He was moved by a missiological goal not a military motivation. He was concerned about permitting the nations to see His glory.

Too many were too much focused on the fight at hand. God was focused on bringing glory to His name! I believe that just as God delighted in using a shepherd boy to bring Him honor in 1000 BC, He delights in letting the shepherds of small flocks bring honor to His name in 2000 AD. God is still moved by the same missiological motivation that prompted Him to use David. His strategy has not changed. He demonstrates His might today as He did then, through those who are weak, so that all the glory can go to the praise of His name among the nations.

If we acknowledge that the battle still belongs to the Lord, we will also affirm that His glory is better revealed in our weaknesses than in our strengths. With that confidence in mind, small church leaders can take to the field and face the battle just as David did. Taking this principle beyond the point of theoretical orthodoxy and putting it into practice, we will vacate the seat of Saul and choose to strategically release modern-day Davids to fight 20th century Goliaths!

Too many were too much focused on the giant: Another observation we can make from the text is drawn from verses 33-37. Saul was skeptical of David's capacity to fight because he viewed the boy and the battle with a professional soldier's preconceptions about warfare. David's point of reference, on the other hand, had little to do with his abilities compared to that of military men or menacing giants. Instead, David's perspective had much to do with God's demonstrated abilities to keep the boy safe in the face of overwhelming adversaries. He had already fought the lion and the bear — and he had won. But defeating the beasts of the field had not proven David's personal prowess. His victories on behalf of the sheep in his fold had proven God's ability to preserve him against all odds. Too many were too much focused on the giant. In the face of this new trial, David was focused on God, not Goliath. The shepherd simply remembered what Saul had forgotten — the battle belongs to the Lord!

Under the stress of conflict, God's appointed king had lost sight of where his confidence should have been placed. So it is often today as we face the giants that taunt the armies of the living God on a global scale in the 20th century. George Otis identifies Islam, Hinduism and materialism as chief among these giants.[1] From our experience in post-Communist Central Europe, we could add extreme nationalism to the list of oversized adversaries opposing the gospel today. Whatever their identity, as we face these incredibly formidable foes, we dare not repeat Saul's mistake by focusing our attention on the giants. If we do, we may well end up presupposing that the "small-church Davids" of the world have no place on the battlefield. In our day as in David's, God can do great things through anyone He chooses. The Lord can handle the giants in our lives if we keep our eyes focused on Him.

Too many were too much focused on the small size of the soldier: A third relevant insight can be inferred from assumptions made by David's brothers, by Saul and by Goliath himself. In verse 42, it is recorded that when Goliath, "looked and saw David, he disdained him." The giant's reaction should be no surprise to us, for by this time in the narrative, similar contempt had already been shown by David's brothers and by the king. Why all the scorn?

To all these men, friend and foe alike, David was not well suited for this battle. He was a boy coming toward a giant with a stick, a few stones and a sling. The soon-to-be hero hardly seemed a worthy adversary. Yet the story teaches us that we dare not assume that only large armies and giant soldiers are fit to fight. Those we disdain may go about the battle in an unconventional way and still prove more effective than professional soldiers. Not much has changed through the ages. Even today, too many are too much focused on the size of the soldiers involved in the battle.

We need not look just to the Bible to learn this lesson. Similar examples are offered by the most imposing superpower governments in our own generation. Military might and technological muscle were well developed when the United States and the Soviet Union marched into their respective debacles in Vietnam and Afghanistan. In both instances, the tenacious toughness of ill-equipped, unyielding guerrilla fighters in these remarkably different contexts demonstrated remarkably similar results. The hugely under-armed "little guys" outlasted the virtually unlimited military strength of these superpower armies and eventually forced them from the field.

This insight regarding the potential success of small-scale challengers has been known for centuries. The bottom line was even captured by Heroditus in his words of wisdom penned in the 5th century BC. He wrote, "It is the gods' custom to bring low all things of surpassing greatness." In the vernacular we might say that the Word of God and the witness of history teach us that "the bigger they are, the harder they fall." It is a timeless fallacy to conclude that natural might always prevails. It is a trendy fallacy to believe that only large churches and professional missionary "soldiers" are fit for facing giants on the world's mission fields.

Too many were too much focused on traditional weapons of war: Finally, we would do well to imagine the scene set in verse 39 when Saul tries to put his armor on David's body. In my mind I see a freckle-faced, red headed boy from a Norman Rockwell type picture. This brave boy's frame is much too small for the equipment being draped about his body. He is more consumed than clothed by the king's armor. The would-be-warrior is made invisible rather than intimidating by this protective covering. Any observer can easily see that the king's battle regalia simply doesn't fit the small shepherd boy. After all, it is hard to walk if your helmet rests on your shoulders rather than your head, and if your breastplate rattles around your knees. David had to help Saul recognize that there were other approaches to warfare, and better tools for a shepherd boy's part in the fight, than the ones the king was accustomed to using. When David faced Goliath, too many were too much focused on traditional weapons of war.

Today the situation is much the same. We must remember that mega-church muscle is not the only weaponry available to God's army. Small church leaders will need to bear these realities in mind as they take up their more meager armaments for spiritual battle in our own day. Never will they match the financial, human or technological resources that better equipped armies from bigger churches bring to the field. But with the weapons small church leaders have tested, and with methods that better suit their smaller frames, these modern-day Davids can still go to war. In the final analysis, the battle will be won not by our wit and wisdom, nor by our power to wage war in our own strength. Victory over the giants will come to us as it did to David — by God's strength alone. The battle still belongs to the Lord!

Applying These Insights to the Mission Enterprise

I hope these insights will free us to allow the Davids of our day their chance to face Goliath. In some respects, a careful reflection on the nature of cross-cultural church planting among unreached peoples should further increase our appreciation of the relative value of including small churches in plans for global evangelism. After all, small church multiplication is the key to saturation church planting. And saturation church planting strategies are the most effective strategies for penetrating unreached cultures. The truth is, many leaders mobilized from smaller multiplication-oriented communities are better prepared to create new churches than are their counterparts from institutionalized settings. This is especially so if the institutionally trained leaders come from non-reproducing mega-church contexts.

Most missionaries mobilized from large churches have never experienced the dynamics of community they are expected to produce on the field. That is, they are tasked to give birth to an animal they have never seen, or felt or touched. The absence of experience and firsthand exposure to small church dynamics militates against their eventual effectiveness in reproducing churches that multiply.

Yet, if conversions are produced among a targeted people, the resulting church is in most cases going to start small. Often they will remain small. This is the case simply because the pace of conversion growth is slow in contexts where no church has ever existed. But "smallness" is perpetuated for other reasons. In most settings, smallness is dictated by the cost of buildings, the expense of operating a new church, and the opposition of governments hostile to the gospel. Persecution in volatile situations necessitates less visible models for emerging churches. The desire to spread the influence of the church through rapid multiplication (remember the saturation church planting strategy) also tends to favor smaller congregations on unreached fields. If missionary leaders being mobilized to unreached peoples come from a context where they have always been encouraged to account for their success by counting and accumulating large numbers of members, a commitment to multiplying small churches can be an unmotivating goal that is difficult to embrace.

Imagine the dilemma of the institutionally oriented leader. If your home church is a 5,000 member mega-church, it is hard to get excited (or to induce excitement in others) by reporting that 150 believers in Mostar have sent a portion of their church family to establish a new work in Tuzla where 35 are now meeting for services. Institutional ears are trained to file such reports in the mental card catalogue under the letter "I" for "irrelevant." For the cross-cultural church planting missionary, however, such small-scale reports of success in multiplication are the life blood of a movement for Christ among an unreached people.

I readily admit that training for missionary candidates can re-orient institutional leaders to expect and appreciate the necessity of focusing on small church development on unreached fields. Training can even help better prepare missionaries to participate in the process of reaching a nation or a people through a church planting movement. But such classroom training is no substitute for actual experience. In my view, a major problem arises when missionary trainers tell their students that they should do this kind of multipli-cation ministry abroad, while at home in the United States, the proponents of saturation church planting are largely not practicing what they preach.

Let me illustrate from my own experience. Some years ago, I attended a meeting to discuss mission strategy at the headquarters of United World Missions (UWM) in Union Mills, N.C. Represen-tatives from UWM, Advancing Churches in Missions Commitment (ACMC), the Antioch Network, AD 2000, Bible Education by Extension, Partners International, DAWN 2000 and the Alliance for Saturation Church Planting were present. I can hardly imagine a group of leaders more committed to saturation church planting than these men. To this group, the concept of small church multipli-cation as a global strategy was an accepted priority. Yet, aside from myself, all of those represented in the meeting were attending large churches. None of them were personally involved in a reproducing church at home in the United States.

I do not want to be critical of these organizations or their representatives because they are all doing much good for the mission world. In fact, many of these men have profoundly impacted my own thinking about mission theory. But this represents an incon-sistency between the principle and practice of missiology. Many of the key spokesmen for saturation church planting are professional theoreticians and not personal practitioners. They are only "theoret-ically orthodox" with regard to saturation church planting. Institutional theorizing must be replaced by a commitment to the kind of functional ecclesiology at home that can reach the world by being reproduced with cultural sensitivity among the unreached peoples of the earth. To be most effective, I believe that mission leaders at home should routinely practice what they preach for application abroad.

Imagine the benefits that can be obtained by sending missionaries from functioning communities of believers meeting in small, reproducing churches. The assigned task for such leaders would simply be to replicate similar communities on the mission field. Such a goal for leaders experienced in reproducing ministries at home becomes a logical extension when applied to the mission field. It is not theoretical. It is tangible. The process is not mysterious and unfamiliar. It is already a part of their personal experience. It is both consistent with their practice of church life, and a reasonable objective. Ordinary people can do this!

The dynamics that make small church life easily reproducible also make small church life well suited to meet the needs of the unreached peoples of the world. Missionaries trained through contextualized discipleship and apprenticeship style modeling in reproducing churches at home will have the right genes to produce the desired fruit on the mission field. Small churches, therefore, should be seen as a valuable source for the kind of seeds needed to produce a harvest of church planting around the world.

Where Do We Go From Here?

By now it should be clear that I believe institutional approaches to Western ministry and to missionary church planting must be overcome if the kind of community life described in the book of Acts is to become a reality at home or abroad. Redirecting the momentum of institutionalization will require substantial change. We will need to repent of faulty thinking in our ecclesiology, and we will need to retool our churches to facilitate multiplication rather than expansion growth. We must also reclaim the priority of releasing laymen to do the work of ministry that God intended them to do as representatives of their communities of faith. The following suggestions may prove helpful to those who choose to dispense with institutional approaches to missionary church planting in favor of pursuing community dynamics. If small church potential for missions ministry is to be maximized we must be mindful of these priorities for change.

1. We must encourage the multiplication of Christian communities in the form of small congregations.

There has always been room in God's economy for David to fight Goliath. When Jesus first challenged the church with the responsibility to be His witnesses to the world (Acts 1:8), He gave that charge to a small group of 120 believers in the upper room. He could have waited to see that number reach 3,000 at Pentecost and then urged them to work from a mega-church base in Jerusalem, but He didn't. Jesus' strategy called for multiplication of small churches throughout the known world. He was looking for the David's of the 1st century. Why should we disdain the Master's plan for world missions? Jesus' approach is, after all, far easier for laymen to implement than the professionalized missionary approach promoted globally today.

I have tried to give some insight into the benefits of community ecclesiology through our own story and through strategic reflection as well. Let me summarize some of the advantages that are inherent in small congregations. These strengths should encourage small church leaders who are searching for a reason to release themselves from the bondage of institutional thinking:

• Small churches generally offer more opportunity for a higher percentage of lay involvement than do larger ones.

• Small churches rely more on volunteer, non-professional leadership than do larger ones. This invites many to be involved in service and adds a dimension to body life that disappears when the pianist, choir director, janitor, secretary, etc. are all part of the "paid staff."

• Small churches generally demonstrate a greater interest in caring for people than for programs. They are more relational than large churches, and therefore offer a greater sense of intimacy to each and every member.

• Small churches experience more of the joys of intergenerational fellowship than larger congregations do. This phenomenon encourages a greater commitment among the generations and fosters deeper appreciation between older and younger believers. Smallness also allows for a kind of "cross pollination" that is not possible when a local body accommodates continued growth by structuring subgroups around age, gender and marital status. Such segmentation generates a measure of separation that deprives members of the benefits of sharing life with others unlike them.

• Small churches are more informal, more flexible in their schedules, more family-oriented in their ministries and often simply easier to fit into. They offer a place for everyone to belong.

• Small churches are less complex. Compared to larger bodies, small churches grow at a faster rate, with greater overall quality, while offering more variety to attract the unchurched populace and to meet the needs of existing Christians.

• Small churches are survivors. They are hardy organisms that can endure stress, strain, oppression, occasional failures and even a succession of disasters. The resilience of small churches makes them especially suitable for attempts at transplantation across cultural barriers. The small church has a unique capacity to adapt, adjust and flourish in new environments. Lyle Shaller has done a good job articulating the merits of small church ministry. Interested leaders should especially study his book, *The Small Church Is Different.*[2]

2. We must apply church growth principles toward the goal of multiplication so that those insights can better serve the mission potential of small churches as well as large ones.

The truth is that small church leaders should think big. Church growth is still the right objective, and lack of growth is not a legitimate option for healthy congregations. A church, whether large or small, that has stopped growing is in decline. So even a community-oriented philosophy of ministry will value growth. Community ecclesiology simply applies the principles of church growth to the end of multiplication, rather than toward the goal of amassing ever-larger numbers in one congregation. Multiplication seems to be the clear priority in Acts where the upper room church of 120 grew quickly to thousands but still found ways to meet regularly in smaller fellowships. Kent and Barbara Hughes effectively express the caution we need to maintain in this respect as they write in *Liberating the Ministry from the Success Syndrome*:

> Certainly there is nothing wrong with the wise use of any of [these church growth] principles. They should be part of the intelligent orchestration of ministry. However, when the refrain they play is numerical growth — when the persistent motif is numbers — then the siren song becomes deeply sinister; growth in numbers, growth in giving, growth in staff, growth in programs — numbers, numbers, numbers! Pragmatism becomes the conductor. The audience inexorably becomes man rather than God. Subtle self-promotion becomes the driving force.[3]

Ultimately, driven leaders who fail to reach their numerical goals will become disillusioned and may drop out of the race. If we acknowledge the value of touching other people's lives for Christ over driving toward institutional goals, perhaps our work in small churches will prove more fulfilling. The crux of Jesus' earthly ministry, after all, was the investment He made in the lives of twelve, then seventy and then perhaps 120. In His life and ministry, quality was consistently valued over quantity, and people were valued over programs. But His deep work in the lives of a few still touched the masses and ultimately turned the whole world upside down. Let us return to the Master's plan for building His church through personal discipleship and multiplication of Christian communities. Numbers simply must not remain our primary measure of success in ministry.

3. We must recognize and respond to the expanding demand for relational ministry and personal approaches to meeting human needs.

The global trend toward urbanization has resulted in disappointment, dysfunction and dehumanization on an unprecedented scale. Never has the need for personal concern and community living been greater. George Barna sees this even on the American scene and makes an observation that may be equally applicable worldwide if we shape our churches appropriately:

> ... the church is better poised than any other institution ... to respond to the rampant loneliness of the American people. In addition to bringing people together on a regular basis, the church has the potential to create lasting bonds between people who can share common interests and common goals. As more and more adults search for opportunities to meet other people, one of the greatest selling points of the church in the coming decade will be the ability to meet other people from the community. Systems, policies, programs and procedures which capitalize upon this felt need will enable churches to grow in numbers, in depth of ministry and in the ability to celebrate the love of Christ poured out through His people.[4]

But such will not be possible unless we move away from institutionalization and restore our capacity for community. Whether in small churches or in congregational groups that subdivide larger churches into meaningful communities of believers, we must give people permission to share their joys as well as their pain. We must provide a place for them to reach out for personal support rather than programs. If relational approaches to ministry are to become a reality, significant changes in our functional ecclesiology are unavoidable. We must retool! Our success in expanding the church's capacity to care will depend greatly upon laymen being prepared to do the lion's share of ministry. As strange as this may sound today, this is exactly what Paul prescribed in Ephesians 4:11-16. It is time to return to this biblical paradigm.

Moreover, to be effective in performing the work of ministry, laymen will need to be well trained by their pastors and elders. For the most part, their preparation will need to be done contextually and not in residential seminaries. Effectiveness in this process will demand a greater appreciation for biblically based methods of ministerial formation and a more realistic appraisal of the relatively weak though more widely accepted institutional approaches to leadership development. All indications are that laymen are hungry for the opportunity to shoulder the load if institutional barriers to their service can be removed. Progressive church leaders will readily clear the way!

4. We must be willing to ask more of the laity than they ever dreamed they could give in time, talent and treasure to serve the Kingdom.

Put another way, **privatization of faith must give way to deeper personal commitment.** We must encourage one another toward a total surrender to Christ. George Barna has spoken to this concern as it relates to the American context but his words could apply equally well to cross-cultural situations. If we are to be taken seriously by lost people in our world, Barna suggests we must prove our own sincerity by putting our faith into action:

> ... we will have to demonstrate the relevance of Christianity in every dimension of our lives. We cannot be Sunday Christians. More emphasis must be placed upon why we believe and how we live those beliefs. As Americans grow increasingly hardened and skeptical, the built-in credibility of Christianity will be steadily reduced in people's minds. Christians must communicate the importance of the faith by exhibiting a lifestyle based upon a Christian philosophy of life. We have to convey our perception that the difference we make in the world is personally fulfilling, but achieved for the benefit of others, not

ourselves. In short, we must be representatives of Christ through more than just the words we speak. Compassion, joy and a sense of mission must shine through us as often as possible.[5]

He also writes about our **need to turn attention from programmed ministry to personal involvement with others.** The times in which we live and the mission targets we are attempting to penetrate simply demand a more interdependent approach to Christian living. As Barna puts it, we dare not downplay discipleship:

> One of the glaring weaknesses of the church has been in the area of discipling and accountability. If we are to make inroads during these next 10 years, we must support each other in deeper, more personal ways. While we may feel threatened by the vulnerability of confession, learning, and sharing needs, there seems to be little chance that the Body can be strengthened sufficiently to progress without the discipline of discipleship.
>
> We will be tempted to downplay the importance of commitment and obedience. We will be tempted to soften the truth so that a hardened generation will give us a fair hearing. There is a fine line between clever marketing and compromised spirituality.[6]

Jesus taught his disciples that the Kingdom of God is like a pearl of great price. Its value is so great that, if need be, we should sell everything we own in order to buy it. Modern-day disciples are not served well if we make the Kingdom seem more like costume jewelry, inexpensive, easy to come by, and as easy to discard as it is to obtain.

5. We must accept non-formal training as a credible route to vocational Christian ministry.

It will be no small problem to wrestle the responsibility of ministry from the iron grip of institutionally trained clergymen, but such must be done. Dr. Ralph Winter has agreed that this is among the most pressing issues facing those involved in world mission today. In his view, **professionalizing the ministry has dramatically slowed the advance of the gospel everywhere in the world!** Under the sub-title, *Recovering from a Professionally Trained Ministry*, he writes:

> Despite the normal perspective of newly arriving missionaries from the United States, the Christian movement on a global level continues doggedly to depend upon informal apprenticeship methods of ministerial training rather than the recent adoption in the United States of a European state-church style of professional education in the residential schools. This is mainly because apprenticeship is more versatile and flexible than the classroom. We must outgrow the kind of "professional" processes of ministerial formation which have been so assiduously cultivated in the past fifty years in the United States. The fact is, wherever seminaries — or other types of lengthy residential programs — have been introduced overseas *and made mandatory for ordination*, the growth of the church has been severely crippled.
>
> Thus, what has in some circles become almost universally hailed as a legitimate goal — a "seminary education" — may become more clearly a questionable goal in the nineties, even in the United States.[7]

We need to understand that our options are not limited to seminary training or no training at all. No one favors a re-amateurization of ministry at home or on the mission field. At the same time, we should openly acknowledge that apprenticeship, non-formal and informal contextualized training and theological education by extension, are in many cases more effective than residential schools in producing qualified ministry leaders. The suggestion here is that our goal be aimed at **better training on a broader level,** a more massive preparation of the body for the work of ministry than the seminary scenario can ever allow. Though we should be cautious to avoid mobilizing poorly trained leaders, we must not be afraid to champion a sincere re-affirmation of the ministry potential of laymen well trained in their home churches.

The need to develop higher expectations for laymen may seem to fit the mission fields of the world more than our own setting in America. But the truth is that until America's potential "missionary laymen" experience the demands and the delights of true Christian community, they will never be able to reproduce the dynamic cross-culturally. Even the Baby Boomers of our culture who have been consistently coddled by parents and pastors alike will need to be challenged to total abandonment to Christ. Leith Anderson offers encouraging insight about boomers' potential to face their responsibilities in this regard. Writing in his book, *Dying for Change,* he notes:

> The baby boomer should feel "right at home" in the church that holds high expectations of its people, including church membership and attendance, devotional disciplines, service inside and outside the church, financial support, social responsibility, and Christian lifestyle. Baby boomers want to be challenged, and many of them will be attracted to such a church even if they won't join, give, or serve. They like the idea of high expectations even if they don't personally comply.

(But) high expectations alone are not enough; in fact, in themselves they will probably eventually drive people away. With these high expectations must come the *provision of enablement* to meet them. Enablement includes teaching, training, counseling, support, discipline, role models, classes, books and other tools. This creates an environment in which the boomers can feel positive about the church and about self, which opens the way to even higher expectations.[8] Perhaps those higher expectations can be channeled toward multiplication of Christian communities among the unreached people of the world!

Conclusion

If Leith Anderson is right and the church is "dying for change," we must begin immediately to alter our thinking about what makes for church sickness or success. My great concern is that institutionalization will continue to deprive small churches of their great missions potential by keeping laymen satisfied with a seat in the bleachers while professional clergy continue to perform on the field for a passive audience. We must not let it be so. And we must face the damaging effect which institutionalization has had on the church in the West. **We must begin to believe that bigger is not better, and we must gain far greater confidence in God's ability to use laymen in ministry.** Our greatest hope for a remedy to institutionalization is to promote community dynamics and church multiplication at home and abroad, whatever the cost.

If we fail to respond to these realities, the mega-churches of America and the rest of the world may soon be as empty and irrelevant to global evangelism as the cathedrals of Western Europe are today. Perhaps Europe is post-Christian because its great churches were allowed to become post-community. This need not be the future for the American church.

The local church was never intended to be a lifeless, impersonal institution. It was meant to be a life-changing community, a family of believers and a context for raising up those who would count the cost and pay any price to win the world for Christ. God will breathe life back into dying churches if we will let Him do so. And He will provide us with indefinitely reproducible models of small church life which common people can operate and multiply if we will affirm their value. The time has come for serious Christians to radically change what they value in the church of Jesus Christ, and for well-trained laymen to take their rightful place in serving the King of kings! There are giants in the land, and modern-day Davids are waiting in the wings to take the field to confront them. They will never do so if we fail to recognize their potential and if we persistently downplay their faith. Church and mission leaders stand today in the place of Saul as we face the latter day insults of the last of the giants. Who among us will be the first to allow modern-day Davids their chance to face these 20th century Goliaths?

Doing the Possible

*"'Not by might nor by power, but by my Spirit,' says
the Lord of hosts."*

Zech. 4:6

No doubt many small church leaders will find the scope of the
missions ministry NCC has developed a bit overwhelming.
It would be easy to see the history of our work in Bosnia as a good
story that is simply out of reach. I want my readers to remember
that we have taken eight years to develop this work. We could never
have considered the kind of involvement and investment we are
presently making when we first adopted the Bosnian Muslim people
as a mission target. Those who will honestly consider their potential
for missions ministry need to recognize that they cannot just "go
into business." They will need instead to "grow into business" just
as we have over the years.

The cry of my heart in this book is not a presumptuous pro-
nouncement that small churches should simply "get busy." Rather,
I am trying to open the eyes of mission leaders and local church
pastors alike to the untapped potential for global evangelism that lies
dormant in 350,000 small churches in America. We don't need to
reach beyond our capacity but we do need to stretch ourselves and
our churches enough to test the limits of our latent potential. We
must not allow ourselves the luxury of failing in our best effort

simply to do the possible. I believe NCC's example demonstrates that major missions ministry is within reach of any small congregation whose leaders will dare to be guided by faith rather than fear.

A Major Lesson From a Minor Prophet

Moving small churches toward a more aggressive mission ministry will, I know, require a boost to get doubtful leaders over the hurdles of institutionalized skepticism. Modern leaders are not the first to need such help. Five centuries before Christ's birth, God provided such a boost to Israel through the voices of his prophets, Haggai and Zechariah. These two great men of God were delivering His decrees to the remnant of Jews who had been the first to return from Babylonian captivity with Zerubbabel. In 537 BC they had laid the foundation to restore the temple but after just a few years' work, they were compelled by force to stop. For fifteen years, Zerubbabel had been idle and no progress was made on the project.

Haggai and Zechariah then arrived on the scene in 520 BC. Under the inspiration of God, they began to declare that the work should begin again. They prophesied that Zerubbabel would complete the reconstruction of the temple. But by this time, the well-intentioned leader's zeal for rebuilding had been eroded by the harsh realities of dedicated opposition. He was no longer reaching for the high road of redevelopment. For a decade and a half he had been stuck in the rut of real-life limitations. Can you imagine how the now aged builder might have responded? I can see in my mind's eye the old, stiff-jointed leader creaking as he rose to his feet with a giant exhale of complacent disbelief.

He had long since accepted the fact that the foundations of the temple would remain untouched. He had grown accustomed to the mountain of rubble that filled the building site. There were no remaining resources to pay for construction materials. Many of the skilled builders Zerubbabel would have earlier relied on had died or moved on while the project sat idle. Zerubbabel himself was now too old, too weary, and too little motivated to respond in the natural to this fresh outpouring of prophetic vision. Zechariah changed Zerubbabel's mind as he spoke for the Lord, providing the impetus God's chosen builder would need to take up his tools again:

> This is the word of the Lord to Zerubbabel, "Not by might and not by power, but by my Spirit," says the Lord of hosts. "What are you, O great mountain? Before Zerubbabel, you will become a plain.... "The hands of Zerubbabel have laid the foundations of this house, and his hands will finish it. Then you will know that the Lord of hosts has sent me to you. For who has despised the day of small things?"... (Zech. 4:6-10)

Overcoming Barriers to Our Belief

I am concerned that too many small church leaders in our day are being held back from the opportunities that exist for their participation in building the body of Christ around the world by a faith that has simply grown fatigued over time. Like Zerubbabel, their days of "dreaming in the Spirit" have passed. Reality has ruled out their grander goals and their vision has shrunk to fit a small building and an even smaller crowd. They, like Zerubbabel, have come to "despise the day of small things." I want us to see how Zerubbabel responded to God's prophetic call to action. His story offers apt answers for our objections to renewed vision today. I see in Zerubbabel's situation three main barriers to moving by faith into a project that he believed was beyond reach. The same barriers hinder our faith today, and the same responses can renew our hope!

Barrier #1:
The Mission Is Impossible!

This objection on Zerubbabel's part is more implicit than explicit in the text. In the initial word from the Lord on the matter we see God's great grace of reassurance coming to light. It is as if

God is saying, "Don't worry Zerubbabel, this work doesn't depend on your strength alone. It is my work to do. I promise Zerubbabel, if you go forward in faith I will finish what you are willing to begin for me. If you will attempt the possible, I will do the impossible. I will do this ... not by might and not by power, but by my Spirit."

As long as we allow ourselves to be limited by our natural capacities and the limits of our known resources, we will never respond by faith to the opportunities God offers us. At NCC, we have experienced God's faithfulness to finish what we began by His great power. He has done so in Eph. 3:20 fashion, exceeding everything we could have ever imagined. We have mobilized, trained and financed more laborers for this field in six years than we had people when we began our journey on the "road to Sarajevo"! Remember the words of II Cor. 8:8-13,

> I am not speaking this as a command, but as proving through the earnestness of others the sincerity of your love also. For you know the grace of our Lord Jesus Christ, that though He was rich, yet for your sake He became poor, so that you through His poverty might become rich. I give my opinion in this matter, for this is to your advantage, who were the first to begin a year ago not only to do this, but also to desire to do it. But now finish doing it also, so that just as there was the readiness to desire it, so there may be also the completion of it by your ability....

II Cor. 9:6-8 adds more impetus for us to do the possible in giving ourselves to God's service.

> Now this I say, he who sows sparingly will also reap sparingly, and he who sows bountifully will also reap bountifully. Each one must do just as he has purposed in his heart, not grudgingly or under compulsion, for God loves a cheerful giver. And God is able to make all grace abound to you, so that always having all sufficiency in

everything, you may have an abundance for every good deed....

Good intentions regarding small church mission involvement will never get the job of global evangelism done. It would be foolish to expect a harvest of fruit in terms of human or financial resources if we have never planted seed from which the fruit can be born. The temple would never have been restored if Zerubbabel had remained idle. He had to act first, putting his hand purposefully to the plow, in order for God to keep His promises. We need to learn from his example and, by faith, overcome our idleness by taking first steps. We won't ever see God multiply the supply of our financial resources unless we first give freely from our limited funds. He won't multiply laborers until we are willing to invest our people. He won't do the impossible until we pray and act in faith to do the possible. If we do our part though, we can trust God to do His part, "'not by might, nor by power, but by my Spirit' says the Lord!" We need to apply ourselves to the task just like Zerubbabel did.

In order to see God accomplish the impossible, church leaders must first be willing to do the possible!

Barrier #2:
This Mountain Is too Big for Me to Move!

Even men of faith and vision sometimes groan when they face the mountains that have to be crossed as they reach toward the goals God sets before them. In Zerubbabel's case, the obstacle was a literal mountain of debris sitting on the construction site of the temple. For Abraham, the mountain was a demand of faith to move from Ur without knowing where he was going. For Moses, the mountain may have been the stubborn resistance of Pharaoh, or the menacing pursuit of the Egyptian armies or the challenge of leading a stiff-necked and rebellious people toward the Promised Land. For the woman with the issue of blood, the mountain was a bleeding body that had not been well for a dozen years.

God's word to Zerubbabel should inspire our own "possibility thinking." Can you hear the Lord saying to 20th century leaders, "Forget the mountain my friend? Don't focus on what you see as a formidable obstacle. I am a mountain moving God! I am a God that can keep you on the way. I am a God that moves the hearts of kings like rivers of water wherever I will. I am a God who parts seas and changes hearts and heals infirmity of every kind." God's assurance to us in the story of Zerubbabel is that He can handle the mountains in our lives.

And what does it take for Him to do so? We need only offer a small response of faith to accept the opportunities He brings our way. *It only takes a willingness to do the possible.* Zerubbabel had to stop looking at the mountain of debris and pick up the first piece of rubble. Abraham had to take the first step westward toward Canaan. Moses had to overcome his speech impediment and make an appointment to speak to Pharaoh. He had to lift his hands and stretch out his staff over the Red Sea. He had to point the way in the wilderness. The woman with the issue of blood had only to touch the hem of Jesus' garment. They all had to do the possible by taking a small step of faith. We don't have to be supermen to do this. We need not be able to leap tall buildings in a single bound. We need only have enough faith to face our mountains and take the first step toward conquering them. If we do so, God promises He will see us through to the end. Jesus could not have made it more clear in the New Testament when He said, "If you have faith as a mustard seed, you should say to this mountain, 'move from here to there,' and it shall move; nothing shall be impossible for you." (Matt. 17:20)

I believe that God will meet every reader of this book personally and powerfully if they are willing simply to seek His face for directions in the first steps they can take to "do the possible" in missions. It takes very little faith to take first steps in obedience.

God will lengthen our stride and quicken our pace once we get underway. My simple plea is that church leaders not be hindered by the obstacles they see ahead. If we are not careful, doubt will lead us all to make mountains out of every molehill. Our testimony is that God has been true to His word as we faced the mountains that challenged our church-based mission effort in Bosnia. Our challenge is for you to test God's faithfulness by taking your own first steps.

Only Mustard Seed Faith Is Required to Move the Mountains We Face!

Barrier #3:
We Don't Have the Resources
to Get the Job Done!

Zerubbabel certainly couldn't see how the Jews following him could secure the materials needed to rebuild the temple. Cyrus, the king of Persia, had permitted the first Jewish remnant to return to Jerusalem in order to rebuild the temple (Ezra 1:1-3). His permission to return was accompanied with a promise to provide all the materials needed to accomplish the work of restoration. Under subsequent rulers, however, the mandate to rebuild was rescinded and Zerubbabel was ordered to stop the building altogether under Artaxerxes (Ezra 4:23). It was during the second year of Darius' reign that Haggai and Zechariah prophetically announced that building should begin again. In Ezra 6:14 we are told that the work was in fact eventually completed. Where did the resources come from? Zerubbabel didn't supply them! Neither did the Jews who followed him.

Instead, God used the decree of Darius to renew Cyrus' earlier pledge of provision. In fact, the work was completed at the expense of this Gentile ruler, under his personal protection and with a full supply of sacrificial animals thrown in for good measure. Ezra 6:7-12 records how God supernaturally intervened to get the job done. Darius decreed,

> Leave this work on the house of God alone; let the governor of the Jews and the elders of the Jews rebuild this house of God on this site. Moreover, I issue a decree concerning what you are to do for these elders of Judah in rebuilding this house of God: the full cost is to be paid to these people from the royal treasury out of the taxes of the provinces beyond the River, and that without delay. Whatever is needed, both young bulls, rams and lambs for a burnt offering to the God of heaven, and wheat, salt, wine and anointing oil, as the priests in Jerusalem request, it is to be given to them daily without fail, that they may offer acceptable sacrifices to the God of heaven and pray for the life of the king and his sons. And I issue a decree that any man who violates this edict, a timber shall be drawn from his house and he shall be impaled on it and his house shall be made a refuse heap on account of this. May the God who has caused His name to dwell there overthrow any king or people who attempt to change it, so as to destroy this house of God in Jerusalem. I, Darius, have issued this decree, let it be carried out with all diligence.

Zerubbabel had little to contribute to the cost of his mission. Small church leaders today can easily relate. It is the norm for small churches to be bankrupt of everything but faith. We are like the widow from Zarephath in I Kings 17 with only a handful of this and a little jar of that to sustain us. Whether we have a little jar of oil, or a few loaves and fishes like the lad in Mark 6 or a widow's mite like the woman in Luke 21 who so impressed Jesus with the magnitude of her gift, we all face the same issue. We must all decide whether we will release what little supply we have into God's hand so that He can multiply it.

In response to our concern about limited resources in every area of life, God routinely asks us to give what we have, trusting Him to work out the process of provision. Remember the words of Luke 6:38, "Give and it will be given to you. They will pour into your lap a good measure — pressed down, shaken together, and running over. For by your standard of measure it will be measured to you in return." Responding as generously as possible to every opportunity in Bosnia, God has reinforced this important lesson in our lives over and over again. Remember the conclusion from the introduction to part I of this book. It is *not the size of our resource pool but the limits of our faith and vision that determines our impact for the kingdom of God.* Zerubbabel did the possible exercising his mustard seed faith and God moved Darius, a pagan king, to give the Jews an unlimited line of credit and a cadre of royal bodyguards to protect them until the temple was finished. If we have trouble believing such can be the case for us today, the Lord stands ready to "help our unbelief" just as He did with Zerubbabel:

> "But now take courage, Zerubbabel, ... and work, for I
> am with you" declares the Lord of hosts. (Haggai 2:4)

God has never committed to doing His work only through the rich and famous. He delights instead in using ordinary people to do extraordinary things for His kingdom. The question is not whether we have enough to get the job done but whether we will invest what little we have to get the job going. *Widow's mites, mustard seeds and little jars of oil are the currency of the kingdom of God.* How dare we withhold even our limited means from the purposes of our limitless God? The keys that will open the door to missions for the world's smaller churches don't lie in the future accumulation of vast riches but in the present release of the little we have.

A Timely Illustration of This Timeless Truth

As I was penning the final paragraphs of this chapter, I received an e-mail message from the pastor who now leads the church in West Mostar. This church has been searching in vain for a building to buy or a lot to develop as a permanent meeting place for their church family. We have invested heartily in an attempt to make this dream a reality for our brothers and sisters in Bosnia's "Antioch Church." To date, all our combined efforts have been in vain. That is, I thought they had been until I received this message today. With minor modifications to make the English communication more understandable, the exciting letter reads:

SUBJECT: Update from West Mostar

Dear brothers, sisters, and friends!

Greetings from Mostar!

Thank you for your support in prayer for our much-needed building. Your prayers have been answered! Yesterday we had a meeting with the mayor of West Mostar (the Croat side of the river), and he openly said that the town will find us property. He also promised to set us free from paying the tax, and he pledged to find the best construction company for building our church. We will know the details at a meeting with the mayor next week. Keep us in prayer.

We had nearly made a contract with another company when we saw the openness of the mayor of the town to help us in all that is needed. This is really a miracle!

God bless you all.
Karmelo Kresonja
Pastor of Evangelical Church Mostar West
Bosnia and Herzegovina

Karmelo's encouraging report reminds us of a principle we dare not forget. God still moves mountains and He still makes provision through modern day Cyruses. The question of our potential in missions is not determined by the size of our resource pool but by the limits of our faith in the One whose power is limitless. No matter how small a church may be, extraordinary experiences await those who will consider involvement in global evangelism as a "mission possible" assignment.

Widow's mites, mustard seeds, and little jars of oil are the currency of the Kingdom of Heaven.

Fierce Commitment — The First Step Toward Your Possibilities in Missions Ministry

So, what should a small church do to open the way for God to move powerfully in the area of world missions? We have come to summarize five key ingredients that are necessary for a small church to maximize its potential in global evangelism. These five ingredients make it possible to build and sustain momentum in doing missions from a local church base.

As a first step, the leaders of the church must develop a *fierce commitment* to mission involvement. Missiologists are universally agreed that the senior pastor is the primary person needed to keep mission vision alive in a local church. If this is a reliable general rule for churches of any size, we must see the senior pastor's personal commitment to missions as an inviolable maxim for small churches. In a context where there is only a single pastor or where the additional staff is limited to one or two specialists, the priorities the senior pastor promotes will normally be the ones that prevail.

For missions ministry to play a large role in a small congregation then, the senior pastor must be vitally committed to the vision for global outreach. In effect, the pastor of a small church following a church-based strategy in world evangelization must add the "missions pastor" role to the other ministry hats he wears. The entire membership of the church will likewise serve as the mission team. Every effort will need to be made to keep the whole body alert to the goals set for missions, the opportunities for involvement on the part of laymen, and to the funding challenges the church will face.

We have used an annual mission conference to help accomplish these communications and "envisioning" objectives at NCC. Each Sunday in March is given to promoting and clarifying the progress of our work in Bosnia. Even the children's ministries are thoroughly involved. The emphasis we place on this annual event makes our mission conference one of the most highly anticipated and exciting aspects of our ministry year.

In these conferences, credible leaders from outside our own church family have supported the fierce commitment our leaders have maintained for the work in Bosnia. These people, drawn from among mission agencies, national partners in Bosnia and other stateside churches, have helped us build confidence among our laymen that "doing missions" as a church is a viable (even preferred) option for us. Our strategic partners have reinforced our fierce commitment to missions in Bosnia and they have each served our vision rather than asking us to serve theirs. Having these "mission professionals" repeatedly confirm over the years that our goals were achievable helped our congregation believe that we were sane as we set our sights on ministering in the context of a nation at war.

Finally, fierce commitment to our mission vision has also been expressed in terms of our readiness to organize or re-organize our efforts in innovative ways as we made progress on the Road to Sarajevo. We did anticipate this need at the beginning of our journey toward Bosnia but it is only in retrospect that we can see clearly how necessary changes came into being along the way.

In 1989, our elders began considering the implications of our church taking responsibility for mobilizing a church planting team to what was then a peaceful (if unfamiliar) republic in former Yugoslavia. Being practical men, our leaders wanted clear answers to hard questions. What will this effort cost our church? Who will we recruit to lead and to staff this team? How long will the process take? Will the communist government in Belgrade resist such an effort? What specific strategy will we follow?

I had few concrete answers to offer these wisely cautious men as they tried to get a firm grasp on what was then a fairly foggy picture. So we waited and prayed rather than plunging ahead. After several months of discussion, dialogue and diligent prayer, I finally found a way to satisfy the board's felt need to know what our commitment to Bosnia would mean for our church. My response to their questions and their cautions was expressed not in an answer per se, but in an analogy.

On April 12, 1961 the Russian space effort scored a significant triumph in the space race by catapulting Yuri Gagarin into a single orbit of the earth. America felt the pain of that public relations defeat when the Soviet effort seemed to trivialize our own first step in space when Allen Shepherd and Gus Grissom made the initial U.S. attempts at non-orbital loops into space on May 5 and July 21, 1961. Between Shepherd and Grissom's flights, then President John F. Kennedy attempted to re-ignite the American public's interest in and imagination for space exploration by offering a dramatic challenge to our citizens. In a joint session of Congress on May 25, 1961 Kennedy set an unimaginable objective for our nation's space exploration efforts, "I believe this nation should commit itself to achieving the goal, before this decade is out, of landing a man on the moon and returning him safely to earth."

This casual statement to our Congress would ultimately create a tidal wave of invention, innovation and inspired development that would touch every facet of life for America's average citizens. Everything from microwave ovens to mini-computers or from fetal monitors to freeze-dried-food technology flowed from this an-nouncement made in the first sixteen months of Kennedy's presidency. No one could have predicted the challenges that would face the United States or the benefits that would inure to our people as this young president turned the tide in the international space race even before John Glenn made America's first manned orbital flight in February 1962. Accepting this goal had huge implications that could never have been calculated when the objective was articulated.

Nonetheless, Congress accepted this challenge to face a new frontier. Less than 18 months later, on November 22, 1963, President Kennedy was assassinated. Deprived of his visionary leadership, and caught up in a great civil rights struggle, the administrations that succeeded Kennedy's were paralyzed at times by the nation's unpopular involvement in the Vietnam War. Still they managed to make uninterrupted progress toward the goal to put a man on the moon by the end of the decade. On July 20, 1969, Neil Armstrong and Edwin E. Aldrin Jr. fulfilled this long sustained national dream by being the first astronauts to actually walk on the lunar surface.

In 1989, I told our elders that this was the kind of sustained effort that would be required if we were to successfully field a church planting team to serve among unreached peoples. We needed to be fiercely committed to the objective over the long haul. We would all need to own the responsibility to see that the job would be accomplished, even if any or all of us should die along the way. None of us would need to go to Bosnia as missionaries, any more than members of the Kennedy administration would need to go to the moon as astronauts. We merely needed to accept the assignment, begin to envision the steps required to reach our goal and recruit the people and resources needed to move us forward one step at a time. No one, least of all an inexperienced mission enthusiast like me, could have calculated the cost in advance. We could, however, calculate the fierce commitment the goal would demand of us.

Somehow, this analogy captured the hearts of our leaders and we jointly agreed to this long-term commitment and signed the title deed of our future stake in evangelizing Bosnia. Now we know that organizing in response to our mission opportunities meant:

1. refusing to be frightened off by the forces of war
2. mobilizing to minister first in refugee settings
3. sending nearly 400 short-term team members over six years
4. building partnerships with national leaders and experienced mission leaders in America
5. developing a churchwide training program that would guarantee a source of well-equipped workers for the mission effort
6. starting a 501(c)(3) corporation to serve as a "church-based sending agency" for long-term workers sent to Bosnia
7. funding additional church staff including a full-time mission director to serve the missionaries we eventually mobilized as long-term missionaries
8. investing hundreds of thousands of dollars in travel, communications, personnel, vehicles, buildings and logistical support needs.

Had we known in the beginning the price we would eventually pay to help establish the church in Bosnia, we probably would have shrunk back in the sinkhole created by a realistic sense of inadequacy. But God didn't ask for money or people or personal enlistments for mission service as a place to begin. He asked only for our fierce commitment to the ultimate objective of seeing His body born in local churches across Bosnia. The task was far less daunting than putting a man on the moon but its benefits to our church have been as astounding as those which America has gained from our country's involvement in the space race. In the words of Winston Churchill, the responsibility we embraced in fighting for the soul of Bosnia was not to "do what we could in this battle" but rather to "do what was necessary in order to prevail." We have promoted a fierce commitment among our leaders and within our church family to our goal of reaching the Muslims of Bosnia for Christ. Fierce commitment is the first requirement for any small church that hopes to be trusted with a major mission ministry. After the commitment is made, the senior pastor must be chief guardian of that trust.

Faithful Laymen

Once our leaders accepted the challenge of reaching toward Bosnia, the next ingredient necessary for our eventual success was the dedicated involvement of **faithful laymen**. The men, women and children of our church family are the ones who have made our mission effort possible. They have consistently given sacrificially of their treasure in order to provide the financial base we needed to reach toward Bosnia.

Beyond the anticipated need for funding, we have also been delighted to discover in our local body much of the professional expertise we required to keep our efforts moving forward. As our laymen recognized that there was room in our mission effort for their vocational skills to play a part, many became personally invested in the project without being required to visit the field. Business counsel, travel expertise, legal representation, accounting support, computer and communication technology, clerical assistance, medical treatment, linguistic instruction, translation services, purchasing strategies and automobile mechanics are just some of the practical contributions made from the array of skills and experience vested in our local church members. It is our conviction that most small churches have huge stores of latent human resources available within their membership to support major mission efforts. Traditional agencies most often are required to pay for such services. Our members have contributed them enthusiastically, being grateful for the privilege of being allowed to enjoy personal participation in our work in Bosnia.

Beyond providing their talent and their treasure, our laymen have also sacrificed their time unselfishly in this effort. Serving in the ways already noted it is obvious that considerable time and energy are often required to facilitate the stateside demands of the mission effort we are sustaining. But laymen who have traveled to Bosnia on short-term teams have gone above and beyond the call of duty in giving of their limited discretionary time as well. Most of our short-term workers have given up family vacation time to visit refugee camps in Bosnia rather than the beaches of a million more pleasant resort alternatives. Some have even taken a leave of absence from their jobs to offer specialized service over an extended period of time. Teachers have surrendered whole summer vacations and students have followed their example. We could never have purchased the precious weeks our laymen have invested willingly in this work.

Finally, our members have accepted the priority of participation in a comprehensive church training ministry that prepares them for service both at home and abroad. We have long recognized the value of apprenticeship-style training that attempts to offer all that is necessary to equip laymen to reproduce churches like ours. This contextualized, non-formal approach allows our members to complete a comprehensive curriculum by investing one night per week and a few Saturdays per quarter in the discipline of progressive development of their character, capacity and sense of calling to ministry. The devotion of our laymen has humbled us as they follow the example of the Macedonian Church giving of their personal resources "according to their ability and beyond their ability of their own accord." Without these faithful laymen, we could have done very little in Bosnia or at home in Atlanta over these years of exciting missions ministry.

Focused Objectives

The advantage of pointing our members toward *focused objectives* in the world of missions should be obvious by now. Failing to point out this important ingredient in the mix of our missions involvement would however, be a disservice to interested leaders. When we determined to focus our energies on traveling down the Road to Sarajevo, we simultaneously determined where we were not going in missions.

The forces of nationalism that opened the door of opportunity for us in Bosnia in 1989 simultaneously opened other doors in the former Soviet Republics and the Eastern Bloc nations as well.

Hundreds of requests for financial support and practical participation in these areas of the world began to come our way in 1990 and have continued coming throughout our Bosnian experience. Because our objective was focused geographically, however, it has been easy to say "no" to other alternatives. As a small church, we simply don't have the capacity to fight a "multiple front war" as some larger assemblies may. Focusing our objective has allowed us to concentrate our forces in an effort to establish a beachhead for the church in post-war Bosnia. The benefits of sustained effort on one primary geographical and cultural objective have been huge for us.

Our strategic commitment to focus our energies has been reflected financially as well. Our church has made the decision to limit its response to support requests coming from outside our church family. Though some exceptions are made, we generally turn away funding appeals from individuals who are not a part of our local church family. We are also more generous in supporting those mobilized to work with us in Bosnia as compared to members serving in other assignments with traditional mission agencies. Given the limit of available finances for missions ministry, members working in traditional agency roles receive $200 or less each month in financial support. By contrast, the church-based missionaries we send to Bosnia receive 20 percent of their total budget from our church. Both types of missionaries are free to raise additional support directly from our membership as their relational commitments, historical service and personal objectives permit.

It may be helpful to clarify at this point that our elders and mission leaders do not insist that our members only serve our corporate vision for Bosnia. We are careful to honor the personal vision of potential mission candidates who have a dream of their own for other ministries and other parts of the world. In March 1998, for example, we commissioned missionaries for our own Bosnia team and for a Caleb Project church planting team in Uzbekistan on successive Sundays.

We are pleased to mobilize missionaries from our church to both fields, but those serving under our church-based corporate umbrella (Ministry Resource Network) will no doubt receive more frequent and more focused attention from our leaders. Our missionary with Caleb Project will receive her team assignments, field training, and general supervision from the leaders of her chosen mission agency. The new member of our Bosnia team will remain under the direct authority of our church leaders, serving in the assignments we determine appropriate and will be trained in the methodology and philosophical paradigms we are pursuing among our special Bosnian priority.

A determination to focus mission energies in smaller churches may also dictate a higher level of financial commitment for candidates aspiring to serve in higher priority roles. In our case for instance, we have made greater commitments to missionaries serving in pioneer mission assignments than to those in domestic roles. We place a higher value on church planting and Bible translation roles than we do on administrative assignments. We are in this sense focused on the strategic merits of church multiplication and evangelism among unreached people groups in general and among Bosnian Muslims in particular.

We are pleased to have one of our members serve Wycliffe Bible Translators in Waxhaw, N.C., in practical support roles like teaching the preschool children of other Wycliffe missionaries or offering guided tours for visitors to this major missionary base. These roles, however, are not as strategic, in our judgment, as those of another Wycliffe missionary from our church who runs a computer translation and transcription department in Wycliffe's SIL offices in Dallas, Texas. More strategic still, is the role our most recently mobilized Caleb Project missionary will play in Uzbekistan. She already has five years' experience in Turkey and speaks the language of several unreached peoples in this region including the Uzbeks, the Kazakhs, and the Tajiks. The cross-cultural experience and language abilities of this missionary will make her service to the Caleb Project Uzbekistan especially strategic. Every church interested in missions ministry will need to determine which items in a veritable smorgasbord of global outreach options its church will choose to pursue.

We firmly believe that focused objectives in missions will make any church more effective in maximizing its potential in global evangelism. Our sense of focus is expressed **philosophically** in our "synergistic" approach to pioneer mission mobilization. It is expressed **geographically** and **ethnically** as we direct our concentrated corporate efforts toward Bosnia. It is expressed **strategically** in our focus on church-planting and evangelistic opportunities among other options available in the wide array of mission activities clamoring for reinforcement in terms of manpower and material support. **Financially** we have a sense of prioritized commitment toward those who serve our Bosnian effort directly. **Personally** we are committed first to our own member missionaries and only in an exceptional circumstance will we support those outside our local assembly. This multifaceted effort to focus our objectives in missions helps us concentrate our energies and our resources on a specific target over an extended period of time.

Financial Provision

In an earlier chapter, a good deal of attention was directed toward making our experience of overflowing financial supply evident. We have always been forced by circumstances to face our certain failure in a mission effort of this magnitude if God did not providentially intervene to supply our need. A brief review may be helpful as this fourth element involved in a church's attempt to "do the possible" needs to be kept in clear view. Our financial capacity has been consistently expanded by our decision to add new development possibilities as our mission ministry grew. In chronological order, the major facets of our financial plan have included:

1. Unitary Budgetary Commitments

From the very outset of our church, when we had a total budget of only $5,000, fully 20 percent of our income stream was devoted to our mission involvement. We no longer routinely fund missions commitments from our general fund but we do maintain a unified budgetary commitment of $12,000 annually to augment regular support needs if other mission fund sources run short. We also make occasional special gifts from our general fund to cover special needs or urgent requests for support from the field. In 1996, for example, we gave $20,000 from our general fund to help purchase a building for the West Mostar Evangelical Church.

2. Designated Gifts

Since all of our short-term workers in Bosnia raise their own support for these special summer teams, we have always encouraged generosity among our members in helping each other fulfill the desire to be personally involved in our outreach to Bosnia. Designated gifts have helped to send hundreds of short-term workers to our field including dozens of teenagers serving on performing arts and street evangelism teams. Using this means we have been able to buy vehicles, offer humanitarian relief and make significant investments in buildings for several Bosnian churches.

3. Faith Promise Pledges

This concept was explained in Chapter One. Our annual faith promise pledge drive has replaced general fund allocations as our primary source of revenues for ongoing missionary and agency support commitments. Our first attempt in securing faith promise pledges raised $4,993 in 1987. In 1997 the total committed by our church family reached nearly $128,000 when our church family numbered less than 400 people. This faith-oriented approach to fund raising which we have used exclusively for missions, has greatly increased our capacity to do the possible.

4. Church-Based Sending Agency Umbrella

When we formed Ministry Resource Network (MRN) as a separate 501(c)(3) corporation, it was our desire to create a church-based sending agency that could serve our broader mission and local outreach interests. We also had a desire to create a "launching pad" of sorts to facilitate the development of other ministries that would emerge from the limitless creativity of our members. The separate identity of this funding entity has removed many of the barriers that would have ordinarily precluded other churches' interest in supporting our effort in Bosnia. In point of fact, many other churches which are more dedicated to the "supporting paradigm" of missions involvement are now valued (if mostly silent) partners in Bosnia.

MRN was formed in 1993 and took in just over $110,000 from individuals and churches alike. In 1997, the total revenues for MRN reached nearly $380,000! There is obviously an advantage to thinking creatively about financial development for missions.

5. Manna From Heaven

Beyond all our attempts to make it easy for individuals, churches, agencies and foundations to share in the cost of our extraordinary effort in Bosnia, God has acted repeatedly to bless our work materially. While we have endeavored to "do the possible," our Heavenly Father has encouraged our hearts and brightened our hopes by doing the impossible, most often providing material blessings we were neither considering nor seeking in prayer. The gift of our present facilities; the "seed money" provided by an unrelated donor through a "coincidental" meeting in the Frankfurt airport; and the contributions lavished on us by the Jesus Film Project, World Relief and the Evangelical Free Church Mission Compassion Ministry are each excellent examples of "manna from heaven." (These were all described in chapter 5.)

I believe that God delights in this kind of supernatural provision as much today as He did when Israel roamed the deserts of Sinai. Though such miraculous material provision cannot be planned in advance, and is inherently non-reproducible from a natural perspective, leaders would be foolhardy not to factor such divine blessing into the funding equation at least as a possibility. Missions-minded churches need to watch for manna from heaven as they move to penetrate the unreached people groups of the earth with the gospel. Instances of such incredible intervention offer tremendous inspiration along the way. As we seek to do the possible, we need constantly to bear in mind the perspective of Eph. 3:20 and apply this paraphrased praise to the One who is still Jehovah Jireh, our Great Provider, "Now to Him who is able to do immeasurably beyond all that we can ever think, or ask, or dream of or imagine according to His power that is at work within us — to Him be glory in the church and in Christ Jesus throughout all generations, forever and ever. Amen."

Faith

The final factor necessary for a church to be released to "do the possible" involves acting in faith. Hebrews 11:6 pointedly declares that, "without faith it is impossible to please God." Applying this truth to church-based missions ministry, we must recognize that small churches will never achieve great things for God if their leaders' eyes of faith cannot focus on the pleasure God derives from our trusting Him to do the impossible. It is only in so trusting God for the personal intervention in our circumstances that we can demonstrate our conviction that He exists and that He rewards those who seek Him. Church-based missions is fundamentally dependent on our having faith enough to motivate significant risks on our part. In our experience, our faith has generated an increasing willingness to risk and we have grown bolder as God has proven faithful to come through for us, time after time. This is a dynamic with clear biblical precedents.

Consider, for example, the men and women of faith portrayed in God's hall of fame in Hebrews 11. Our faith, no less than Noah's, requires a response of *duty* in seeking to reverently obey God's mandate to save people from impending destruction. Our faith, no less than Abraham's, requires that we face the *dangers* of going without knowing what awaits us on the unreached fields of the world. Our faith, no less than Sarah's, demands that we stare down the intimidating giant of unbelief made more powerful by our personal *doubts* in order to receive resources beyond our known reserves to do God's will on the earth. Our faith, no less than

Joseph's, needs to fuel our sense of *destiny* and a resolve to be "vision-driven" regarding things to come. Our faith, no less than Moses', requires that we relinquish our *dignity*, embracing ill treatment and the reproach of men in order to promote our Lord's glory among the nations.

Those whose faith must wait to act until all dangers, all doubts and all difficulties are removed from the way will never dare take the first necessary steps of faith modern missions requires. I am praying that this chapter will inspire you to be willing to risk great things for a great God and for the completion of the Great Commission. More than we can imagine is possible for small church mission efforts if we are willing to combine a fierce commitment, with faithful laymen, financial provision, and faith to reach toward a focused objective. Mustard seeds and widows mites are all your church needs to make a down payment on your own personal mission adventure. Let me encourage you with four reminders as you begin the journey toward your own "Mission Possible."

1. Begin by dreaming in the Spirit as you prayerfully seek God for clear direction.

2. If you are faced with the possibility of making a serious mistake along the way, err in the direction of being aggressive for the kingdom and choose the path that demands the most faith. Be bold for God!

3. When opportunity knocks, resist the temptation not to open the door. Be opportunistic as you travel the road to your mission objective.

4. Expect that God is abundantly able to bless any risk you are bold enough to take for His glory.

As we choose to trust in God's ability to do the impossible for His people and His purposes, we should act with great expectation. The Lord has always taken pleasure in showing himself strong on behalf of those whose hearts are fully dedicated to Him. It matters not if we are bankrupt, barren or burdened by the shame of past failures. God offers us all a new beginning, a fresh chance to "do the possible" for His glory. If you could ask Zerubbabel he would tell you so! His testimony is simple. **We can do the possible but only God can do the impossible.** The impossible part comes about "'not by might, nor by power but by my Spirit,' says the Lord." Zerubbabel did not learn this lesson the hard way by persevering in the strength of his flesh. He learned it the holy way — the only way anyone can — by doing the possible one step at a time. Why not follow in his footsteps? Take your first steps by doing the possible today and keep your eyes peeled for the intervening hand of God. Nothing is impossible for Him!

Trained to Be Trusted

"Everyone, after he has been fully trained, will be like his teacher."

Luke 6:40

The single verse noted above offers the essence of Jesus' perspective on training. The principle is simple and its lesson was not lost on the disciples as they grasped the significance of their responsibility to reproduce after their own kind once Jesus ascended to the Father. Accepting the mandate to evangelize the world, this handful of ordinary men drew on three short years of daily fellowship with the Savior to motivate and inspire their own ministries in discipleship and leadership training. Life to life contact with Jesus offered in the context of an apprentice style training environment proved effective in preparing them to bear fruit that has since covered the full expanse of the globe, enduring for 20 centuries.

They reproduced themselves in the lives of others not by sharing materials and not by teaching a carefully designed academic curriculum. They multiplied leaders in the first century by investing themselves and all that they learned from Jesus in a life to life exchange that imparted character, conviction and a call to reach the entire world with the message of the gospel. Nurturing the personal capacity of each individual who followed them, the disciples invited others to join them in suffering for the sake of the kingdom as an expression of their devotion to Christ.

Apostolic Apprenticeship

The ministry of these first apostles was intensely practical. It involved prayer, intimate personal exposure and preaching of the word. It also relied upon the same apprenticeship methodology Jesus had used to prepare them for the responsibilities of leadership. Approaching the Christian life like a relay race, these men transferred one baton after another until their disciples could repeat the process with others who would come after they were gone. They had been trained by Jesus to be trusted with the future of world evangelism. Before their lives ended, they too would need to train others who could also be trusted to carry the message of the great commission to the next generation. Faithful handoffs that passed the baton of leadership from one person to another have allowed the church around the world to multiply continually for nearly 2,000 years. Personal access to proven leaders — and not just academic proficiency — has been the secret of sustained growth over this entire span of church history.

Jesus never intended that His disciples would simply "minister to others" who believed He was the Messiah. He trained them, often without their full awareness or cooperation, to "minister through others." Paul captures this idea in Ephesians 4:11-12, "And He gave some as apostles, and some as prophets, and some as evangelists, and some as pastors and teachers, for the equipping of the saints for the work of ministry." In the context of life in the local church, gifted leaders were to help others learn how to build up the body of Christ. Through this kind of contextualized training, committed disciples equipped others who served as spiritual apprentices until they were able not only to minister effectively but also to multiply their capacity for leadership in the lives of others. II Timothy 2:2 gives the sense of the kind of personal and purposeful preparation

1st century leaders felt responsible to reproduce in their followers. Speaking to his own disciple, Timothy, Paul wrote, "the things which you have heard from me in the presence of many witnesses, these entrust to faithful men who will be able to teach others also."

Paul's method was not, however, reduced to a series of core courses or to a set of academic objectives. He imparted his life along with his lessons about faith and church leadership. Speaking of his relationship with Timothy, Paul wrote in II Tim. 3:10-14, "You followed my teaching, conduct, purpose, faith, patience, love, perseverance, persecutions and sufferings ... continue in the things you have learned and become convinced of, knowing from whom you learned them."

This great apostle trained Timothy to be trusted with the responsibility for leadership in the church and with equipping others for ministry. He knew Timothy intimately and impacted his life at a personal level. That's why Paul could affirm his disciple's readiness for a role in leadership. He praised Timothy in Philippians 2:20-22, "I have no one else of kindred spirit who will genuinely be concerned for your welfare. For they all seek after their own interests, not those of Christ Jesus. But you know of his proven worth, that he served with me in the furtherance of the gospel, like a child serving his father."

Timothy learned about the Christian life and about leadership in the church by sharing life and ministry with his mentor. In the context of an apostolic apprenticeship, he proved his worth by serving well in practical ministry, not by performance on an oral or written exam. In the same way, Barnabus learned from the 11 apostles who had been with Jesus during his earthly ministry. Paul learned from Barnabus in the context of the Jerusalem church, in Antioch and on the mission field as they served together under the direction of the Holy Spirit. Paul in turn, trained Timothy, Silas, Epaphroditus, Priscilla and Aquila, Onesephorus and others. Leadership training in the 1st century was church-based, multiplication-oriented, and accessible to anyone willing to faithfully prove their worth by serving others alongside established leaders.

Going Back to the Future

Because the harvest is still plentiful and the laborers are still few (Matt. 9:37-38), we need to return to a training methodology that is also church-based, multiplication-oriented, and available to faithful men and women everywhere. Our presently preferred alternative, professional credentialing through academic study in residential seminaries, is simply not getting the job done. We need to design better training for laymen and make it available on a broader level. Remember, as I noted earlier, wherever seminary training is required for leadership formation, the progress of the gospel and the growth of the church are severely crippled.

In former Yugoslavia, for example, most national pastors have been trained primarily through the ministry of the Evangelical Theological Seminary (ETS) in Osijek, Croatia, or through a similar but smaller Baptist Bible school in Novi Sad, Serbia. The Bible school and seminary in Osijek offers both undergraduate and master's programs to approximately one hundred students at a time. If we assume that emerging pastors are generally encouraged to pursue at least a four-year undergraduate theological program, only 25 pastors can be released for ministry each year.

In 1990, on my first visit to ETS, Dr. Peter Kuzmic, the school's president, indicated that Yugoslavia (which now represents five separate nations since the Yugoslav federation disintegrated in 1991) could immediately make use of 2,500 church planters. I asked how long the seminary would need to produce that many church planters. We agreed such a goal could not be reached in our lifetimes. Acknowledging the time demands that formal theological education makes on aspiring leaders in the church, it would seem that apprenticeship approaches to pastoral formation could do the job more efficiently and effectively. Of course this would require that informal and non-formal training regimens be accepted as viable alternatives to seminary education. Unfortunately, 1st century apprenticeship-training models are not widely appreciated by modern church and mission leaders.

De-Professionalizing the Ministry

I argued in Chapter 9 that accepting the institutional pressure to "professionalize" the ministry has tremendous negative ramifications for both local church ministry and for world mission mobilization. By accepting formal academic credentialing as the essential standard for service in the church or in missions, we effectively define laymen who have not had the opportunity to attend seminary out of the ministry. I believe church leaders should consider finding ways to "de-professionalize" the pathway to vocational Christian service without diminishing our concern for adequate preparation.

Dr. Ralph Winter is both a consummate missiologist and a formally trained scholar. In spite of having paid his dues earning his advanced academic degrees, however, he has been a vocal opponent of a strictly academic approach to developing leadership for the global church. Several major issues fuel his concerns in this area:[1]

1. Requiring undergraduate (and often graduate level) education prior to vocational service in a ministry setting can delay an individual's availability to the kingdom for as long as a decade. Those patient enough to pay the price of achieving proper academic credentials are often arriving at their ministry posts too late in life to adjust easily and well to their new roles.

2. Residential academic training is expensive! Educational loans related to formal Bible school and seminary training can create such a huge financial burden for students that service in ministry (especially in mission roles overseas) must often be further delayed after graduation until these school related debts have been repaid. Requiring academic credentials, in effect, creates a double barrier to the ministry involving huge amounts of time and money. The result is frequently an inordinate delay in finding the freedom to faithfully obey God's call to a vocational ministry role.

3. Proven lay leaders serving churches at home and abroad are often faithful folks with established families and demanding careers in full swing. The pressures of domestic responsibility and relentless job requirements will most often make seminary training an impossible dream for even the most gifted among mature lay leaders. The capacity, character and calling of these leaders are lost to the church because the classroom route to vocational ministry is out of reach for mid-career men and women.

4. Unable to train the more mature and proven lay leaders who are functioning in ministry roles without the benefit of adequate education, academic institutions often turn to younger, unqualified and untested students to fill their classroom vacancies. Consequently, they end up training nice but not necessarily gifted people. Often such students have no definite sense of direction or calling when their academic regimen is completed. They also often lack the invaluable support of their local churches because their academic preparation is allowed to precede proven ministry at home.

5. The academic pursuit of a theological degree is a far different process than the long-term acquisition of wisdom and character. The biblical standard for leadership in the church has always been defined biblically by personal discipleship, giftedness, integrity and spiritual passion. Academic achievement is an inferior standard often better suited to the development of scholars than shepherds.

6. As Peter Wagner suggests, leadership in the church is not only learned, it is also earned and discerned.[2] A balanced process of leadership formation that includes all three aspects Dr. Wagner deems important in identifying emerging ministers cannot be accomplished solely in a seminary classroom.

Other voices are beginning to join a host of credible critics like doctors Winter and Wagner in a chorus of complaint about our seminary system. Jeff Reed, writing as the Executive Director of BILD International in 1992, declared that, "Theology lost its soul (when) the orientation of study changed form ... laying a foundation for the lifetime pursuit of wisdom to an intense mastery of academic disciplines."[3] Dr. Jonathan Chao wrote an exhortation for the 1974 Lausanne Conference on Evangelism that said in part, "It is not possible to 'improve theological education' as suggested by the covenant, in isolation from the ministerial context. Rather, a complete, integrated approach to the development of indigenous leadership with the church must be undertaken.... What we need is not renovation, but innovation"[4] in the process by which we train leaders.

In 1978 Anal Solanky, then dean of Union Biblical Seminary, Yvatmal, India, offered a clear call for renewal of theological education when he wrote: "What we need is not just innovations or better methods but radical change in our concept of education: learning as experience, **versus** gathering content, a body of information. We must treat students as persons, not as boxes to be filled little by little, with little, logically arranged, packets of information. We must expect them to develop abilities, to grow in their experience of the Lord."[5]

Jim Engle also touches on this same point urging a higher priority for Christian character formation as an integral part of theological education and training for ministry. In developing his argument that a need exists for massive retooling among North American mission agencies, he suggests that, in the face of significant changes occurring in the global church, wisdom would dictate that we substitute a more practical standard for training ministry leaders to replace traditionally respected academic credentialing. His suggestion — replace the seminary criterion with a "demonstration of successful ministry, making use of talents and gifts in challenging situations which require acceptance of diversity, mutual submission and integrity."[6] In short, make training a personal, practical, contextual process.

Dr. Winter encourages his readers to accept the challenge to change our approach to leadership preparation without fear. He reminds us that the reality is, many capable church leaders, even in the United States, don't have formal seminary training. He notes surprisingly, "50 percent of the 25,000 newest churches in America don't have seminary trained pastors ... there is no clear connection between the seminaries and the gifted local leaders of these new churches."[7] Dr. Winter makes it clear that somehow, these newest North American leaders were trained to be trusted with vocational ministry responsibility apart from formal theological education in residential schools.

His point is not that serious theological and missiological training is unimportant but that such preparation is often not adequately available to the people who need it most. We must recognize that "the accessibility of training is just as crucial as the content."[8] Too often, seminary opportunities are so far removed from the people who should pursue them they tend to filter out truly gifted leaders in the local church rather than facilitating their service.

The Danger of Re-Amateurizing Christian Leadership

Recognizing the urgent need to make high quality training more accessible to more of those already serving in key ministry roles in the world's churches does not mean that seminaries are not valuable. Neither does the desire to offer better training or a broader level indicate that training is unimportant. In fact, Dr. Winter expresses an almost equal and opposite concern about ministerial formation as he urges us to consider the dangers that attend the process of de-professionalizing the ministry. Somehow, we must balance the serious priority for making better training more broadly available with a caution that we not, at the same time, re-amateurize our leadership — especially leadership on the world's mission fields.

A certain level of tension comes to those who try to hold both these concerns in balance. The priority of church-based mission ministry promoted by this book is one of the emerging realities that magnifies Dr. Winter's concern about what he calls "creeping amateurism or drive-by missions."[9] The massive mobilization of short-term workers — a significant part of our own strategy in Bosnia — only adds to his anxiety on this point. It can easily be seen that OM, YWAM, Frontiers and other agencies promoting short-term mission commitments among young people are succeeding in a massive level of mobilization. But many of those being released for ministry have no college degrees at all. Is the trend toward short-term ministry in missions a move toward releasing the ill prepared? Dr. Winter seems to think so. If the motivation behind this kind of large-scale student mobilization is simply the result of combining Western affluence with a romantic zeal for adventure, he could be right. We may be trading enthusiasm for experience, downgrading our mission staff to a cadre of religious tourists in the process.

I would argue however, that the long-term effectiveness of "short-term agencies" like those noted above should prompt us to reject a panic response at this point of concern. The truth is, emotional energy and romantic idealism fade quickly in the midst of real life ministry demands. This is especially true when the intense heat of interpersonal team dynamics magnifies the pressures of vocational service in the kingdom of God. The simple fact is that vocational ministry — whether one serves as a missionary or a domestic church leader — is no vacation. The challenges of ministry quickly cull out under-committed workers.

My experience has been that those serious enough to sustain their desire to serve Christ vocationally will keep seeking to grow both professionally and personally along the way. No one wants to promote amateurism among the leaders of God's global army. But neither do we want to torture the spiritual vitality out of potential leaders by requiring them to tread water for years before we let them take a turn at swimming in the sea of unevangelized and unreached peoples. There must be a better way to train leaders to be trusted with ministry.

Viable Options Are Available

Looking for alternatives to residential seminary training quickly leads to a wide range of available options. Many academic institutions are now offering extension programs that allow students to study at home in their own context while in pursuit of the much valued end of earning a suitable degree for their efforts. The U.S. Center for World Mission embraces this option and, though not a seminary per se, provides missiologically sensitive degree programs on an extension basis.[10] The U.S. Center's program allows students to earn both undergraduate and master's degree credit without leaving home. Their "seminary in a suitcase" makes it possible to mobilize leaders now and to finalize their academic preparation over time. Such "in-service" options can be valuable vehicles for those who balk at more typical "extractionist" educational models. These contextualized alternatives are especially effective when they provide seasoned mentors who can facilitate informed interaction over course content. Personal mentoring effectively roots the lessons learned in real world experience.

Still, these options provide a curriculum designed to achieve a liberal arts foundation or a basic ministry orientation built around a systematic approach to theological education as an academic discipline. The winds of change seem to be urging a more full orbed transition in our training methodologies. Satellite schools and TEE programs often do not go far enough toward attempting to facilitate more flexible and more accessible models for leadership training. Bolder innovation will be required if we are to broaden the availability of ministry training on a global scale. Risking more innovative approaches to training cannot be avoided if we are serious about reaping an adequate harvest of qualified leaders for the global church.

A Call for Renewal in Theological Education

Dr. Robert W. Ferris, a career missionary and internationally experienced Christian educator has written pointedly that "powerful forces have been — and are — at work to press the need for renewal of theological education."[11] His book documenting those forces does not claim to be making a novel observation. In fact, he represents in part, the concerns put forward as early as June 1983 by the

International Council of Accrediting Agencies for Evangelical Education (ICAA) in a formal "Manifesto" on the subject.[12] Framed in the format of explicit points of repentance and corresponding recommendations for change, the Manifesto speaks on behalf of its global array of member agencies and theological schools expressing these key concerns among others:

> We are at fault that our curricula so often appear either to have been imported whole from abroad or to have been handed down unaltered from the past.

> We are at fault when our programs operate merely in terms of some traditional or personal notion of theological education (without regard for) the needs and expectations of the Christian community we serve. Our theological programs must become manifestly of the church, through the church and for the church.

> Too long we have been content to serve the formation of only one type of leader for the church, at only one level of need, by only one educational approach.... We must attune ourselves to (serve) the full range of leadership roles required, ... to take into account all academic levels of need, and ... we must embrace a greater flexibility in the educational modes by which we touch the various levels of (church) leadership. We must learn to employ ... both residential and extension systems, both formal and non-formal styles as well as short-term courses, workshops, night school programs, vacation institutes, in-service training, traveling seminars, refresher courses and continuing education programs.

> We are at fault that our programs so often seem little more than Christian academic factories, efficiently producing graduates. It is ... biblically essential that the whole educational body — staff and students — not only learn together, but play and eat and care and worship and work

together.... (We must nurture) modes of community that are biblically commanded and culturally appropriate.

We are at fault that we so often focus educational requirements narrowly on cognitive attainments, while we hope for student growth in other dimensions but leave it largely to chance.... Our educational programs must deliberately seek and expect the spiritual formation of the student and achievement in practical skills of Christian leadership.

We are to be blamed that our programs so readily produce the characteristics of elitism and so rarely produce the characteristics of servanthood. We must actively promote biblical leadership through modeling by the staff, and through active encouragement, practical exposition, and deliberate reinforcement.

Our programs of theological education need urgently to refocus their patterns of training toward encouraging and facilitating self-directed learning. We need to design academic requirements so that we are equipping the student not only to complete the course but also for a lifetime of ongoing learning, and development and growth.

This revealing series of confessions and suggestions would likely have been offensive had someone outside the accredited academic community offered it. Made more poignant considering the source of the ICAA Manifesto, these comments nonetheless lose considerable force when we note that they were articulated fully fifteen years ago. Unhappily, little meaningful change has actually occurred, though the clarion call for substantial reform is still being sounded — and still by accredited educators committed to equipping leaders theologically and missiologically.

Dr. William D. Taylor for example, has edited a 1991 collection of articles addressing the need to reform our approaches to educating

Christian leaders. These articles were written as an outgrowth of the triennial World Evangelical Fellowship Consultation on Missionary Training held in Manila just prior to the Lausanne II Congress on World Evangelization in July 1989. In Chapter 1 of his book, *Internationalizing Missionary Training*, Dr. Taylor notes that we are too often releasing workers who are theologically educated but, for all practical purposes, untrained for leadership. He writes,

> One of the greatest tragedies I have seen on the mission field is the missionary who has formal theological training, but for all practical purposes is giftless and has never had any practical ministry before going to the foreign field. These cases invariably demonstrate the candidating process failed when it did not evaluate the ministry experience of the then-future missionary. The price tag for such cases is terribly high for all involved...."[13]

This obvious dilemma is created in part by the tacit assumption made by many searching for qualified leaders to serve the church and the mission field, that a seminary credential certifies preparedness for ministry. Such a conclusion flows from what Dr. Edgar J. Elliston of the School of World Missions at Fuller Theological Seminary calls the "Information Myth." He says, "We tend to believe that, if we know more, we will be more ... Jesus did not command, as some of us mistakenly read, to "teach all things." That is a serious problem many churches, Bible colleges and seminary programs now face. It is a growing problem as Two-Thirds World churches are influenced by Western theological education. We strive to "teach all things" rather than "teach obedience in all things" He commanded. To know is not to be. To describe is not to do. To list is not to apply. *Information will not save us.*"[14] (emphasis added)

The simple point is that formal education alone does not a qualified leader make. Dr. Elliston makes the point that the apostles of the 1st century were primarily uneducated laymen in our modern sense of that term. (See Acts 4:13) "Among the early apostles, only the apostle Paul had a formal theological education. However, even he had to have a year of in-service training in Antioch before he could be sent out under the supervision of Barnabus."[15] Dr. Elliston's concern is that we may err by reading our formal approaches to modern leadership development into the New Testament account without due justification.

Legitimizing Church-Based Training

In spite of serious institutional opposition to actual reform of the processes by which we pursue leadership development, a global movement in that direction is under way. Emerging alternatives to formal accredited residential schools are attempting to improve our appreciation for non-formal and informal models of Christian formation. These approaches are especially well received in the Two-Thirds World because they are more effective, less costly and require less time — usually also with no need for those undergoing training to be extracted from their ministry setting.

Dr. Taylor's book gives considerable detail about alternative schools functioning in Asia, Africa, South America and even in the United States. In the shifting landscape of leadership training, Dr. Taylor admits that, in the Two-Thirds World, "Some trainers frankly harbor grave suspicions about formal education. They have observed the weaknesses of formal training. They also want to avoid further exportation of the Western dominated model of equipping. With the opportunity to create something new ... they are designing the program solely on the non-formal system. Those who prefer formal training suspect that the non-formal is simply a cover for inferior education. They feel that non-formal training simply cannot meet all of the needs. They also minimize the role of the community (in the training process). This is unfortunate."[16] It would seem that traditionalists who would invalidate alternatives for formal education are supporting a view that is increasingly untenable. Alternative approaches are simply producing too much good fruit to be denied or ignored any longer.

Dr. Taylor's conviction, and my own, would encourage a marriage of formal, non-formal and informal methods of leadership development. Integration of this sort will allow leaders to get the training necessary for ministry effectiveness without their being required to pursue academic credentials in every case. We must remember as Robert Ferris has noted in designing ministry training regimens, "appropriateness is a curriculum issue,"[17] while "accreditation is a philosophy issue."[18] If the philosophy of ministry in a particular context demands no academic credential, it is absurd to pursue extractionist models of formal training to that end. The developing leader may well do better in his context if he were to "learn while doing" through non-formal or informal training processes. Far too often we have so over-educated Two-Thirds World national leaders in Western contexts that we have rendered them irrelevant to their original place of service. Worse yet, we have so acculturated them to a Western setting over four to ten years of academic processing that we have purged them of a passion to return to their own people. In the final analysis, we must simply acknowledge that better training can be done on a broader scale if we deliberately define more pragmatically and more flexibly what constitutes "good education" for the ministry.

Dr. Paul Pierson has suggested, for example, that acceptable training needs to focus on two critical issues, training and experience on the one hand and personal spiritual formation on the other. A developing leader in Dr. Pierson's view needs training and experience in at least four areas: maturity in their relationship with God; biblical and theological understanding; technical competence in their area of specialization; and appreciation for the necessity of experiencing the positive aspects of community life in Christ.[19]

We should take care that Dr. Pierson's last point not be lost on our traditional perspective shaped by a bias for formal preparation for ministry achieved apart from participation in a local body of believers. For too long, mission leaders as well as pastors, teachers, evangelists and prophets have been permitted to labor as lone rangers having little or no meaningful accountability within or credible connection to the local church. With a limited sense of ecclesiology and a philosophy of ministry effectively untouched by the real benefits of rootedness in a specific congregation, ministers of all stripes have been allowed to value their independence more than the important dynamics of interdependence in the Christian community.

Many who are devoted to training emerging Christian leaders assume that successful completion of a seminary degree program is, by itself, adequate preparation for all types of ministry. Elliston disagrees noting that, "Existing Christian leaders have often assumed that spiritual formation, growth in Christlikeness or spiritual ministry and maturation would automatically result from studying the Bible, theology or ministry courses. Some success can be seen. However, the more emerging leaders come from broken or troubled backgrounds and from a less churched society (the more) direct attention is required."[20] On this point Dr. Pierson concurs, observing that too many leaders come "out of church experiences that were negative, (or) churches which were not open to the missionary movement. *If we are to avoid the creation of churchless missions and missionless churches in the future, it will be important for (leaders) to have a positive experience and a personal as well as a theological appreciation of the body of Christ and life in Christian community* (emphasis added)."[21] This perspective has emboldened us to consider the benefits of a church-based approach to developing emerging leaders in our church and in our mission work in Bosnia. From our experience church-based training options are proving to be completely adequate for multiplying ministries both at home and abroad. Our experience is, thankfully, not unique in the world today.

Church-Based Leadership Development

Dr. Edgar Elliston notes in his book, *Home Grown Leaders*, "A trend among rapidly growing churches is the meeting of most of their leadership needs by "local" or "internal" ... development processes.... Local churches provide the primary arenas for identifying, selecting, and developing the whole range of Christian leaders. A person may attend a Christian college, university or seminary for a training interlude ... but his "home" congregation continues to provide the proving ground for continuing development and lifelong service.... What happens in the local church precedes, complements, supplements, and legitimizes what happens in Christian higher education."[22] I would add that the local church also sustains a leader's capacity to minister at home and on the mission field by providing the primary source of ongoing spiritual, emotional, financial and practical support for lifetime service.

William Taylor seems to agree when he notes, "It must be a church that evaluates gifted individuals, gives them territory and time to exercise their gifts, including the right to fail and try again."[23] He then qualifies his pro-church perspective regarding training for mission candidates by writing, "the local church can and must develop a training program for its future ministry.... However, the local church alone is not a substitute for (formal education). And a church can think too highly of itself when it assumes that in its own context it can handle all the equipping for effective cross-cultural ministry."[24]

Dr. Taylor's view offers a reasonable caution but we would do well to bear in mind that local churches vary as greatly as formal educational institutions and not all are mono-cultural. Even in our own small congregation, for example, though we are situated in a North Atlanta suburb, we have a tremendous ethnic and cultural diversity among our members. In our local assembly, we have had regular attenders and members who have immigrated from India, Germany, Russia, Japan, China, Thailand, Singapore, Indonesia, Ghana, Uganda, Kenya, Bosnia, Macedonia, Montenegro, Serbia, Austria, Iran, Romania and South Africa. Our small part of the "global village" is probably as ethnically diverse as many university settings in the United States and we really can offer cross-cultural exposure to our emerging leaders. The larger urban community around our church offers even greater cultural diversity.

So do most other urban and suburban settings around the world. The truth is, cross-cultural exposure which is so valuable for preparing mission leaders is available to almost any local church willing to pursue options close at hand. In our case, for example, several thousand Bosnian refugees now live within easy reach of our church. Prospective missionaries for our target group need not go overseas to experience the culture or to work on language skills. Bosnian Muslims now literally live in our backyard.

For this reason, we refuse to labor under Dr. Taylor's apparent presumption that local churches necessarily lack the capacity to prepare people for cross-cultural ministry. Moreover, we would never assume that any single training context should attempt to provide all the training input that any developing leader would ever need. From our perspective, the Holy Spirit plays the key role by controlling an emerging leader's training regimen, guiding the individual to a lifelong variety of learning experiences, ministry opportunities, mentoring relationships and challenging contexts where growth in character, capacity and a sense of calling are made possible.

The Spirit's delivery system may include informal educational opportunities that provide unplanned and relationally intensive occasions for spiritual development. In our view, **informal** lessons learned at significantly teachable moments usually offer the most important and continuous source of instruction in every believer's life. **Non-formal** education is also a viable delivery mechanism for the Holy Spirit's influence. Non-formal training processes provide a planned and proven regimen involving seminars, workshops, conferences, conventions and on-the-job apprenticeship settings. Though most often not suitable for providing degree accreditation, non-formal instruction is still perhaps the most widely available path to leadership formation in the global Christian community. This approach to training is contextually relevant, inexpensive, highly personal and easily within reach of laymen. Non-formal training is especially effective for enhancing practical ministry skills in a potential leader's home setting.

Of course, the Holy Spirit may also use **formal training** in developing the life of a leader. But, as we have already noted, relatively few gifted leaders — even in the West — are able to access this alternative which is characterized by highly demanding academic processes in expensive residential schools. Formal education may be the most prized vehicle for leadership training, but I am arguing here that it is not the most practical. We dare not avoid the real possibility that professional degrees earned in formal training settings may well not adequately equip a student for ministry. In any case, formal education does offer a standardized exposure to material believed by many to be highly relevant to spiritual formation. For this, formal approaches to training are useful.

No matter how initial training for leadership is pursued, we believe the development of a leader must, in every case, extend beyond a focus on increasing knowledge. Effective leadership development must go beyond mastery of content to facilitate maturity of conduct and character. We must not lose sight of the important truth that the progress of spiritual formation is not to be measured merely in informational terms. It is more importantly transformational, marked by growth in godly wisdom, spiritual fruitfulness and Christlike qualities observable in the life of the developing leader. Combining spiritual gifts with God-given capacity and ministry experience superintended by the Holy Spirit, laborers were continuously produced for the kingdom of God long before seminaries ever came on the Christian scene. Over the centuries the church has been the usual setting for developing leaders. My argument is that churches still offer a more viable context for training than do academic classrooms. I believe that reaffirming the church's role in training may be the key to our developing adequate capacity to meet increasing needs for qualified leadership in the 21st century.

Even if formal education were deemed the most desirable methodology for training leaders (a point I am not prepared to concede) we must acknowledge this approach alone cannot be expected to get the job done in the days ahead. Seminary style education will simply not be able to produce leaders rapidly enough to supply the demand the global church is making for trained laborers. Looking at the trends in missions alone demonstrates the problem. From 1980-1988, the missions movement in non-Western settings mobilized 22,686 new missionaries — an increase indicating a phenomenal decadal growth rate of 248 percent. During the same period, the Western mission force grew by only 48 percent per decade. *"This means that the Two-Thirds World Missions movement has grown approximately five times faster than the Western missions movement during the (decade of the '80s)....* If the Two-Thirds World missionary movement continues at its present rate of growth, ... there will be 162,360 (workers mobilized) by the year 2000 ... This would make the non-Western missionary force 54.4 percent of the total Protestant (missionary force by the end of the present decade)."[25]

Such unprecedented growth in missions will likely create a corresponding unprecedented need for additional local church leaders around the world. Present formal education models of ministerial formation will not be able to get the job done in supplying this demand for missionaries, pastors and trained leaders of other sorts. These changing realities dictate a change in our approach to training regimens. In the 21st century, we will be required to do better training on a broader level at a lower cost in a shorter amount of time than ever before.

The answer to this challenge lies in our coming to grips with the true value of the local church as an incredibly fruitful seedbed for rooting and raising up reproducing leaders. As a training setting, the context of a community of believers surpasses the relevance of an academic educational institution in the same way that a biological family surpasses the "brotherhood" of a college fraternity. The relationships and resources offered by a family are simply more accessible, more genuinely committed, more long lasting and more formative than those rendered by an artificial Greek society. In essence, trainers serving the global body of Christ, and most especially those serving in the context of local churches, must change their minds about the biblically mandated mission of evangelists, prophets, pastors and teachers. These gifted leaders (and I would include elders and deacons in this respect) must accept responsibility for equipping others for the work of ministry within their local congregations. We simply have no right to farm out a ministry so fundamental to the future of the worldwide Christian community.

In my view, it takes little reflection to realize that real life lived in the context of a local church is a better teacher than classroom case studies covered artificially in an academic setting. Professors can't hold a candle to the lasting spiritual light brought to bear by parents, pastors, peers and parishioners working together in the local church. Life's learning experiences are simply richer than the challenges of the classroom because they are more real. Education, experience and exposures that can be provided by the classroom can be reproduced in the context of the local church. The converse is not so generally true. Even a small church has great advantages over an academic setting if our training goals transcend simple educational achievement. This is even more dramatically so if the academic professor has no ongoing personal and private exposure with students outside the classroom. Academic training void of personal discipleship is unfortunately the limiting rule in academia rather than a liberating exception.

The local church has more capacity to balance the "zeal to know" with the responsibility "to do and to be." Local fellowships offer a context to practice and perfect new skills, to exercise legitimate stewardship and to actively endeavor to combine serving with the concept of sharpening one's leadership skills. In sharing with emerging leaders the actual shepherding responsibility over a local congregation, gifts can be confirmed, released, and legitimized in the real world by already proven leaders. Developing leaders can thus be empowered for ministry in the church in ways that are out of reach in the classroom.

Rosabeth Moss Kanter suggests four ways that emerging leaders are empowered to minister. Existing leaders can authorize and legitimize new leaders as they:

1. Give people important work to do on critical issues
2. Give people discretion and autonomy over their tasks and resources
3. Give visibility to others and provide recognition for their efforts
4. Build relationships for others, connecting them with powerful people and finding sponsors and mentors.[26]

In pursuing these avenues of empowerment in the context of a local assembly, opportunities to demonstrate the capacity to lead and influence others redemptively abound. Through personal mentoring with public and private blessing, the confidence, competence and commitment of emerging leaders is developed. Under the personal care of capable pastors and elders, emerging leaders learn to serve, to shepherd others and to be effective stewards over God's church. They therefore become increasingly capable and their comprehensive training allows them to be trusted with the responsibility to reproduce themselves and their local church communities. Following Paul's example, this has always been the church's global goal — a goal that has not changed for 2,000 years.

No Formal Credentials Required

If Robert Ferris is correct in observing that appropriateness should determine curriculum and philosophy of ministry should dictate the need for accreditation, we should not be surprised to find that many leaders around the world can serve the cause of Christ effectively without the benefit of formal academic credentials. In our setting for example, our church exists for the purpose of multiplication here at home and among the world's unreached people groups. Our purpose statement is codified in a single sentence. *Northside Community Church exists for the purpose of multiplying Christian communities through the contribution of every member to the ministries of worship, edification and mission.* This statement is sloganized in the declaration that, in our local church, *"Every Member Is a Minister."*

For our assembly to be successful, our leaders — vocational and volunteers alike — need to know how to create and multiply the body life dynamics of a highly relational church family. They must be committed to mastering the dynamics of personal discipleship, small group leadership, and congregational leadership that govern the life of our community. Our leaders must also maintain an ongoing personal and corporate priority to emphasize the word, prayer, evangelism, mission, worship and blessing as core values which shape our environment.

Our leaders don't need to know Greek and Hebrew to reproduce themselves or our congregation. But they do need to know how to think theologically and how to discern truth. They must also know how to share their faith, how to shepherd others, how to assimilate newcomers, how to nurture spiritual growth at a variety of levels and how to mobilize our members to meaningful ministries. They need to know how to use their homes as a base for ministry and how to touch the lives of others through intercession. In our context they need to know how to pray for physical healing, for deliverance from demonic strongholds, and for inner emotional healing. They need to know how to commune with the Holy Spirit, how to seek His face, to hear His voice and to release His gifts.

Appropriate to our context is a broad-based curriculum we have developed to equip laymen for service that honors our unique sense of ecclesiology and our philosophy of ministry. A scope and sequence chart is provided on pages 252-255, as one example of the kind of credible church-based training I am recommending.

Northside Community Church
August 1996

Active Members	Aspiring Leaders	Ministry Leaders (Shepherds, Ministry Team Leaders)
Abiding in Christ Prayer Fasting Worship Devotional Life Meditation Priority of Relationships	**Abiding in Christ** Prayer Fasting Worship Devotional Life Meditation Priority of Relationships	**Abiding in Christ** Prayer Fasting Worship Devotional Life Meditation Priority of Relationships
Small Group Experience Commitment Class (CC) Ministry Team Involvement Personal Prayer Life/Intercession 2:42 Group Growing Kids God's Way Personal Spiritual Life Living in Community Foundations of Faith	Bible Study Methods (BS) (Discipleship Dynamics) Small Group Dynamics (SG) Crown Ministries (CM) ACTS — BILD Material (AB) Experiencing God (EG) Short-term Missions Training	Mission/Evangelism/Discipleship (BTCL) Teaching Principles and Methods (BTCL) Pauline Epistles (BILD) Accountability Groups
Classes/Seminar Basic Christianity (BC) New Members Class (NM) Personal Evangelism Training (PE)	Congregational Dynamics I(CD I) Mission Policy Personality Profiles (PP) Spiritual Warfare (SW) Spiritual Gifts (SPG) Family Life (FL) Communication Skills (CS)	Applied Ecclesiology (AE) Short-term Missions Trip Conflict Resolution (CR) Peer Counseling (includes Deliverance/Inner Healing) (PC) Family Ministry (FM) Congregational Dynamics II (CD II) Spiritual Leadership (SL)
Character Issues Commitment Generosity Submission Forgiveness Fruit of the Spirit Faithfulness Availability Teachability	Servanthood Flexibility Stewardship Purity Spiritual Discipline Humility Honesty Gratitude	Responsibility Self Denial/Self Control Compassion (Grace/Mercy) Discernment Diligence Contentment Hospitality Integrity

Training Scope and Sequence

Congregational Leadership	Mentoring Leaders (Elders, Mentors, Wise Women)	Church Planters
Abiding in Christ Prayer Fasting Worship Devotional Life Meditation Priority of Relationships	**Abiding in Christ** Prayer Fasting Worship Devotional Life Meditation Priority of Relationships	**Abiding in Christ** Prayer Fasting Worship Devotional Life Meditation Priority of Relationships
OT Survey (BTCL) NT Survey (BTCL) Bible Doctrines (BTCL) Church Ministry (BTCL) Advanced Small Group Leadership (AGL) Leadership Orientation	Church History (BTCL) Church Administration (BTCL) Pastoral Ministry (BTCL)	New Atlanta Fellowship Church Planters Fellowship Preaching (BTCL)/(BILD)
ACMC National Conference Teaching Practicum (TP) Celebration/Worship Dynamics Mission Conference Planning	Antioch Network National Conf. EFCA General Assembly Preaching Practicum (PR) Advanced Christian Doctrine	Advanced Church Growth (ACG) Cultural Anthropology (CA)
Capacity Boldness Initiative Passion for God Wisdom Calling Balance Discretion	Godliness Temperance Fidelity Prudence Virtue Gentleness Selflessness Alertness	Trustworthiness Vision Faith Decisiveness Persuasiveness Balance Dependability Reverence

Northside Community Church

Active Members	Aspiring Leaders	Ministry Leaders (Shepherds, Ministry Team Leaders)
Required Reading List *Basic Christianity*-Stott (BC) *Called & Committed*-Watson (CC) *Witnessing without Fear*-Bright (PE)	*Descending into Greatness*-Hybels (CD I) *The Christian Family*-Christiansen (FL) *Knowing God*-Packer (CD I)	*Spiritual Leadership*-Sanders (CD II) *The Community of the King*-Snyder (CD II) *In Search of Guidance*-Willard (PC) *Assimilating New Members*-Shaller (CD II) *Your Church Can Grow*-Wagner (AE) *Your Church Can Be Healthy*- Wagner (AE)
Recommended Reading List *As You Sow*-Bright (NM) *The Holy Spirit*-Bright (NM) *The Quiet Time*-IVP (NM) *Too Busy to Pray*-Hybels (NM) *The Hallelujah Factor*-Taylor (NM) *The Bible Study Handbook*-Nav Press (CC) *Excel In Global Giving*-Jensen (NM)	*The Man in the Mirror*-Morley *Disciplines of the Beautiful Woman*-Ortland *Experiencing God*-Blackaby (EG) *Master Plan of Evangelism*-Coleman (BS) *Fire in the Fireplace*-Hummel (SPG) *The New Reformation*-Ogden *How to Win Friends and Influence People*-Carnegie (CS) *Manage Your Money*-Blue (CM) *I Want to Enjoy My Children*-Brandt (FL) *What the Bible Says About Child Rearing*-Fugate (FL) *Spiritual Warfare*-Warner (SW)	*Celebration of Discipline*-Foster (SL) *Ordering Your Private World*- McDonald (SL) *7 Habits of Highly Effective People*-Covey (SL) *Growing Adults on Sunday Morning*-Larson (AE) *Your Home a Lighthouse*-(FM) *At the Heart of a Matter*-Brandt (CR) *Communication-Key to Your Marriage*-Wright (FM)

Training Scope and Sequence
(continued)

Congregational Leadership	Mentoring Leaders (Elders, Mentors, Wise Women)	Church Planters
Required Reading List *Making of a Leader*-Clinton (ET) *Body Life*-Steadman (ET) *Living By the Book*-Hendricks (AGL) *The Gospel of the Kingdom*-Ladd (ET)	*Paul, the Spirit and the People of God*-Fee (ET II) *This We Believe*-Olsen (ET II) *Missionary Methods, St. Paul's and Ours*-Allen (ET II) *Developing the Leaders Within You*-Maxwell (ET II)	*Understanding Church Growth*-MacGavran (ACG) *Cultural Anthropology Course*- Kraft (CA) *Developing the Leaders Around You*-Maxwell (ACG) *Leading your Church to Growth*- Wagner (ACG)
Recommended Reading List *Systematic Theology*-Grudem (BTCL) *7 Laws of Teaching*-Gregory (TP) *Dynamic Bible Teaching*-Wilkenson (TP) *The Purpose Driven Church*-Warren (ET) *A Tale of Three Kings*-Edwards (ET)	*Church Discipline and the Courts*-Buzzard/Brandon (ET II) *Sharpening the Focus of the Church*-Getz (ET II) *Biblical Preaching*-Robinson (PR) *Demon Possession and the Christian*-Dickason (ET II) *Desiring God*-Piper (ET II)	*Perspectives*-Winter (ACG) *Power Evangelism*-Wimber (ACG) *The Frog in the Kettle*-Barna (ACG) *Dying for Change*-Anderson (ACG) *Let the Nations Be Glad*-Piper (ACG) *The Open Church*-Rutz (ACG)

This chart summarizes the levels of training and the course sequences we use to prepare leaders to effectively serve our unique purpose. We are training small church leaders to value the strengths of small church life and to reproduce them at home and abroad. As we offer these courses on Wednesday evenings and one Saturday per month over three calendar quarters each year, it is possible for our emerging leaders to complete the full training regimen we offer in 36 months time. Classroom teaching, small group experiences and seminar settings combine with constant in-service mentoring and practical application to balance acquisition of knowledge with ministry skill development. Personal discipleship and accountability groups encourage commitments to devotional disciplines as we seek to achieve a balance between knowing, doing and being in our approach to leadership development.

While we have seminary-trained leaders among our church-based faculty, our goal is not to offer a seminary style curriculum. Our goal is rather, to offer a curriculum that will prepare our leaders to participate in small church leadership and small church reproduction at home and, in some cases in our mission context. Our training effort is augmented by occasional seminars and workshops offered by mission agencies and educational institutions. We draw from these outside sources only the specific training we need, not the full range of options they offer. We are aiming at contextual and personal relevance not academic achievement per se. Our philosophy of ministry simply does not require or depend upon formal education, academic accreditation or seminary credentials to function effectively. Our goal is not graduation but the gradual formation of Christ-like character and capacity over time. Our testing comes at the point of contact with people, not in a final written or oral exam.

We are training men and women to be trusted with the members under our care not simply to be proficient with the particular curriculum a seminary might offer. We are training stewards as well as students, shepherds as well as theologians, and servants grounded in truth and intimacy with God not just a cadre of educationally elite graduates. We are serious about this responsibility because we will one day answer to God for our faithfulness in obeying His command to equip the saints for the work of service (Eph. 4:11).

If we can succeed in this goal, we believe other small church leadership teams can as well. We believe that it is time for local church leaders everywhere to take their training responsibilities seriously. Deferring to professional academicians and referring emerging leaders to seminaries and Bible schools is not enough. We must learn again to trust those we train at a local church level for meaningful ministry. At Northside Community Church, we are trying to do just that.

On the mission field in Bosnia, we are encouraging national church planters to trust their capacity to train emerging leaders at a local church level as well. We are coming alongside our national partners to help them equip laymen for effective ministry in their own congregations. When vocational ministry seems an appropriate option for developing leaders, we are helping to provide comprehensive non-formal training in a Bible school operating in Mostar. Offering two-weeks of intensive classroom, training six times a year, those being trained spend most of their time in contextual application at home. In practical application, these leaders adapt what they are learning to their own unique contexts and pass their increasing expertise along to people in their own church.

Only occasionally is formal credit afforded a student. That accreditation is provided by the Evangelical Theological Seminary in Osijek on a special arrangement basis negotiated by the student. Our intention in helping to operate the Mostar Bible School is to encourage the rapid development of leaders through an in-service process. Credibility of student leaders is more important to us than offering credit for our courses. Practicality of our curriculum options is a higher priority than progressive theological education. Effective reproduction of leaders and churches is a higher goal than official recognition by professional educators. We are seeking to accomplish our part of the great commission — a task that foresees no need for an eventual commencement ceremony. We are trying to train leaders who can be trusted to win their culture for Christ and mobilize missiologically to touch other near neighbor groups in Albania, Kosovo, Turkey and Bulgaria. We are excited to be pioneering alternatives to formal seminary training regimens both in the United States and in Bosnia.

Institutional pressures will always militate against liberating the laity for leadership. Professionalizing the ministry will always marginalize the masses of people God intends to release to serve His kingdom. Amateurizing the ministry at home or abroad will always serve to accentuate already complex barriers that hinder completion of the Great Commission. These objections to releasing leaders trained outside residential seminaries will always be raised but they must also be overcome. If they are not, qualified leaders will always remain in short supply.

Before the Exodus, Moses was dispatched to Pharaoh to proclaim God's sovereign demand, "Let my people go that they may serve me." Today, that same call is going forth again. In our day though, the call to release God's people for service is not directed to recalcitrant secular leaders like Pharaoh, but to reluctant church and mission leaders around the world who are holding much needed laborers back because they are not sufficiently educated. We must change the way we define good training and reaffirm the suitability of apprenticeship in informal and non-formal processes. God has made it clear that He gave gifted leaders to His church for the purpose of equipping the saints for the work of ministry.

It is time to take that mandate more seriously at the local church level. It is also time to make better training available on a broader level. It is time to allow God's gifted people to go about His ordained business. It is time to put our reluctance to release others aside. Around the world throughout the ages, church leaders have been called to train others so that they may be trusted to carry out and to reproduce responsible ministry. Failure to trust those we train violates God's trust in us. For the sake of the kingdom we must be willing to let God's people go that they may serve Him.

13

Two Are Better Than One

"Two are better than one because they have a good return for their labor..."
Eccl. 4:9

Solomon's wise observation from Eccl. 4:9 begins a passage which expands on the value of working together toward a common goal. The larger context of this verse, drawn from the heart of the Old Testament's wisdom literature, offers easy application in the arena of modern mission ministry. The benefits of laboring together in strategic mission partnerships can be summarized under four general headings. In global evangelism as in other aspects of life, joint efforts promise the advantages of:

Synergy: *"Two are better than one because they have a good return for their labor."* (Eccl. 4:9)

Often the increased productivity derived from partnership with others doesn't just add incrementally to our results, it multiplies them. This kind of synergy, in which the whole product is greater than the sum of the parts invested, is observable in a variety of arenas. One example is found in God's promise to Israel concerning the battlefield results which He prophesies will come from His people's choice to face their foes together. Leviticus 26:8 anticipates that a geometric increase will result from cooperative efforts in warfare. Here Moses writes, "five of you will chase a hundred, and a hundred of you will chase ten thousand, and your enemies will fall before you by the sword." By increasing the number of warriors twenty-fold, God's promise was that Israel would become a hundred times more effective. Partnerships create the possibility of such synergistic results. Working together is especially important when opportunities are great and manpower is limited. Shared commitment to common objectives almost always offers dramatic increases in our effectiveness.

> **Support**: "*For if either of them falls, the one will lift up his companion. But woe to the one who falls when there is not another to lift him up. Furthermore, if two lie down together they keep warm, but how can one be warm alone?*" (Eccl. 4:10-11)

Partnerships are all the more practical when the project at hand is inherently difficult. Who has not been blessed by the availability of a helping hand, an encouraging word or a faithful friend who hangs in until the job is completely finished. The practical support gleaned from having a fellow laborer at your side almost always lightens the load and improves performance. This reality is readily observable in the world of track and field. Relay teams always generate faster results than individual competitors produce by running an entire race alone. Performance is improved because each runner brings fresh legs and full energy to his personal portion of a given event. The support generated by four runners sharing a race simply outstretches the capacity of a single person to perform alone. These verses confirm lessons taught in real life. When the task is daunting a duet beats a solo every time! Perhaps this is why Jesus sent His disciples out to minister two by two.

Security: "*And if one can overpower him who is alone, two can resist him.*" (Eccl. 4:12a)

Solomon's wisdom next declares the simple but significant truth that reinforcements increase our ability to stand against our enemies. Danger is diminished when others stand ready to fight at our side. My twin brother has been a policeman for more than 20 years. I have always been amazed at the courage men and women in his profession display in their daily assignments. They routinely venture into troubled areas of the city or into tense circumstances that I would be afraid to face alone. Think of the risks that come with unruly mobs, or barroom brawls, or domestic disturbances where angry spouses have come to blows. Policemen walk into such settings every day with cool heads and unshaken confidence. Riding along with cops on their beat, I learned the secret behind their amazing sense of security. It lays in the constant availability of a "code three backup." Whenever the chips are down, or the situation seems to be getting out of hand, a simple call for reinforcements brings other policemen with "code three" urgency — lights flashing and sirens blasting to announce their approach. A beat cop's confidence is magnified by the certain promise of instantly available support whenever the need arises. Partnerships in the kingdom of God can bring a similar reassurance. Committed cooperation in serving common goals was the secret behind the success of some of the most famous pairs in scripture. David was made more secure by Jonathan's commitment. Paul was emboldened by his brother Barnabus. Aquila was freed to accompany Paul because his willing wife Priscilla was eager to go along. When dangers lurk in our walk of faith or in our work among the nations, there is no substitute for the committed companionship of fellow soldiers in Christ.

Strength: "*A cord of three strands is not easily broken.*" (Eccl. 4:12b)

Finally, this text tells us that working together makes us predictably stronger as we face imposing foes. The principles of "collective security" have long guided the affairs of nations as treaties link one government to another for mutual defense with the intent to ward off would-be aggressors. It was this kind of strength born of mutual commitment which allowed the North Atlantic Treaty Organization to provide a sufficient show of strength to forestall Soviet ambitions in Europe during the cold war.

In the international arena of diplomacy, collective security has long been encouraged because of two significant advantages it promotes. First, cooperative security agreements create a measure of external protection flowing from the combined strength of peaceful partners. Allies, pledged to act in concert against aggression, discourage opportunistic enemies who might otherwise resort to force of arms. Collective security agreements also create an internal impetus for selfless action. As Henry Kissinger has suggested, commitments to common action are "fatal to selfish aims."[1] Partnerships make us more daunting as we stand against our enemies and more determined as we stand with our friends. Formal partnerships, whether formed between countries bound by treaties or by colleagues bound by trust, make us stronger to face the dangers that come our way.

Two are better than one because partnerships generate synergistic potential, increased support for challenging tasks, enhanced security in the face of danger and magnified strength for the battle. Solomon's wisdom is too obvious to be ignored in the pursuit of global evangelism.

Competition Must Give Way to Cooperation

These lessons from Ecclesiastes offer a firm foundation for strategies that could enhance the results of mission activity through cooperative efforts on the field. Unfortunately, cooperation has been a relatively rare dynamic in the history of world mission. Perhaps this is because so many missionaries view their counterparts who serve with other agencies as competitors rather than colleagues. (Review the faulty rationale behind competition among Christians presented in Chapter 9, "Seeing As God Sees.")

Whatever the cause, cooperation has been consistently overshadowed by competition in many mission settings. This reality is evidenced by the early development of "comity agreements" among sending agencies which were intended to insure mutual respect for prearranged "territorial boundaries" on shared mission fields. It is equally apparent in the more recent attempts at domination (and even denigration) of Protestant missionaries by emerging Orthodox or Catholic "state churches" in nations which once were part of the Eastern Bloc. From the days when Hudson Taylor could garner no support at home for mission work in China to the current evidence of institutional opposition to intentional evangelism in Central Europe, genuine cooperation in missions has for too long been in short supply.

In the arena of global outreach, one would think that partnerships would be especially appreciated for the advantages they offer. Instead, they have been assiduously avoided by many and difficult to sustain in the best of instances where they have been attempted. But the world missions scene is changing. Western agencies are facing emerging realities on the field as well as at home, which are making fruitful alliances more necessary and, at the same time, more difficult than ever to achieve. Missionary executives and church leaders alike must grasp the changes that are already upon us if they hope to find a way to survive in a new era of mission enterprise. The historical dynamics of competition among Christian missionaries must give way to a more passionate commitment to cooperation and to the development of just partnerships. Shared ministry cannot be avoided if we Westerners are to have a viable role to play in 21st century mission. Formal partnerships allow us to display more strength as we stand together against our enemies and more heart as we stand together with our friends.

Changing Relationships With Nationals

Some of the difficulties that have diminished the potential for partnership with nationals have existed for centuries. They stem from four common concerns. In some cases, missionaries have had legitimate desires to honor serious doctrinal differences that distance them from national leaders. Sometimes, philosophical incompatibilities are more imposing than doctrinal issues. In other instances complex cultural/religious realities make cooperation a unique challenge in a given mission context. Too often, the most significant issue is unabashed missionary ethnocentrism that alienates capable and willing national partners. Our experience has exposed us to all four of these barriers.

In Bosnia, the challenges of sharing the gospel vary greatly depending upon whether one is ministering to an ethnic Croat who is a nominal Catholic; or to an ethnic Serb who holds to Orthodox traditions; or to a Muslim who knows nothing of the Koran but is certain that "Orthodox Christians" have destroyed his country and his way of life. Barriers to evangelistic ministry in these three instances are raised more by cultural realities than by religious convictions. In effect, many of the barriers to effective evangelism in our mission context are secular problems that wear a spiritual mask. The marriage of national identity and a nominal religious faith make former Yugoslavia an especially complex mission field.

These contextual realities complicate the potential for partnership with nationals as much as they frustrate efforts in evangelism. Croatian Protestants are carrying most of the burden for national leadership in our mission work directed toward Bosnia's Muslims. They can do so because, for the most part, Croats fought with Muslims to withstand Serb aggression in the recent war. Serb evangelicals, on the other hand, have far more difficulty ministering in Bosnia because they are still seen as deadly enemies there. In some areas, Croats fought Muslims as they each battled Serb forces. In these areas, Croats are sometimes as bitterly opposed as Serb evangelicals would be. Mostar, is one such example. Muslims and Croats live on opposite sides of the Neretva River and Croats still practice ethnic cleansing with impunity. In Bihac, the one city where Muslims fought each other as well as their common Serb opponents, evangelism has been especially slow. Intense hatred has not yet given way to a serious hunger for the gospel in these areas. No short-term solutions or simple schemes will soon be able to overcome the complexities of ethnic and nationalistic barriers to evangelism or to forming just partnerships in Bosnia.

Among Croat missionaries working in Bosnia, two major thrusts have been made by separate groups of indigenous Protestant evangelicals. The Pentecostals, under the banner of the Evangelical Church, and the non-Pentecostals, represented primarily by the Baptist Union, are separated by sincere theological distinctives. The doctrinal differences between these two groups have militated against their cooperation in mission ministry in Bosnia just as they have in other parts of the world. A more congenial working environment is being developed as serious attempts are made toward forming "evangelical alliances" to benefit all Protestants who are likely to remain a hopeless and helpless minority if they refuse to stand together. In spite of those positive steps however, deeply held doctrinal positions still cause Christian co-laborers in these different doctrinal camps to act more like strange bedfellows than like brothers joined in strategic partnership. Divergent beliefs about the ministry of the Holy Spirit have for too long, in too many places, made holy communion between members of God's family nearly impossible. Too easily we murder the mandate to love one another with our commitment to maintain our personal or denominational doctrinal perspectives. In heaven after all, the One Who is Truth will surely settle this earthly failure.

Philosophical perspectives also have complicated the mission landscape in Bosnia. Some agencies aim at serving in this troubled territory by aggressively recruiting nationals to work as "agency staff" there. These national workers are being lured away from a handful of infant churches that offer a very limited supply of often newly converted leaders. As "the best" churchmen are recruited to serve Western mission agencies rather than local congregations in Bosnia, national pastors can easily develop resentment over what seems to be self-serving recruiting tactics.

Other agencies, seeking to provide humanitarian relief in Bosnia, do so in the name of Christ but with a firm commitment not to proselytize actively among the three ethnic groups which make up the population. On the surface, such an eclectic commitment may seem noble. But to national pastors who are serious about reaching their neighbors for Christ, the agreement not to take evangelistic advantage of the opportunity relief efforts bring can be seen as an indefensible accommodation to culture.

This issue is a special problem on this field because of the historical realties unique to the context. More nominal than noble, the decision not to evangelize has for centuries been an accepted cultural norm in Bosnia. In 1990 for example, a Catholic priest told our team that there was no need to develop a strategy for evangelism in Sarajevo since all of that great city's citizens were essentially monotheists. He seemed to be quite content in his conviction that the Jewish, Orthodox, Catholic and Muslim communities could be equally well served and equally secure for eternity practicing whichever monotheistic faith they embraced. He betrayed no sense of struggle in acknowledging that people from each of these faith communities were acceptable as worshippers in his small chapel. Proselytizing was an unnecessary and confusing affront for religious leaders in pre-war Bosnia and, apparently, an unwelcome intrusion being encouraged by newly arriving evangelicals like us.

Such "peaceful coexistence" free from the turmoil which efforts to evangelize might bring, has long been the "religious rule" in Bosnia. As some missionaries embrace and respect this perspective, national evangelicals are not so encouraged. They are concerned that while the public peace in Bosnia has been shattered by the war, the "religious rule" that has always discouraged evangelism may still be fully in tact.

The issue is of legitimate concern for national leaders. If "the rule" against proselytizing that was once enforced by Communist leaders is now to be reinforced by emerging democratic politicians with the full support of "broad-minded" Western diplomats, the post-war scenario for evangelicals could be worse than ever in Bosnia. This issue is made more serious in the face of opposition against evangelicals being promoted by religious leaders serving state churches. Dr. Peter Kuzmic summarizes the concern clearly, "National churches, especially the Orthodox church in several republics of the former Soviet Union, Romania, Bulgaria and Serbia, and the Catholic church in Poland, Hungary and Croatia, are reasserting their claims of monopoly on religious life and activity in their nations. In these countries, belonging to the national church is becoming less a question of theological persuasion and allegiance to Christ and more a question of patriotism, and bona fide citizenship. Protestantism in general is looked upon with great suspicion as a radical movement which in the past has divided Christendom, and as a modernized, western faith, and thus a foreign intrusion which at present, in its various fragmented forms, threatens the national and religious identity and unity of the people. Democratically and ecumenically illiterate clergy and militant fanatics among laity, are frequently opposed to Protestant evangelicals as disruptive sectarians involved in dangerous proselytizing and unpatriotic activities. Violent clashes, legal and illegal discrimination, and cultural marginalization are not excluded. It is not inconceivable that some evangelical and other leaders of religious minorities could become the new 'dissidents' of the post-Communist era in Eastern Europe."

Withholding ones personal witness may be important if the goal is to be politically correct but it is an impotent gesture if the goal is personal conversion. Which goal is right for Bosnia? How should evangelicals partner together when they are faced with such a variety of convictions? These philosophical issues make cooperation genuinely challenging.

The historical barriers to cooperation born from divergent views on doctrinal issues, philosophical preferences and respect for other faiths encountered on this field are only intensified when cross-cultural dynamics are added to the mix. Western missionaries have always struggled with the challenge of developing just partnerships with national leaders. Too often, we end up patronizing our national brothers in the process or pursuing our own global mission goals. We Westerners somehow assume that our insights are more sophisticated, our methods more meaningful and our strategies more efficient and effective than those put forward by leaders who come from "underdeveloped, third-world" cultures. Has it not been blatantly presumptuous for us to divide the earth into "the East and the West and all the rest"? Is it not more demeaning yet to intrinsically assume that of these three, "the West is best"? Such descriptive language alone carries sufficient ethnocentric arrogance to make my point about this barrier to just partnerships with nationals. The modern reality of Western material wealth and military might have left us convinced that cultures from the "two thirds" world are no match for our own. Our ethnocentric language conspires with our ethnocentric logic to magnify our inherent attitudes of superiority. These cultural issues are real and they are not easily resolved as we make attempts to work more fairly and more effectively with national partners on the mission fields of the world.

Agreements That Define Inherent Inequalities

Think of the issues traditional partnership agreements attempt to clarify in written form. Often they serve to reinforce the inequities among potential partners rather than delineating truly equitable terms for shared commitment in ministry. They deal with concerns about the source of **funding** for the mission enterprise. Who will pay for the programs the partnership envisions for a given field? They also address the issue of ultimate **authority** over the means, the methods and the missionaries involved in the project. Who, in the final analysis, will have the **right to rule** the partnership?

A partnership agreement also generally conveys a sense of **ownership** of the vision and strategy being pursued by the parties involved. Whose agenda will be served in the joint commitment of people and resources? The **identity** of the fruit produced by the partnership effort is also usually clarified before the work begins. If churches are to be planted, for example, to what denomination will they belong? Few Western denominational mission agencies are neutral on this point. Moreover, the preferences of national leaders are seldom afforded overriding consideration. Too often, public relations issues facing Western partners at home are asserted to rule the day.

Finally, traditional partnership agreements stipulate who has the prerogative to set the pace and exercise **initiative** on the field. As callous and crass as it may seem, implementing a partnership with nationals generally boils down to a clear declaration of who holds **power** in the partnership and who ultimately **controls** the collaborative effort. Not surprisingly, nationals have most often been left with the short end of the stick in the process of negotiating for much needed Western resources.

This reality is now changing dramatically. National churchmen are increasingly assuming their rightful place in the more influential positions of leadership in the global Christian community. Some experts are predicting that, by AD 2000, more than half the world's mission force will be mobilized from the Two-Third's world. Thus, emerging national leaders are no longer timid in wrestling for an equitable arrangement with Western partners who have, for far too long, dominated their arenas of influence. It is encouraging to see most missiologists from the West applauding the emergence of these powerful national personalities. It is right to welcome their influence in the worldwide Christian movement.

Even when they are greeted warmly, however, the growing influence of capable national leaders is putting tremendous pressure on traditional approaches to partnership with the West. No longer do expatriate missionaries have room to assume it is their divine right to rule in cooperative relationships with nationals. Western paternalism simply has no legitimate place in the changing world of mission partnerships.

National leaders are no longer willing merely to assume the role of "junior partners" in global evangelism. They want to offer leadership in evangelizing unreached people groups that are more culturally proximate and more receptive to them than to Western missionaries. Financial resources and seniority in the world mission movement notwithstanding, Westerners are being forced to reconsider the rules of engagement in global outreach.

Embracing a New "Enabling" Role for Westerners

Paul McKaughan President of the Evangelical Foreign Mission Agencies (EFMA) sees America's shifting place in world mission as an example of the redefinition of roles now underway. He has said, "Without a massive reordering of the U.S. missionary enterprise, and a dynamic movement of the Spirit of God renewing His church in the United States, the structures and industry which we missionaries represent could, in the not too distant future, appear analogous to an abandoned ship buried by the tides on a seashore, with only its weather beaten ribs as visible testimony to far better and more useful days."[2]

McKaughan's observation is shared by other progressive Western mission leaders. James Engle, for example, expresses a similar conclusion when he writes, "A dominant, controlling mode (of mission leadership) ... might have been applicable in an earlier period. Now we are reaping the fruit of discontent and resentment sown among competent overseas leaders who deserve acceptance as our peers in every sense of the word...."[3] Engle sees an international environmental shift toward Two-Thirds World leadership in global evangelism which demands "a radical reassessment of fundamental paradigms accompanied by adaptation and change."[4] He concludes that failure to change will have catastrophic results for North American mission agencies. Engle speaks to the pressing need to reassess and retool our mission organizations pointedly, "I contend that the prospects for survival of world missions as a central driving cause in the North American evangelical church are increasingly bleak. It is time to remove our head from the sand and face reality."[5]

Realistic reappraisal will, in Engle's view, drive Western mission leaders toward a new "enabling role" in global evangelism. Conceding that mature and experienced nationals will increasingly set the agenda for world mission activity, Engle recommends that Western missionaries aim at coming alongside agreeably and aggressively in a supporting role. He suggests we should do so in a manner that demonstrates our commitment to participate with no desire to dominate, or to control, or to patronize our national partners. We must learn to be their servants offering all that we can in the way of resources and assistance to enable them to be all they can be for the kingdom of God.

Full Support Means Funding Too!

As this change in roles for Westerners takes place, I believe that we cannot avoid the difficult challenge of learning how to continue bringing the lion's share of financial resources to the table while remaining in a predominately supporting or enabling role. Missiologists are rightfully cautious about creating a national church dependent upon Western material support for its continued existence. Traditional mission thinking would dictate a maximum effort to make national churches self-governing, self-supporting and self-propagating.

In the face of changing global realities however, this accepted strategy should not be allowed to justify the status quo. Western mission leaders simply cannot afford to perpetuate a "fiscal golden rule" that effectively presumes that "the ones who have all the gold get to make all the rules." Dr. Chris Marintika offers an Indonesian example of the excellent world mission leadership nationals are increasingly providing. Dr. Marintika directs the Evangelical Theological Seminary of Indonesia that has a vision for planting 20,000 new churches by the year 2015. He addresses this fiscal issue straightforwardly by recommending a revised perspective on traditional missiological monetary policy. He suggests that we all learn "to pray together, play together and pay together" in our joint efforts to reach the unreached peoples of the earth for Christ. In his model of cooperation, every partner would bring every possible resource to assure every possible success in every possible mission effort. Dr. Marintika is proposing that, this kind of unreserved trust and commitment offers the people of God the best opportunity to enjoy the delights of reaching unreached peoples on the kingdom playgrounds around the world.

Traditional thinkers will no doubt respond with concern over Westerners footing the bill for ongoing Third World initiatives. In the face of such concerns, Chuck Bennett, president of Partners International, points out that we would do well to remember the simple truth that, "Paternalism is an attitude not an amount of money. If the indigenous worker feels like a trusted, equal partner, then financial subsidy is not a problem. If he or she is made to feel like an employee, then paternalism and resentment can result."[6]

Sensitivity on this point has allowed us to work in Bosnia with maximum generosity in partnership with Croatian and Bosnian national leaders without creating undue concern over our giving birth to a crippling dependence or a compromising lack of financial accountability with our partners. We understand that a relatively small Western church like ours has little possibility of paralyzing a long-term church planting movement of national scope like the one we serve in Bosnia. Our pockets are simply not deep enough for us to represent a serious threat in this regard. This would be true even if Bosnia's economy were sound — but it is not!

Bosnia has been made bankrupt by the war and suffers from an unemployment rate exceeding 80 percent of the population. In such a society where humanitarian relief is the primary sustenance for the vast majority, our national partners need all the financial help we can offer. Material resources are far more available to us and are therefore one of the "enabling investments" we can and must contribute to our partnerships. Failure to do so would mean denying one of our obvious strengths to our partners. Such a failure may well validate traditional mission theory but it would violate the truths of scripture which call us to be aggressively responsive in the face of genuine need (James 2:14-17, I Jn. 3:17-18).

Does the Enabling Role Really Work?

The outcome of our pursuit of the kind of enabling role that Engle's envisions and that Marintika recommends has been a genuine blessing to us and to our national partners in Bosnia. Reflecting on the results of our partnership with nationals, Phill Butler, President of Interdev, offered an objective report on our work. After facilitating a combined meeting of Croatian nationals and Western mission leaders who were seeking a mutually agreeable model for cooperation in the pursuit of mission strategies for Bosnia he wrote to Dr. Paul Cedar, then the president of our denomination,

> While in Zagreb I had a chance to personally see how the Croatian church leadership views the work undertaken in Bosnia by Northside Community Church and their partner churches in Atlanta. Again and again the Croatian church leaders pointed to John Rowell and his team (field leadership and rotating teams of workers) as a model of the kind of partnership they respected and appreciated most deeply. Clearly, the Northside Community-led initiative in Bosnia has not only captured the attention of other churches in the U.S., it has captured the hearts of the Croatian leaders themselves.... It is good news that Northside Community and their partner churches in Atlanta have managed to avoid the worst and demonstrate the best (in partnership efforts with nationals).[7]

These significant changes occurring in the world of missions present increasing difficulty for Western agency leaders who insist on remaining entrenched in methodologies that no longer suit the environment. But agency challenges are not limited to the nuisances created by more demanding national partners. Mission leaders also struggle with sea changes taking place in partnership dynamics at home. Even in the familiar surroundings of their Western sending bases, traditional mission leaders are being forced to consider shifting realities that affect their partnerships with supporting churches at a foundational level.

Changes on the Home Front

We have already noted that Western agencies have traditionally struggled with releasing a full measure of material support to national initiatives if they cannot enjoy a commensurate measure of control. Now they are facing their own fiscal crisis born of similar dynamics at home. In Jim Engle's recent book, *A Clouded Future,* he writes about the reality of the financial crisis facing North American mission agencies, describing it in unmistakable terms. "In general, giving for benevolent causes (all activities beyond the local congregation) has decreased by 33 percent as a percentage of income between 1968 and 1992. Furthermore ... two thirds of the pastors (surveyed) agreed that global missions is in sharp decline as a focus of today's church."[8]

What is creating this trend away from a serious missions interest in North American churches? Engle would place the blame on the boomer generation that is coming of age and exerting an unsettling influence on the entirety of church life. Engle's point is important to note — even at the risk of joining the "boomer-bashers" who would it seems lay most of our pressing church environmental problems at the feet of the post-World War II generation as if it were some sort of ecclesiastical El Nino. Baby boomers, Engle says, are changing our traditional paradigms by introducing influences that consistently undermine missiological zeal. Among the unsettling trends Engle sights are boomer penchants for:

- **Individualism.** As a whole, boomers tend to reject the status quo and are entrepreneurial in outlook. Life is characterized by a search for meaning, identity, fulfillment, and self-gratification as they question the values of earlier generations.

- **Pluralism.** There is a greater tolerance for diversity and formerly taboo practices and lifestyles. Legalistic practices and outlooks are questioned. Previously accepted theological premises are subjected to scrutiny, an example being that Jesus is the only way to know God.

- **Skepticism.** Existing institutions are subjected to the searchlight of relevance, and many, including missions in the traditional sense, are found to be wanting. Denominational and institutional loyalties are suspect and even rejected unless a clear rationale can be found for their justification.

- **Holism.** Any remnants of historic evangelical dichotomy between evangelism and social action are totally rejected as unbiblical and outmoded. There is a full expectation among boomers that both dimensions will be addressed in outreaches that ask for support.

- **Activism.** Boomers are characterized by a willingness to tackle issues and to seek new solutions — especially when they are given full opportunity to make use of their spiritual gifts, talents, and abilities. As a result, they stand out among all other segments of society when it comes to financially supporting and volunteering for causes which they feel are providing real solutions to real problems. This is far more true however, of secular causes and local initiatives than it is of world missions.

- **Isolationism.** While knowledge of world issues may be relatively high, initiatives to meet world need often are rejected as nonproductive. There is growing disdain toward causes which are seen as throwing resources at world problems with little return for the effort. Furthermore, world problems are seen as being of such a magnitude as to defy solution, especially by outsiders. This is less true on the local scene where there often is a brighter and more immediately positive prognosis.[9]

Engle adds to this list an additional, albeit unintentional, missiological impact that has resulted from a shift toward seeker sensitive methodologies in the North American church. This philosophy of ministry tends to treat worshipers as consumers and orders church programs to fit the felt needs of a constituency conditioned by our culture to be highly sales-resistant and particularly reluctant to respond on the basis of passionate appeals to duty. Engle concludes, "When programs and (missions) emphases fall on such resistant ground, there is less incentive to persevere, no matter how important the cause or issue. Nothing can be more discouraging than large numbers of worshipers expressing their disaffection through withdrawing their presence and their pocketbooks. There is no question that the global outreach of the church can be sacrificed on this altar of felt needs."[10]

The consequent fiscal implications are telling and create what Engle has called "a clouded future" for North American missions. The signs of the times for traditional mission leaders include these realities:

· Large numbers of overseas mission agencies, big and small, have plateaued in growth — both in terms of personnel and financial resources.

· Mission revenue is stagnant or declining and falls far short of meeting the challenges of growth.

· Existing funding sources are eroding. Donor bases are aging and new donor acquisition is falling far short of needs.

· Financial realities are forcing many agencies into the trap of reliance on percentage subsidies from missionary support funds as the primary revenue stream.

· Growing numbers of churches are looking beyond existing agencies to find new and more productive ways to meet the challenge of world evangelization.[11]

The disturbing climate Engle is conveying indicates that many local churches in the West are no longer merely wrestling with a traditionally passive role in missions. His message is urgently clear. North American Churches are increasingly moving away from missions altogether. This is thankfully, not a universal reality, but the days of finding easy partnership with "missions generous" churches seem to be fading fast.

The Game Has Changed
Even if the Players Remain the Same

Among the churches which choose to remain involved in missions, there is a perceptible move away from nominal participation as world mission "resource providers." More churches want to share an active partnership role on the world's mission fields. This philosophical impetus for change is like a fire in the belly of some churches that would dare to assume the primary role of mission leadership when suitable agency partners are uninterested or unavailable to show the way. Some churches may even demand to take the lead when agencies are willing to fulfill their traditional role. Such churches are pressing agencies to share in the mission enterprise in an enabling rather than a leadership role. Advances in information technology, cross-cultural exposure due to the forces of a global economy and the ease of international travel are adding fuel to the fire that is warming local congregations to the possibilities of church-based missions. As this new activism takes hold and local churches get more eager than ever about direct mission involvement, they are less responsive than ever to the old paradigms that asked them simply to offer support and to facilitate agency-led professional mission ministry.

The phenomenon of church-based mission initiatives is helping to create the mission agency fiscal crisis Engle is identifying. Churches are viewing partnership with agencies with the same reticence that agencies have expressed toward nationals. In effect, churches are beginning to withhold traditionally reliable sources of support if agencies are not offering more active options for direct involvement. The message seems clear, churches will no longer invest generously if they have no hope to influence broadly. Agency leaders are clearly feeling squeezed as this trend develops. They are being held at bay by the very reasoning they have used historically to hold nationals in their place.

Churches Acting Like Agencies

The dual pressures of increasingly scarce financial resources and increasing interest on the part of a declining number of activist-oriented churches are providing the force for this transition from the traditional assumptions governing agency-church relationships in mission. Dr. Bruce Camp was among the first to focus attention on this paradigm shift which is putting a new face on the mission enterprise and calling for radical change in agency strategies for partnership development at home. Dr. Camp contrasts two traditional "resource oriented" paradigms with a third more active alternative which is gaining popularity among North American churches that choose to remain passionately committed to global evangelism.[12]

- **The Supporting Paradigm** represents the most passive approach for mission involvement at a local church level. In this form of relationship with mission agencies, churches provide financial and prayer support for global evangelism while leaving strategy, implementation, training and mobilization decisions to the professional missions community. Most churches interested enough to remain involved in global evangelism have long since been educated away from this paradigm as a singular approach to global outreach. Unfortunately, mission profession-als who helped point the way out of such passive participation continue to rely on the "supporting paradigm" for the bulk of their financial resources. As churches have become less willing to partner passively however, this paradigm has begun to play out like an overmined vein of gold. Agencies of necessity have therefore, shifted the weight of support generation from the local church to individual Christians. In seminar settings, Tom Telford who now serves with United World Mission has identi-fied this shift away from local church partnerships as one of the "Top 10 Mistakes Mission Agencies Make." He estimates that 25 years ago 75 percent of Western agency funding came from the local church and 25 percent from individual donors. Now, those figures are exactly reversed and "supporting church" partners make up only 25 percent of the donor base for most agencies.

- **The Sending Paradigm** provides a more active alternative for church participation in the "resource-oriented" approach to missions. In this model, churches are encouraged to become "mission mobilizers" investing not just their prayer and financial support in global outreach but their people too. "Sending Churches" are encouraged to become actively involved in selecting, motivating, training and sending their missionaries. Most often, they do so under the auspices of traditional agencies.

ACMC (Advancing Churches in Missions Commitment) has served the North American church dramatically in educating local church leaders into this more participatory option. This organization's national and regional conferences have provided a much needed forum to put church and mission leaders in a common networking environment. The sending paradigm gives local churches both a voice and a vote in the development of mission candidates and mission field strategies. Because tradi-tional agencies largely retain control of partnerships developed under this model, the sending paradigm is an alternative that has been widely accepted and encouraged among mission professionals.

• **The Synergistic Paradigm** represents the "sea change" we are describing in the Western mission environment. This may be the most significant new development for missions in the 21st century. In this partnership option, the roles of the local church and the agency are largely reversed. Synergistic churches make a proactive commitment to world missions (often adopting an unreached people group target in the process) and aim at mobilizing and directing their own initiative to get the job done. The local church maintains ownership of the vision God has given it, looking to traditional agencies only for support along the way.

Jim Engle calls congregations operating in this paradigm "mission-focused churches" and applauds this trend as a valuable emerging reality for world mission. The mission-focused church he writes, "presents the best overall scenario for the cause of world evangelization. The church now takes its rightful place in the kingdom of God and is committed to strategic use of its resources following our Lord's priorities. The starting point lies with world need and moves from there to the explanation of ways in which a congregation can utilize its resources to make a strategic impact. This is often done through participation in strategic alliances and partnerships in various parts of the world. In doing so, the church is being proactive in the best sense of the word. This paradigm presents major challenges to mission agencies which are still functioning in the (sending paradigm).... No church or agency can ignore the fact that (the synergistic paradigm) will rapidly become more common place, especially among larger change-oriented churches.... I contend that all agencies committed to a long range role in world evangelization will have no choice but to wrestle with the implications of (this) paradigm. After all, it seems to embrace everything that our Lord envisioned for His church."[13] Not all mission leaders share the enthusiasm Engle and Camp reflect as they see the synergistic paradigm growing more popular among mission-minded churches. Some leaders feel it is absurd to think that churches would presume to pursue this paradigm, daring in the final analysis to act like mission agencies on their own accord.

Mission Professionals Struggle With Changing Partnership Dynamics

Referring to three examples of mission leaders who don't like all that they see in this paradigm we can develop a clear sense of the mixed reviews the synergistic paradigm is receiving in the mission community. Chuck Bennett, president of Partners International, conveys predictable agency frustrations and resistance to this trend when he says, "Those of us who have spent a lifetime in the complex world of cross-cultural missions wonder why those churches (large American churches which have become sending agencies themselves) will no longer just give their money and trust us like they used to do. Now they want to be equal partners."[14]

Bill Taylor, Executive Secretary of the Missions Commission of World Evangelical Fellowship, is also the editor of Kingdom Partnerships for Synergy in Missions (William Carey Library, 1994). Though generally positive about agency partnership with churches, he warns pastoral leaders about the perils of a single church trying to do too much in missions without involving other entities. He suggests, "Extremely rare is the single local church that can effectively and fully train the missionary prior to field service. Rarer yet — if non-existent — is the church that can effectively shepherd, strategize and supervise missionaries on the field.... The more thoughtful sending churches wisely enter into field partnership with experienced agencies who have personnel and history."[15] Taylor's concern is born in part from an institutional expectation that high turnover of mission committee leadership will ultimately undermine a church's ability to sustain a long-term capacity to meet the ongoing needs of mobilized missionaries. His perspective is telling as he suggests we pray that God would deliver the mission community from such "lone ranger" churches.

In reality, few synergistic churches desire to "go it alone" in their effort to serve global outreach to their full capacity. Rather, they are looking for agency partners who will not insist on the church remaining in the traditional "limited partner" position. Rare is the mission agency leader who is genuinely excited about the local church initiating its own mission vision rather than responding to agency driven agendas. Rarer yet is the agency leader who stands eagerly in the wings ready to serve enthusiastically in a limited partner, "enabler" role on the field. A future painted with bright congregational colors and bold church-based mission strokes just doesn't suit the taste of many professional missionary leaders.

Dr. Sam Metcalf, President of Church Resource Ministries, is another example of an agency executive who is less than excited about the synergistic paradigm. He reflects a limited appreciation for this "modern art of missions," as he expresses serious reluctance to accept the church-based trend. He writes, "History shows that whenever the local church exercises control of the missionary enterprise, or seeks to become a sending agency in and of itself, the mission effort eventually is impaired."[16]

Dr. Metcalf was obviously not thinking of the historical evidence that the Moravian Church offers as a positive example of the benefits of the synergistic paradigm. From a church base that never exceeded 600 souls, the Moravians mobilized more missionaries in 50 years than the rest of Protestantism did over three centuries. One Moravian out of sixty was a tent making missionary when only one in five thousand other Protestants were serving in global outreach. This 18th century local church fellowship demonstrated that it could reach to the four corners of the earth and effectively spread the gospel to previously unreached fields. Why shouldn't 20th century churches aspire to do the same? History simply does not prove Dr. Metcalf's intended point that church-based mission is a bad idea!

Dr. Metcalf and I were mission agency colleagues for years and together hammered out the philosophy of ministry that resulted in the birth of the agency he still serves. I have great personal respect for him but, in fairness, his obvious frustration with "churches which act like agencies" offers anything but a fresh look at church-agency partnership dynamics. He openly objects to what he calls an all too common "muscularity" exercised by local churches in their relationships with agencies. The emerging trend toward increased church initiative and control of the mission agenda is, he believes, hamstringing agencies and creating an adversarial environment that militates against partnership potential. He concludes that, "cross-cultural mission is far too complicated, as well as geographically distant from the supporting church, for the (mission) committee to exercise responsibility for field strategy and supervision.... Churches are actually slowing down (agency) opportunity to respond to ripe harvests and unique opportunities for evangelism."[17] Dr. Metcalf is clear and uncompromising. He disagrees with this trend ecclesiologically, missiologically, theologically, historically and practically!

Pushing the Synergistic Envelope Further

In spite of the reluctance of many agency leaders to embrace and encourage the synergistic paradigm, I agree with the future Dr. Camp and Dr. Engle envision. I believe this model of mission partnerships will continue to gain momentum and become the driving force for missions for the 21st century. I am an enthusiastic advocate for this alternative to the supporting and sending para-digms that have consistently relegated small churches to a marginal role in missions. For too long, the missions potential of smaller churches has been altogether overlooked by agency leaders. They have pursued the supporting and sending paradigms by looking almost exclusively to larger churches for resources. In effect, they logically choose to fish in mega-church oceans rather than in small church ponds. They have done so for obvious reasons. If mission leaders are only looking for financial support and potential mission candidates to serve their agencies, it makes sense to go where more of both resources exist in greatest measure. Large churches can spare the "extra dollars and a few key bodies" far more easily than small ones can.

But if we are looking to mobilize the entire body of Christ on a massive scale, every church, regardless of size, should be urged to be involved in missions at a level that will demand the personal energy and combined resources of all its members. If we want to release the full measure of the financial and human resources latent in the body of Christ, we must recognize that the task is as effectively done in smaller congregations as in large ones. In fact the synergistic approach to missions may be especially effective for small congregations. The full membership of a small church is a more easily motivated and mobilized group than is the massive membership of a mega-church. A small church is able to stay better focused than is a larger one. Our experience demonstrates that the synergistic paradigm is tailor-made for the small local church! The Moravians demonstrated this in the 18th century and Northside, among other smaller synergistic churches, is doing so again today!

Don't Overlook Small Churches!

I am passionately concerned that institutional thinkers in the mission community will encourage each other to conclude that only mega-churches have partnership potential in this emerging mission scheme. This is already effectively occurring. As Sam Metcalf, for example, writes disparagingly of the synergistic model, he assumes that "the view that the church should, in effect, operate as a mission board is being embraced *mostly by mega-churches*, and by other churches that can afford missions pastors."[18] Chuck Bennett's quote noted above laments the trend which is allowing "*large American churches*" to become sending agencies themselves. Jim Engle praises the trend and declares it will become "more commonplace," but he sees this reality arising *"especially among larger change-oriented churches.* (emphasis added)

Gary Cowin, an S.I.M. missionary who also serves as associate editor for the Evangelical Missions Quarterly has gone so far as to suggest an alternative term for the synergistic paradigm. His term inherently reserves this approach for larger congregations. He coins the phrase "missiomega churches" and writes positively of the phenomenon. "Missiomega churches represent the largest single pool of human and financial resources available to the missions enterprise.... Smart agencies are working hard to relate effectively to them."[19]

Equating this dynamic to church size, however, Cowin joins other missiologists drawing the unfounded conclusion that a church should be large if it wants to adopt this approach to missions. He is overt on this point, "Size isn't everything! But, as most basketball coaches would be quick to add, it sure doesn't hurt and you sure can't ignore it! Something like that is true when it comes to churches active in the world missions enterprise: The big ones can do a lot of things that the small ones can't, and they have their own way of going about it."[20]

I want to argue here against Cowin's "missiomega church" label as a term to describe this trend. In my view, the body of Christ will only repeat regrettable errors from the past, relegating small churches to a marginal role in missions, if we accept the notion that "synergistic churches" must be big. Other terms have been used which don't carry this anti-small church bias. The leaders of BILD, International for example, speak of "church-based missions" as the new paradigm.[21] Bruce Camp has offered the phrase "entrepreneurial mission focused perspective" as an alternative that is too cumbersome to gain popular acceptance in the parlance of mission literature. George Miley, Director of the Antioch Network, has suggested "entrepreneurial churches" as a term to describe these mission-minded congregations. He leads perhaps the most synergistically oriented association of churches in the world, so his optional terminology no doubt has merit. Synergistic church leaders invariably manifest entrepreneurial and apostolic tendencies. Jim Engle uses "missions-focused churches" as he offers his own abbreviated description to explain Camp's synergistic paradigm. The U.S. Center for World Mission is using the term "congregation-direct missions" as yet another alternative.

Proliferation of jargon has been in vogue in mission circles as much as in any other area involving technical expertise. Technical terminology is not, however always useful in serving the interest of clear communication. I prefer Camp's "synergistic" terminology because it stands in such easily recalled contrast to the "supporting" and "sending" alternatives which are nearly self-explanatory. I also think he deserves credit for first pointing to this emerging trend. Whatever term we ultimately adopt to identify this dynamic throughout the mission community, I want to strongly urge us to avoid a label that inherently presumes small churches can't fit into the paradigm. We must discipline ourselves to "see as God sees" and to make the conscious decision to find methodologies which will "allow David to fight Goliath."

Painting By the Numbers — Becoming a Synergistic Church

Bruce Camp suggests that the three paradigms he has articulated are not progressive developmental stages in the mission history of a church. In fact, he assumes that a church could begin its mission involvement from the synergistic paradigm as well as either of the more traditional options.[22] This observation reinforces my conviction that even a small church can pursue this model for missions. This is not, however, the road by which our church arrived at this methodology. We were not nearly so clever! We arrived at this paradigm simply through "painting by the numbers."

The first seven chapters of this book detail our mission journey. I want to offer a brief recap here only to emphasize that we painted our picture one color at a time as others in the professional mission community pointed the way. Our success has come from believing that the challenges mission leaders presented our congregation were intended to be taken seriously. We accepted the responsibilities missiologists declared were ours and we acted on them. Traditional mission leaders critiqued us, coached us and counseled along the way. As these mentors helped us to do the possible, God did the impossible.

We began in a traditional sending paradigm giving 20 percent of a $5,000 monthly budget to world missions. We were guided by ACMC's "How to Write a Missions Policy Handbook" in developing the procedures by which our available support would be assigned. ACMC's conferences offered ongoing education as our church developed and, under the influence of mission professionals frequenting their conferences, we learned from ACMC how to increase our impact as we matured in our missions interest.

As described in Chapter 1, we added faith promise to increase our capacity to give — and the faith promise system worked dramatically well for us! We also sought to build relationships with reliable national leaders as we made early support commitments in an effort to maximize the impact of our limited funds. That is not to say that we were trying to find a "cut-rate" way to do missions. We simply wanted to be as cost effective as possible with our small mission budget.

You will recall that our church decided early in its history to devote the full month of March each year to our annual mission conference. We still maintain this commitment in an effort to keep our congregation on the cutting edge of developing mission theory. In such a conference, Keith Brown from OC Ministries eventually challenged us to become a sending church. Within a few months we mobilized our first missionary with Wycliffe Bible Translators.

Ongoing exposure to ACMC eventually led to my first opportunity to travel overseas on a short-term vision trip. This was a much heralded priority for a seriously missions-minded senior pastor. I had the privilege of going to Romania with Bill Waldrop who would later become the director of ACMC. Today he directs

Joshua Project 2000, a ministry of AD 2000 and its Mission America project. Bill Waldrop's influence on our progress was tangible. My trip with him led to a growing appreciation in our church for short-term team visits to Eastern Europe. Eventually it also paved the way to our prayerful adoption of the Bosnian Muslims as an unreached people group target.

Once we adopted a particular unreached people group, we appealed to our denominational leaders in the Evangelical Free Church Mission (EFCM) for help in getting started. Though our mission had AD 2000 goals which made mobilizing a team to a Muslim people group a priority, administrative and logistical limitations in our agency's headquarters' staff as well as in the field made opening a new work impossible for EFCM. We were consequently left to advance our vision on our own.

Along the way, I also continued in serious personal study of missiology. Eventually, I took all the D-min courses in church growth offered at Fuller School of World Mission. But I did not take the courses for credit because I lacked the prerequisite Master's degree. While I was growing in my own missiological understanding, ACMC conferences and our annual mission month speakers helped educate my congregation. These non-formal training contexts prepared us as a congregation to press the initiative that has since become our work in Bosnia. Most of our "partners" have come from networking opportunities discovered in the context of ACMC.

When the EFCM could not respond to our appeal to assume the leadership of our initial mobilization toward Bosnia, God sovereignly put us in touch with George Miley and Antioch Network. If ACMC was uniquely used of the Lord to educate us in missions and to introduce us to the global missions community, Antioch Network was especially critical in encouraging and developing our confidence that even a small church like ours could "do missions" on a global scale. George Miley and his associates increased our sense of commitment to team ministry, to contextualized training and to an expectation that existing agencies could be expected to enthusiastically support our vision for Bosnia without subordinating our participation in the process. Antioch Network's mentoring has been a crucial, ongoing catalyst to our progress. I strongly urge leaders from agencies and churches alike, who want to understand church-based approaches to missions to make Antioch Network's annual conference a primary priority.[23]

Under the ongoing tutelage of ACMC and Antioch Network, we eventually established incredibly beneficial partnerships that facilitated our work in Bosnia. The influence of forward thinking leaders also helped us set a goal of facilitating our national partners' vision for the region rather than insisting on our own strategies. Again, earlier chapters of this book offer details about a variety of partnerships we have enjoyed with the Evangelical Theological Seminary, the Jesus Film Project, World Relief, the Evangelical Free Church Mission Compassion Ministry, ACMC and Antioch Network among others. These agencies facilitated our vision and helped us discern what to do each step along the way. They willingly became "enablers" for our work before this special role had been articulated for them by Engle. They taught us to paint by the numbers.

Trained to Be Trusted in Missions

My point in offering this summary is to demonstrate that my church was gradually educated into the synergistic paradigm over an extended period of time. With constant exposure to missions professionals our preparation ultimately required more than a decade. As a congregation, we enthusiastically submitted to a long-term, non-formal training process conducted largely by mission agency leaders. As we committed ourselves to be learners, we believed we were being "trained to be trusted" as qualified partners in global evangelism. We eagerly accepted every challenge, dutifully tried to implement every insight new to us and aggressively committed ourselves to apply the unreached peoples prioritization urged upon us by virtually every credible missiologist we encountered.

We have, in effect, now arrived at precisely the destination we were directed toward by the best mission thinkers we could find. In the process, we came to illustrate the synergistic paradigm of partnership though it had not been articulated until we had already adopted a "church-based" missions strategy. We never intended to present a challenge to traditional mission agency leaders. After all, what they told us to do worked brilliantly for us. Our success, however, seems to have surprised our mentors in the professional missions community. Having "painted by their numbers" we are confused that these very leaders now find the resulting picture such an anomaly. We are even more confused that we, as church-based mission leaders, are so little trusted by our fellow laborers in the world missions community. Shouldn't the confidence of those who have coached us in credible service be the logical outcome of their efforts? Having been trained, we believe we should be trusted.

Ours is not an independent, arrogant church. We have been blessed into a posture of genuine humility as we look back on all that God has done in, around and through us. We don't resent or reject partnerships with mission agencies. Agency partnerships of all kinds have made critical contributions to our progress in Bosnia. Even today we need all the help we can recruit to our field. We are still actively searching for partners in Bosnia — partners who believe churches can work as equal peers alongside mission professionals.

Most of our partnership arrangements have been informal and temporary, meeting particular needs for a limited span of time. Some have been more enduring. One partnership is unique in our experience. Among our greatest delights has been the culmination of a formal written partnership agreement with the EFCM. In the spirit of partnership reform this chapter is encouraging, our denominational mission has truly come alongside us to enhance our vision without presuming to take over our work. We welcome their experience, their expertise and their critique as we go forward together. They are now serving in exactly the enabling role Engle recommends and we are impacting Bosnia more effectively because of their help.

Our Partnership With the EFCM

Forming the partnership with the EFCM was difficult for us both. Neither the denominational leadership nor our church had ever committed to so fluid an arrangement. We each had to grow in our mutual confidence in the other's integrity, capacity and long-term commitment to our joint effort. Like all our other more informal partnerships, we eventually arrived at an arrangement that produced a relationally oriented agreement rather than one based on strict terms specifying lines of authority and carefully delineated rights to resources. The document governing our partnership (reproduced in Appendix III) contains a number of unique features that demonstrate our mutual trust, our joint commitment to mutual success and a healthy appreciation for our respective sense of vision. The chart on page 292 attempts to capture the somewhat flexible structure of the agreement.

As shown in that diagram, our church has a formal partnership with the Evangelical Church in Bosnia-Hercegovina, the Pentecostal denomination in Bosnia. The EFCM does not have that direct partnership linkage with the Evangelical Church but enjoys a strategic relationship through our church's formal agreement. Instead, our denomination has a formal partnership solely with our local church and with other EFCA churches which may join us on this field at a later date. Our country leader, David Lively, leads our staff under the banner of Ministry Resource Network, the 501(c)(3) corporation we formed to facilitate fund raising for the long-term missionaries we mobilize. You may notice that the chart places David Lively under the EFCM's European Director, Rick Burke. In our agreement, David is officially under Rick in a chain of counsel rather than a strict chain of command. This distinction is important since David is not officially a part of EFCM's staff.

BOSNIA PROJECT ORGANIZATIONAL CHART
Northside Community Church Relationships

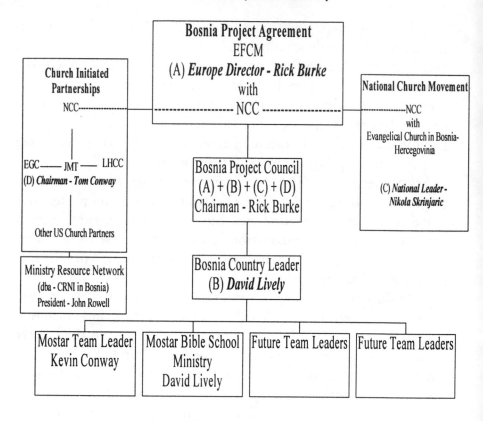

EFCM = Evangelical Free Church Mission   EGC = East Gate Congregation   MRN = Ministry Resource Network
NCC = Northside Community Church   LHCC = Living Hope Community Church   dba in Bosnia, CRNI = Church Resource Network, Int
JMT = Joint Missions Team

EFCM teams mobilized to Bosnia will in a similar way serve under David's leadership until, or unless, the Lord raises up a logical EFCM replacement to fill the country leader's role for the partnership. Conceivably, David could eventually have responsibility for overseeing numerous EFCM team members with whom he has no "official" staff relationship. It is also possible that a future EFCM leader could later oversee our teams. We all are trusting God to direct our mutual acceptance of appropriate leaders as they emerge on the field.

Other U.S. churches in the EFCA are free to follow our lead in sending church-based teams "synergistically" to Bosnia. Such churches would become a part of our "Church-Initiated Partnership" Network. EFCA churches may alternatively mobilize their mission candidates under EFCM in the more traditional "sending paradigm." All future team members mobilized to Bosnia from our church will submit to EFCM's training process, though like David Lively, they will not be officially a part of the EFCM staff. David has already gone through our denomination's country leader training. All our church-based staff serving long-term in Bosnia are participating in EFCM regional meetings in Europe. Rick Burke has also attended our staff retreats and training events in Bosnia.

As you can see, our partnership is highly flexible, highly fluid and based on a significant degree of mutual trust. Either partner can initiate activity on the field as we coordinate efforts and keep communication open with each other. Ultimate control, final authority and ownership of the vision are not issues that trouble us as synergistic partners. Consequently, none of these issues is specifically addressed in our written agreement. We are each less concerned with control than with a maximum commitment to do all we can to ensure mutual success on this field. As God blesses our combined efforts, our partnership hopes to stimulate a church planting movement of local churches that will identify with the Evangelical Church of Bosnia-Hercegovina, Northside's Pentecostal national partners. Though the EFCA is clearly not itself a Pentecostal denomination, we have agreed to allow Kingdom issues to outweigh the doctrinal distinctives which would traditionally have kept us and the EFCM from cooperating with the Evangelical Church leaders in Bosnia. We are, in this respect, deferring to the wisdom of indigenous leaders who believe that introducing another "brand" of evangelical faith would only serve to more deeply divide an already deeply divided nation.

Conclusion

We think this agreement is illustrative of the kinds of creative "enabling" partnerships that will be needed to accommodate the respective missions interests of nationals, and local church leaders in the West, and mission agency professionals alike. I am excited to see the EFCM take the lead in risking the release of latent mission potential through this kind of synergistic partnership. Dr. Ben Sawatsky, the EFCM International Director, deserves special affirmation for his bold and creative contribution to this unusual agreement. I hope other denominational agencies will learn from his innovative example.

I am also pleased that the EFCM has permitted our church to open a new field for the entire denomination. Dr. Sawatsky's trust in us and his cooperative spirit have made me more enthusiastic for other, unrelated EFCM initiatives. Though I am a synergistic mission leader focused in Bosnia, I am genuinely excited about supporting my denomination's larger mission effort which reaches around the world.

I believe that I am a better pastor and a better mission leader because of the accountability and support my denomination is providing through our partnership. At the same time, the denomination's goals are being more effectively achieved as we are released both to multiply churches in the United States and to do missions synergistically in Bosnia. We have been made to feel that all our efforts fit neatly into the national and international goals of our denomination. But beyond the benefits that inure to us, our national partners in Bosnia are able to advance their own denominational mission interests with the help that the EFCM and our church are offering together. Our partnership's assistance is being provided to Bosnian churches with "no strings attached." Refusing typical institutional conditions to cooperation, we have been delighted to find that we are consequently becoming more relationally credible to national leaders. Indigenous pastors recognize that our partnership with the EFCM is genuinely serving the agenda they have set and not our own.

Our experience has proven that small churches can release inordinate resources for the cause of world missions by pursuing the synergistic paradigm. Our joint efforts with our denominational mission and other traditional agencies has proven that the synergistic approach can be a partnership paradigm that includes healthy agency involvement in a manner that is potentially more powerful than either the supporting or sending methodologies. Our national partners are demonstrating that Third World leaders can effectively point the way if we Westerners are willing to come alongside to facilitate, to follow, and to serve in a spirit of genuine mutual submission. Our partnership is producing results with obvious benefits of synergy, support, security and strength which could never have been generated if we had labored in Bosnia on our own.

I hope that by working well together, our congregation and its synergistic partners are offering a credible example that other churches and agencies will want to emulate. And I pray that our experience will prove to skeptics that churches don't have to be bound by traditional approaches to missions partnership. I believe that agency leaders can adjust to the demands of changing times to play an ongoing vital role in fulfilling the Great Commission. The face of mission partnerships may well be changing but the fact that working together has incredible value is not. The simple truth is that local churches in the West, mission professionals and national leaders really do need each other as they seek to serve the cause of world evangelism. Our experience has convinced us that genuinely just partnerships can pave the way to greater effectiveness. I hope that we are also proving that local churches pursuing the synergistic paradigm are not anti-agency or opposed to partnerships. They are simply passionate about promoting the maximum release of local church potential for the cause of world missions. We believe that partnerships which can embrace the emerging synergistic paradigm are especially strategic.[24] Drawing on our experience in Bosnia, we are more convinced than ever that indeed, two are better than one!

14

I Will Build My Church

"I will build my church and the gates of Hades shall not overpower it."

Matt. 16:18

Our experience sharing the gospel in the midst of the brutal war in Bosnia has given us a glimpse of God's faithfulness to Jesus' unqualified promise to build His church — even in the face of the most horrific opposition hell can muster. We have been amazed to find the conflict opening rather than closing doors for evangelism. We have seen ethnic hatred create a hunger for healing that has softened hearts rather than hardening them. The enmity of men really can be overcome when people encounter God's love in a personal way. Our faith has been built as we have come to expect the Spirit of grace to overpower a grudging desire for revenge — a natural response from those suffering the atrocities of genocide.

Observing firsthand God's obvious presence even in the most perilous times and the most pitiful circumstances, it has been our privilege to incarnate the gospel of Christ in refugee camps, in bombed-out buildings, and in cities void of the most basic services necessary for living. We have been blessed to offer the light of God's word and the living water of God's Spirit where water and power were not available. We have huddled with hurting people under the hardships that come with sustained shelling and indiscriminant sniper attacks. Never did we sense we were in the wrong place at the wrong time. It seems to us, even with 20-20 hindsight, that we like Esther of old, were raised up by God for just such a time as this.

On reflection, we have come to recognize four guiding principles that may help direct other small churches as they dare to choose their own road to synergistic involvement among the unreached peoples of the earth. We developed a deep conviction regarding the priority of these principles as we went about our work in Bosnia — not as a prelude to our service there. As I have said before, we were not clever enough to see our path so clearly before we got involved in this effort. We have simply learned by doing while we painted by the numbers. I want to close this book by sharing these final insights gleaned over our years of mission ministry. My hope is that other church leaders can benefit from them before they begin a similar journey of their own.

The Principle of Primary Responsibility: Acts 1:8

Much of what I have already written here explains how Northside Community Church embarked on the road to Sarajevo attempting to play a small part in reaching the unreached Muslims of Bosnia. We did not intentionally set out to do this work on our own initiative following the synergistic paradigm. As we were sovereignly led into this methodology however, we have become increasingly committed to the principle that **mission ministry is the primary responsibility of the local church and only secondarily the purview of professionals serving in mission agencies**. The nature of "para-church" ministries should dictate that agencies come alongside the local church, not supplant it.

The assignment of primary responsibility for global evangelism is not left unclear by scripture. In Acts 1:8, for example, Jesus repeats the mandate of the great commission by reminding the apostles leading the Jerusalem church, "You shall receive power when the Holy Spirit has come upon you; and you shall be my witnesses both in Jerusalem, and in all Judea and Samaria, and even to the remotest part of the earth." This reiteration of God's call to take the gospel to all nations and to advance the church throughout the world, was issued to a handful of leaders presiding over a local assembly of only 120 people. Jesus' audience on this occasion was not comprised of hale and hardy workers, eager for the challenge of global outreach. These 11 men were ordinary, uneducated people who were in no way confident of their competence for the task. They were frightened by the events of the immediate past, uncertain about the security of their present circumstances and timid about taking the future by storm. Their response to Jesus' words was not to hurl themselves headlong at a hostile world. Instead, they hid themselves in a secret upper room. Even after the Spirit's power came at Pentecost, they ministered only in Jerusalem — apparently apprehensive about mobilizing to take the gospel to the four corners of the earth.

Their reluctance is understandable. What local church, especially a small one, would be bold enough to presume that a worldwide scope of ministry lay within its reach? Like these early leaders, even in the 20th century, most of us who lead small churches feel ill-equipped, unprepared, under-resourced and overmatched when we are urged to consider taking a full share of responsibility for the remaining task in world mission. Contemporary small church leaders are able to easily identify with the reticence of these first apostles and their followers.

But we should also be urged to identify with the eventual success enjoyed by that first small church in Jerusalem. In spite of their meager numbers and the enormity of the task to be done, God's Spirit empowered them to serve His purposes and Jesus proved faithful to His promise to build His church through them. I firmly believe the Lord Jesus wants to do the same through us today whether we are part of a large church or a small one. Churches everywhere have the potential to be effective just as the Jerusalem and Antioch assemblies were in fulfilling the great commission.

Local church potential will never be realized however, unless ordinary people like you and me begin to believe that major mission ministry is, and always has been, the primary responsibility of our congregations. Obviously, there is a role for specialized mission teams to play in completing the task of world evangelization. But the church is still primarily responsible to get the job done.

This "principle of primary responsibility" flies in the face of traditional missiological thinking, which has been conditioned by a separation of duties between modality and sodality structures. In modern mission jargon, modalities are broad-based church structures open to everyone regardless of age, sex, training or level of maturity. Modalities are typically associated with local assemblies that care for anyone willing to attend and whose doors are open indiscriminately to all comers. These structures are maintenance-oriented by necessity.

Sodalities on the other hand are second commitment structures. They are formed for special purposes, usually to perform a particular task. Because of their special focus, they normally restrict participation to individuals who, because of special qualifications, are uniquely useful in serving the task at hand. Participation in a sodality structure is dependent upon meeting special criteria that can include minimum or maximum age limits, gender requirements, specified training and prior related experience. In most cases, service in these task-oriented organizations is made possible only by invitation. That is to say, one must be recruited to a sodality rather than simply choosing to join its ranks. Most mission agencies fit the profile of sodality structures.

Mission agencies are usually formed for the express purpose of extending specialized Christian ministry beyond the local area or to provide specific services (like Bible translation or humanitarian relief) to others in the name of Christ. Only with a "second commitment" to standards, which often reach far beyond normal church membership requirements, can service in a mission sodality be achieved. Distinguishing between the maintenance roles of modalities and the specialized functions of sodalities helps us understand how the church has advanced through the ages.

The unique sodality (mission team) and modality (local church) function which missiologists have dated from the 1st century forward also offer helpful insights into the kinds of ministry leadership and strategy necessary to move the influence of the gospel from culture to culture in our own times. We must acknowledge and respect the different dynamics involved in winning new converts to faith and in preserving the fruit of our evangelistic efforts until Christ comes again. Sodalities have traditionally been affirmed as the most effective structures for performing evangelistic and service-oriented functions of the church while modalities are acknowledged to be best suited to maintain the fruit of outreach and service ministries.

But in accepting the validity of modality and sodality concepts it need not follow that modalities should characteristically lack concern for specialized mission or evangelistic tasks. I believe we are dead wrong to conclude that mission agencies have an exclusive or preemptive claim on cross-cultural ministry efforts just because they specialize in these areas. In fact, that notion has in my opinion, been nearly fatal to the mission interests of countless churches, especially smaller ones.

The scriptures repeatedly portray local churches taking the lead in promoting the extension of the body of Christ from one culture to another. Acts 8:4-25 shares in brief the experience of the Jerusalem church in sending Philip, and subsequently Peter and John, to Samaria when the gospel was first extended beyond its initial seedbed in Judea. Essentially, members of the first church ever to exist almost accidentally bridged to this neighboring culture, making disciples without having been clearly directed to do so. In response to this "unauthorized mission effort," the Jerusalem congregation dispatched established apostolic and elder leaders to manage the conversion fruit being produced by the Spirit of God.

The same pattern is repeated in Acts 11:19-30 when believers from Jerusalem shared the hope of salvation with other Jews in

Phoenicia and Cyprus and Antioch. Men who were natives of Cypress and Cyrene also preached the Lord Jesus to Greeks in Antioch, apparently doing so more spontaneously than strategically. As a consequence of their cross-cultural witness the church spread from its Hebrew origins to take root in the Hellenistic community. The leaders in Jerusalem, taking responsibility again for this additional unintentional fruit from a spontaneous mission effort, dispatched Barnabus to oversee the impromptu "sodality" effort, which had inadvertently founded the church in Antioch. Thus the Jerusalem church gave accidental birth to its first daughter congregations. Barnabus so enjoyed his "midwife" role in Antioch, he soon recruited Saul from Tarsus to join in the fun.

The Antioch example makes church planting look a lot easier than we expect it to be today. Perhaps we are making the task of reproducing churches harder than it should be — even when we are planting new churches cross-culturally. Antioch surely seemed to follow the pattern of the Jerusalem church with relative ease. Once it was established in Syria, the Antioch church also extended the influence of the gospel to other nations. In this case, however, the mission effort was to be an intentional initiative for the local body of believers. The best of Antioch's leaders were put in charge of the effort after being specially selected by the Holy Spirit for the task.

Acts 13:1-5 describes this first strategic mission mobilization effort. As the Antioch church matured, its leadership core included a multi-ethnic mix of gifted men including prophets and teachers. While they were ministering to the Lord, the Holy Spirit handpicked Barnabus and Saul to purposefully carry this local church's ministry to the world. This was the first deliberate attempt a local church modality ever made to form a specialized sodality team for the express purpose of taking the gospel to the uttermost parts of the earth. Paul and Barnabus would eventually recruit many other "ordinary people" to expand their mission agenda throughout the known world. I believe God wants us to develop similarly gifted leaders in our churches today! And as churches, I believe we have the capacity to raise up and release modern mission teams like the ones Barnabus and Paul led. Such is the responsibility of the local church if we take the command of Acts 1:8 and the model of the Jerusalem and Antioch churches seriously.

In each of these instances, the local church proved its capacity to respond to the challenge of extending itself in mission The formation of mission teams was a strategic development undertaken to better facilitate the advance of the gospel beyond the immediate community. That pattern was then followed in "leap frog" fashion as churches in Philippi, Ephesus, Thessalonica and other cities contributed people and financial resources to keep the mission advance of the church going.

Such was the foundation for the Roman Catholic model of mission. In the Catholic approach, the local church diocese was charged with caring for members of each Catholic parish at a local level. Reaching beyond the confines of the local community, Roman clerics developed the monastic tradition, which provided a sodality structure capable of extending the influence of Catholicism to previously unchurched regions. Monastic teams of Franciscans, Jesuits and monks from other pioneering orders explored new worlds, won native peoples to faith and planted new modality structures in far away lands. These new modalities then produced their own sodality workers, adding monks from newly converted cultures, to extend the church still further. In this way, the Catholic church eventually touched much of the world reaching from Europe into North and South America, the Pacific Islands, Asia and the four corners of the earth.

Throughout the history of mission, this same "leap frog" dynamic has been of major importance. In the modern era, however, it is interrupted at two critical points, which highlight failures on the part of sodalities and modalities alike. The post-World War II proliferation of mission agencies operating independently of churches has greatly increased the scope of Christian ministry around the world. Yet, this enhanced "mission productivity" is like the magnified crop yields stemming from hybrid plants which have been genetically engineered by agricultural scientists. On the farm, hybrid seeds now routinely produce more hardy plants that bear up better under adverse climates, resist pests more effectively and require less fertilizer than ever before. Hybrid plants also often produce higher quality fruit in larger quantities than do plants germinated from natural seed. But there is a significant drawback. Many hybrid plants don't reproduce at all. They simply lack the capacity to generate seeds with fruitful potential for the next generation.

In modern missions, we see a similar scene. Productivity is up dramatically but reproductivity is down and an unfortunate kind of sterility has become commonplace. Many agencies acting exclusively in specialized sodality roles are fruitful in their own right (providing humanitarian aid, building schools, caring for orphans, encouraging agricultural development, etc.). But many no longer even attempt to produce local church modalities in the process. Correspondingly, most local church modalities have ceased producing the very sodalities needed to extend their impact beyond their immediate context. The complementary role that sodalities and modalities have historically played in extending the church globally has broken down. The sodality/modality frog just doesn't leap any more!

Even when Ralph Winter first introduced the sodality/modality concept in 1974, he saw this problem and spoke to it specifically. He wrote then, "Without being critical of the vast plethora of mission 'service agencies,' I believe to be highly significant two closely related emphases of the church growth movement. First of all there needs to be deliberate, intentional effort to establish (church) fellowships of believers no matter what else is being done in a given situation.... Thus, even if an agency specializes in medical work, or orphan work, or radio work or whatever, it must be aware of, and concerned about, the interface between that activity and the church-planting function.... But, secondly, in addition to this older, well known concern for the establishment of churches, there have appeared in church growth circles a number of ... articles which indicate very clearly the need for the intentional and deliberate implantation of mission sodalities."[1] Both sodality and modality structures are necessary and both can be generated by a local church, if its leaders are focused on that objective. On the local church side of the equation, we must see the formation of mission sodalities as a legitimate and logical local church responsibility.

At NCC, we have been influenced by Dr. Winter's perspective and we have accepted this sodality-generating role. Our Atlanta-based modality has, for this reason, created its own sodality structure which partners with other para-church and denominational agencies to facilitate more effective and efficient funding and management of our mission effort in Bosnia. We have done this because we hold two strong convictions in tension. The first maintains that the local church has the primary responsibility for pursuing global missions. The second compels us to see a vital role for sodality structures in accomplishing our vision. We have therefore, concluded that we need not forfeit our local church's primary role in missions to make room for sodality structures on the field. We are creating sodalities in order to increase our capacity to extend our ministry beyond our local area. In our view, too many churches have failed to capitalize on such opportunities and have consequently lost all their impetus for serious mission ministry.

The Principle of Providential Provocation

As noted above, the Jerusalem church did not immediately move toward the mission fields of Judea, Samaria and the uttermost parts of the earth just because Jesus conveyed that responsibility in Acts 1:8. Instead the apostles, and those who followed them, timidly remained in the familiar confines of Mt. Zion until persecution literally pushed them out of their city. In Acts 8:1, following the martyrdom of Stephen, we are told that all the members of the Jerusalem church (except for the apostles) were scattered throughout Judea and Samaria. Saul, and probably other Jewish zealots who opposed the early church, used intimidation, incarceration and brute force in an attempt to extinguish the light of the gospel before it could penetrate the world's darkness.

In effect, God used government and religious persecution to get the Jerusalem church involved actively in the mission mandate. **We have come to believe that such instances of "providential provocation" should be viewed as divine direction toward doors which have been sovereignly opened for ministry effort. This principle points the way toward people and places where potential for fruitful ministry is enhanced by God.**

Returning to Acts, for example, we can observe that the Lord sovereignly imposed harsh circumstances in order to interrupt the status quo. He forced His people to flee for their lives and made Jerusalem's early believers into beleaguered refugees and reluctant missionaries at the same time. Driven from home by persecution, Philip became the first to preach the gospel in Samaria. Guided by the Spirit, he also shared Christ with the Ethiopian eunuch who took his newfound faith to the court of Candace, introducing Christianity to North Africa in the process. Some members of the Jerusalem church were apparently evangelizing in Syria as well. They did so with sufficient success that their momentum became known back in Judea. Saul of Tarsus sought permission from Jewish authorities to move toward Damascus in an effort to continue his aggression against the emerging church. On the way there, Saul himself encountered Jesus and began his own journey toward a career in missions.

The apostles were not idle during this period of persecution. Peter, for example, was supernaturally directed to Caesaria to introduce the gospel of Jesus to Cornelius and his household. Others from Jerusalem carried the good news of salvation in Christ throughout the coastlands of the Mediterranean Sea and to Antioch. Thus, it was not brilliant mission strategy formulated by bold church leaders that prompted the initial steps in 1st century global evangelism. Rather, it was God's providential provocation that pushed the church through divinely opened doors. It was only under duress that Christian refugees became ambassadors to lost people in these other cultures.

Providential provocation would once again open doors for mission ministry in Acts 16 when Paul and Barnabus answered the Macedonian call. On that occasion, when Paul and Silas were beaten and bound in stocks in Philippi, the hand of God shook the earth hard enough to open the jailhouse doors and the jailer's heart. The Savior thus moved with sovereign control to provoke the salvation of the jailer's entire household. Providential provocation was, therefore, the key to Paul's ultimate success as an intentional missionary to Macedonia.

In the 20th century we have seen similar providential provocations pointing our way to opportunities for ministry in Bosnia. Reversing the Acts 8:1 motif in our case, God made refugees of the mission target rather than the mission force. In the refugee context, the way was opened for our missionaries to reach Bosnian Muslims effectively. The special evil of ethnic cleansing literally moved millions of Bosnia's Muslims from their homes to accessible locations in relative safety where Christians could share the love of Jesus with them.

Bereft of family and friends, facing an uncertain future, suffering the sudden loss of property, possessions and any hint of personal security, we found incredible openness among these displaced masses. Many responded eagerly accepting the gospel as they grappled with the inadequacies of their nominal faith in Islam. By meeting real needs in critical circumstances and by caring enough to share the sparse and temporary shelter of the refugee camps, we offered a personal, incarnational message of God's love. As we shared in the reservoir of despair that wartime refugee centers represented, the Spirit opened floodgates that released rivers of living water. Thus personal faith was produced from the providential provocation which forced the dislocation of multitudes.

Circumstances which the natural eye could only see as disastrous proved to be the divine intervention God intended to advance His church. We have come to believe that our eyes of faith should be able to discern this kind of providential provocation in a variety of circumstances that can make unbelievers uncharacteristically open to the truths of the scripture. Political upheaval, military conflicts, economic reversals, relational stress, famine, and natural disasters are some of the events that magnify human suffering and heartache around the world. Such hardships often work to open the hearts of those who most need the love of God and who have been historically most closed to the message of salvation available in Jesus' name.

Let me be clear as we talk about the impact of providential provocation. I am not recommending an opportunistic strategy that would make missionaries into professional proselytizers capitalizing on other people's pain. Rather, I am urging mission-minded church and agency leaders to be spiritually discerning about the circumstances God is using to create a special openness to His Spirit's offer of healing, hope and eternal life. In the hardest of circumstances, Christians should commit themselves for the long haul, incarnating the gospel and introducing unreached masses to the power and purity of the Master's message of saving grace.

Where needs are most urgent, Christians should be most eager to offer aid in Jesus' name. Where hatred is most intense, Christian love should be most intentional and sustained. Where the lies of the demonic hosts have people bound in darkness, we should be living as children of the light, showing firsthand the way to spiritual freedom rooted in truth. Where we find men and women suffering under heavy loads, weighed down by years of oppression or wayward living, Christians should boldly intervene to help shoulder the burden. Our commitment to such long-term incarnational service for Christ is not opportunism. It is the means by which we can help hurting people overcome their alienation from the only One who can truly relieve their distress and redeem their situation.

In the face of providential provocation, Christian missionaries are not short-term intruders but long-term investors. Our presence and God's power should improve the lot of broken people's lives wherever we go. In needy circumstances, our help should come with no strings attached. As we share our lives, our strength, our resources, our love, and our capacities, we will naturally have opportunities also to share God's love and His truth. With His blessing the church will be built as it demonstrates the ability of God's kingdom power to overcome evil with good. At the same time, the cities we dwell in will be better places to live and even those who reject our gospel will accept our good intentions to serve them. Taking note of God's providential provocation has kept our effort in Bosnia pointed in the right direction. Perhaps this principle can serve as a spiritual compass to direct others toward effective mission ministry too.

The Principle of Preeminent Grace

I had never viewed Romans 5:20 as a verse with missiological implications until we began our work in the midst of Bosnia's war. But involvement in the context of this conflict soon changed my mind. From the very beginning, we encountered military force, ethnic cleansing, mass rapes, concentration camps, torture, genocide, war crimes, ethnic hatred and religious animosity. All these horrors came our way before we even began to imagine how we might move our people into this war-torn mission field. The overwhelming evil amassed in this bedeviled place made the obstacles in our path unimaginably difficult. Even the secular media discerned the uniquely desperate context Bosnia had become. One ABC television news special dubbed Bosnia, "The Land of Demons."

But demons should never deter the determination of our missions priorities! We entered Bosnia in the name of Jesus, the Lord of Hosts. We went forward with His authority and His power. We were serving the purposes of the One who purposes to offer deliverance from every stronghold hell can devise. I am embarrassed to admit how feeble my faith was as we took our first steps on the road to Sarajevo. We advanced only with timid caution always feeling concerned that the Spirit of God was speeding the pace of our journey beyond our comfort zone. By His might, however, every crooked way was made straight and every obstructing mountain and hill were made low. By His grace we made steady progress.

We have now sent hundreds of workers into this region. Every one has been thrilled with their experience and we have never had anyone seriously exposed to harm's way. Our yoke in Bosnia has felt easy and our load has seemed light, even as we have been stretched continually to meet needs for people and resources that have always exceeded our capacity to supply. The simple truth is that we have experienced an overwhelming outpouring of grace from God at every turn in our road to Sarajevo. In retrospect, the results of our efforts far exceed any sense of cost to us.

Reflecting often on the unmerited favor God has demonstrated on our behalf, we have come to recognize that Romans 5:20 has definite missiological implications. The verse says simply, "Where sin increased, grace abounded all the more." This English rendering of the Greek words Paul chose to use here doesn't do full justice to the contrast the apostle is trying to communicate. Paul uses two different words for increase in this phrase. Where sin "increases" (pleonazo), grace is caused by God to abound — or to increase all the more (huperperisseuo). More literally, the text might read, "where sin increases incrementally, grace is lavished." Grace multiplies geometrically wherever sin is added to the environment. Kenneth S. Wuest catches this nuance as he offers an alternative rendering of this phrase in his helpful work, *Word's Studies from the Greek New Testament*. He translates this part of the verse, "where sin increased, grace super-abounded, *and then some on top of that.*"[2] (emphasis added)

Think for a moment about the point Paul is making here. This verse promises that, wherever demented men or the demons of hell sow evil on the earth, and in whatever measure, we can expect God to produce a far greater supply of grace. That is to say, the harvest of wheat sown from heaven will always outstrip the yield of tares sown from hell — if the church will simply till Satan's ground in the power of the Spirit. **This principle from Romans 5:20 teaches us that wherever sin is poured out, grace can be released in preemi-**

nent proportions. But God's guarantee of preeminent grace is often contingent upon the mediating presence of His people. Sin can't win in situations where Christians sustain their witness for the kingdom of God. If we are willing to take our message of saving faith in Jesus to the hellholes of the earth, grace will overcome evil every time That's the missiological promise inherent in Romans 5:20. It is the persistent hope of those who believe in God's ability to provide preeminent grace.

Our experience in Bosnia has proven this principle and verified this promise over a period of years. This nation has been riddled by war, filled to overflowing with fierce ethnic and religious animosity and made the focus of global attention to the point that Bosnia has become a byword for brutality at the end of this century. Post-Persian Gulf prophecies predicting a "New World Order" free from bullies and brutes were dashed in this desperate place. International hopes for lasting peace were strangled out by the suffocating grip of intentional hatreds harbored in this region. Former Yugoslavia did not disappear in a civil war. It was destroyed by deliberate design born in the hearts of evil man.

As Peter Kuzmic has observed, the Yugoslavia we once knew disintegrated when Slovenia, Croatia and finally Bosnia fell pray to Serbian aggression expressed in the interest of blatant territorial aggression. The evils of this war were promoted intentionally by political leaders with sick ambitions to enlarge their personal span of control without regard to the costs in terms of human suffering.[3] Sin has thus been intentionally encouraged to abound here. It is time now for grace to "much more abound" through the agency of both natural and supernatural means. By God's design it is time for true Christians to incarnate Jesus' ministry and for our Father in heaven to release His power, offering peace and provision and healing in Jesus' name. Such healing can only come, however, with an outpouring of grace born of an equally intentional long-term labor of love by God's people. The need of the hour is an expression of supernatural love and commitment offered by people of God who choose to live on the sites of the greatest savagery perpetrated in Bosnia.

It is in this spirit that we have sustained our work on the road to Sarajevo. In spite of the daunting threats of the Serbian war machine and the reality of genuine danger, we have waded cautiously into the sea of troubles in Bosnia. To our surprise, God has parted the waters and kept us safe and secure throughout the war. By His grace many Bosnians have come to faith in Jesus while living as refugees in Croatia and Slovenia. Others have met the Lord as they immigrated to the safety of Western European nations, the United States, Canada and Australia. We have seen God's cup of blessing keep pouring out grace in this land otherwise littered with land mines and laden with an overwhelming weight of grief, and grievance and gratuitous violence.

We believe our presence has been a part of God's plan to have His grace super-saturate the blood-soaked soil of Bosnia. Only the blood of Jesus can wash the stain of wartime sins away. We have the promise that the blood of Jesus will speak better than the blood of the sons of Adam (Heb. 12:24). As we offer our witness to the power of the Savior's blood to re-establish a peace that passes understanding, we can go on being a part of God's means for fulfilling the promise of Romans 5:20. God wants to release grace in far greater measure than the volume of sin that has victimized Bosnia. He wants His grace to be preeminent.

If we want to be effective in missions today, if we prefer to do mission service where the Spirit of God is most anxious to break down barriers to faith in Jesus Christ, we should remember the principle of preeminent grace. It teaches us that we should be looking not for easy assignments but for opportunities in the places where evil is being visited upon the helpless with unprecedented viciousness. Where satanic forces and sinister men are most malevolent, the grace of God's Spirit promises to be the most magnificent. It is in the heart of darkness that God's light will shine the brightest. The demonstration of God's ability to overcome evil with good is one of the special fruits of His special favor. The principle of preeminent grace should give missionaries boldness to choose the most difficult places to serve. It is in the haunts of hell that heaven will most clearly prove its power. In such places, the grace of God will grant us victory — if we will abide persistently, suffer patiently and stubbornly refuse to lose heart.

The Principle of Prophetic Investment

While we labored in Bosnia with the confident expectation of spiritual victory, military victory on a natural plane came to no one. Serbs, Croats and Muslims merely exchanged blows like punch-drunk boxers until none of the combatants had energy enough left to gain a real edge. Thus, in 1995, a tentative and uncomfortable peace was restored to the region under the Dayton Accords engineered by U.S. Assistant Secretary of State, Richard Holbrook. The agreement was facilitated by force as NATO bombing raids on Serb-held targets proved to be the only motivation that could lead Milosovic and his Serbian colleagues to end hostilities.

The final agreement was itself enforced militarily by the rapid introduction of tens of thousands of NATO ground troops. This well-intentioned "implementation force" replaced ineffective "U.N. peacekeepers" with more pragmatic "IFOR peacemakers." Thus, the NATO presence provided the serious military muscle that had always been needed to press all parties in Bosnia's war to work for a lasting peace. But peace produced at gunpoint holds the same dubious hope that stems from shotgun weddings. There is an immediate expectation of fruit to be gained from the marriage, but the long-term potential for unity is tentative at best.

We were nonetheless grateful for this visible witness to the West's often declared, but consistently delayed, resolve to intervene forcefully to stop the bloodshed in Bosnia. In our view, hundreds of thousands of lives could have been saved had the same moves been made by NATO years earlier. We had been shamed by the obvious vacuum of leadership and the absence of moral resolve that persisted in Washington D.C. for the early years of the Bosnian conflict. Now we were grateful that the United States had finally taken its rightful role in putting leashes and muzzles on the wolves of war.

Even though IFOR troops seemed suddenly omnipresent in Bosnia by early 1996, lasting peace was not yet assured and Sarajevo was not yet safe. It was in that uncertain moment that a new ministry opportunity was presented for our consideration. We had been in touch with the Evangelical Church leaders in Sarajevo for over a year by this time. This small but stalwart assembly of a handful of believers had survived the war together and had managed to continue meeting for Bible study and encouragement all through the years of siege. Under the threat of constant shelling, they had taken refuge in the shadow of the cross and had even led others to faith while fighting raged on day after day.

Now that the war was over, this growing assembly needed a place to meet. More importantly, it needed a visible location to be identified with the church and its Agape Humanitarian Aid ministry. We were asked at that time to raise $125,000 to purchase property for the Sarajevo Evangelical Church. They had chosen a building in the center of the city. Before the smoke had completely cleared from recent shelling, this church's vision had come sharply into focus. I remember visiting Sarajevo in January 1996 to inspect this proposed church site.

The three-story building filled only one quarter of the plot of land it occupied. The structure was one of very few in Sarajevo showing no damage from the years of bombardment that had scarred so much of the city. Sheltered by surrounding high-rise blocks of flats, the small community of believers believed this was the perfect place for them to establish a tangible presence for their tenacious congregation.

I wondered about the wisdom of making a real estate commitment in the most beleaguered city in the world. As we wound our way to and from the proposed church property, the roads were still lined with empty cargo containers, burned-out buses and disabled tramcars stacked like cordwood three and four high. These makeshift walls lined streets throughout the city making use of the useless wreckage of war to provide important protection from indiscriminate enemy fire. The building was just a block away from sniper's alley. It was hard to believe that this was really a reasonable proposal to consider. Soon I was to see that God's ideas don't have to be reasonable in order to be wise and right.

As I thought and prayed about the request being made of us, I was led to review an unusual passage in Jeremiah 32. The story this text recounts occurred in the final days before the fall of Jerusalem and the beginning of the Babylonian captivity. Jeremiah had long since been prophesying the imminent overthrow of the Holy City and the coming deportation to Chaldea. The prophet's faithfulness to his message of doom and gloom had evoked the personal wrath of King Zedekiah. Jeremiah was therefore being held under house arrest in the king's court while Zedekiah tried desperately to avoid the fulfillment of Jeremiah's vision of impending disaster.

The circumstances Jeremiah faced were very similar to those in Sarajevo in 1995. Both cities had been under siege for an extended period of time. Both were surrounded by hostile armies whose intentions were anything but good. Neither city was a safe place to be making long-term plans — especially not long-term plans for real-estate investment. But for Jeremiah, that is exactly what God had in mind.

Jeremiah 32:6-15 records the prophetic direction that God gave regarding this 6th century BC land deal.

> The word of the Lord came to me, saying, behold, Hanamel the son of Shallum your uncle is coming to you, saying, buy for yourself my field which is at Anathoth, for you have the right of redemption to buy it. Then Hanamel my uncle's son came to me in the court of the guard according to the word of the Lord and said to me, buy my field, please, that is at Anathoth, which is in the land of Benjamin; for you have the right of possession and the redemption is yours; buy it for yourself. Then I knew that this was the word of the Lord. I bought the

field which was at Anathoth from Hanamel my uncle's son, and I weighed out the silver for him, seventeen shekels of silver. I signed and sealed the deed, and called in witnesses, and weighed out the silver on the scales. Then I took the deeds of purchase, both the sealed copy containing the terms and conditions and the open copy; and I gave the deed of purchase to Baruch the son of Neriah, the son of Mahseiah, in the sight of Hanamel my uncle's son and in the sight of the witnesses who signed the deed of purchase, before all the Jews who were sitting in the court of the guard. And I commanded Baruch in their presence, saying, thus says the Lord of hosts, the God of Israel, take these deeds, this sealed deed of purchase and this open deed, and put them in an earthenware jar, that they may last a long time. For thus says the Lord of hosts, the God of Israel, houses and fields and vineyards will again be bought in this land.

On the surface it seemed that a city under siege was a bad choice for making an investment in property. This was especially true because God had been so clear in His word to the prophet. Jerusalem was going to fall to Babylon. Seventy years of captivity were on God's immediate agenda for the people of Judah. So certain was the prophet about the yoke of bondage that lay ahead for his people, he could barely believe that God would be directing him now to buy land there. Buying land just before everyone is to be taken into captivity is like buying a season pass to Sea World the day before you are scheduled to move to the Mojave Desert. According to human logic, the opportunity to invest is simply **ill timed**.

So strange was this prophetic command, Jeremiah apparently couldn't fully accept it until his nephew, Hanamel, showed up to offer the field in Anathoth for redemption. Only when events occurred just as God had said they would did the prophet know for certain that he had heard the word of the Lord. Apart from this confirmation, it would have been altogether **illogical** to buy property that had already been effectively condemned by divine fiat. But the logic of men is often overruled by the revelation of God. Acting on the language of heaven, Jeremiah faithfully performed all that God had directed him to do.

It seems obvious to me that Jeremiah never assumed he would enjoy a vacation home in Anathoth when he bought this lot. *His interest was in posterity not in prosperity.* The passage makes it clear. Jeremiah purposely made the closing on this real estate transaction a very public and profound event. Gathering witnesses and long-lasting clay pots, the prophet had the deeds signed, and sealed, and stored away as a testimony to God's promise for the future. The city would indeed fall. Its inhabitants would indeed be in captivity for seventy years. The surrounding land would indeed become a complete desolation. But, houses and fields and vineyards would be yet bought there again. God was confirming His promise to that end by causing Jeremiah to act in a manner that confounded his countrymen.

Jeremiah's "prophetic investment" was a divinely designated **illustration**, a token of the promise that God's plan for Israel's eventual return would surely come to pass. The nation would be punished but by God's power His people would also be preserved. The Lord was sending them into captivity but He would also call them back again in due time. Was such a sequence of events possible? Jeremiah 32:17 gives an unflinching answer for anyone lacking faith in this prophet or in the word of the Lord. "Ah Lord God!...Thou hast made the heavens and the earth by Thy great power.... Nothing is too difficult for Thee."

God could do it. He would do it. Jeremiah proved his personal trust in his personal prophecy by betting his personal investment in Anathoth on the oath of God. He did this purposefully and publicly so that everyone would know his confidence in God's promise of a future without calamity. **This text from Jeremiah opened my eyes to the principle of prophetic investment. Somehow, in God's economy, it is prudent to acquire property in perilous places. As God wills, such purchases can have prophetic impact.**

As our elders prayed over this text and our invitation to invest in what seemed to be an inappropriate place at an inopportune time, our faith was enormously strengthened. We claimed God's promise expressed in Jeremiah 32:40-44 beseeching the Lord for an end to chaos in Bosnia,

> And I will make an everlasting covenant with them and I will not turn away from them to do them good; and I will put the fear of Me in their hearts so that they will not turn away from Me. And I will rejoice over them and do them good, and I will faithfully plant them in this land with all my heart and all my soul. For thus says the Lord, Just as I brought all this great disaster on this people, so I am going to bring on them all the good that I am promising them. And fields shall be bought in this land of which you say, "It is a desolation, without men or beast."... Men shall buy fields for money, sign and seal deeds, and call in witnesses ... for I will restore their fortunes declares the Lord.

From Jeremiah's example, we concluded that we were being allowed a genuine privilege to follow the prophet's example. We were blessed in being asked to consider making a "faith purchase" in a land mostly flattened by the forces of war. Inspired by Jeremiah, we chose to act in the interest of posterity and not for our own prosperity. In fact, we raised the $125,000 needed for the transaction in Sarajevo and intentionally retained no title or vested interest in the property for ourselves. In the eyes of the world, our investment, like Jeremiah's, was **ill-timed** and **ill-logical**. But to us, this purchase served, as Jeremiah's did, to offer a divine **illustration** of God's outpouring of grace and of His promise of good will for the days ahead. Our "prophetic investment," like Jeremiah's, was meant to be a testimony. We wanted to send a message of hope to an infant church in a nation too long hopelessly acquainted with the ways of war.

By God's grace, the money for this first building in Bosnia was raised in less than 30 days! By this time we were not even surprised at God's miraculous provision. He had provided manna from heaven again and again on the road to Sarajevo. As others have seen who have tested God's ability to supply, the Lord really can pay for everything He orders. We believe in the principle of prophetic investment. More importantly, we believe other churches should gain courage from our confidence and consider making faith purchases like this in other tragically condemned corners of the world. By doing so, perhaps we can magnify hope among the nations and open more doors for missionary intervention.

Conclusion

As I draw this book to a close we are raising funds for the acquisition of property for a second church building in Sarajevo. We are thrilled that God is still challenging, still blessing, and still rewarding our faith in Him! The body of Christ in Bosnia is not just growing — it is multiplying. So is our full-time staff in the country. By the end of 1998, we hope to have two teams helping to plant churches among our target people. Other churches and agencies are also now operative in this arena. We expect to see this nation reached for Christ in our lifetime. When that task is completed, should the Lord tarry, we will undertake yet another road to reach another unreached people with the gospel. Our will to keep working in an intentional mission outreach is based in part on the four principles set forth above.

Our acceptance of *primary responsibility* for serving God's mission mandate has allowed us to enjoy a level of mobilization that far surpasses what might be expected for churches many times our size. Our unique pilgrimage on the road to Sarajevo has been made possible by God's *providential provocation* more than by our peculiar abilities. Our experience of God's *preeminent grace* has been overwhelmingly consistent along the way. And the returns flowing from our *prophetic investment* have made us eager to test this principle again and again. Our eyes as well as our pocketbooks have been opened by our firsthand experience of God's power to make much of the meager resources we release for the sake of His kingdom.

The major lesson I hope readers of this book will have learned from our journey is summed up in the initial observation made in the introduction. Like the disciples who helped Jesus distribute loaves and fishes to 5,000 hungry souls on the shores of Galilee, we are walking away from this good work not with empty hands, but with baskets heavy laden with an abundance of leftovers which benefit us. We are richer for risking this incredible trip on the road to Sarajevo. Any blessings that we have brought to the people of Bosnia have been far exceeded by the grace poured into our lives along the way. God has opened the windows of heaven and His rain continues to refresh us deeply to this day. Scripture tells us that the disciples of Jesus' day failed to gain insight from the incident of the loaves and fishes (Mk. 6:37-44). We dare not make the same mistake today. Incidences like these are intended by God to teach us faith — faith that dares to act. I am praying as I close this final chapter that you will have been provoked to greater action for the kingdom by what I have written.

As you reflect on what has transpired for us in Bosnia, be assured that your church really can enjoy a similar experience. The place to begin is simply to believe, without any doubting, that *it is not the size of our resource pool but the limits of our faith and our vision that determines our impact for the kingdom.*

Maybe I can emphasize the point one last time by referring again to the words of God's great prophet, Jeremiah. It doesn't matter how small our store of resources may be. It doesn't matter how few our numbers are. It doesn't matter that our confidence and our capacity seem limited in the extreme. No matter how timid we feel about taking God at His word, God's word should overrule our reluctance to dream in the Spirit. **The truth is that nothing is too difficult for us when we truly believe that nothing is too difficult for Him.** This is Jeremiah's defining declaration.

The nations will be blessed in greatest measure when all churches everywhere — no matter what their size — come to fully comprehend and act on this truth. I firmly believe that God wants to build His global church and that He wants to use ordinary people like you and me to do it. I hope I have encouraged your faith along this line by sharing our story. I hope I have inspired you to reach higher than ever before to spread the gospel among the nations. I hope I have made you bolder to risk walking in God's power, and working in God's strength while watching for God's supply. I hope that I have broadened your vision so that you are better able to walk by faith and not by sight.

By now you know I believe our Heavenly Father really does want us to live and to minister beyond the limits our natural perceptions and capabilities. Doing so will require that we develop a capacity for "seeing as God sees." It is my prayer that this book has helped you develop the kind of "spirit eyes" that will allow you to transcend your natural limitations. If it has, I have I have succeeded in my desire to magnify your vision for the small church!

Appendix I

Eight Reasons I'm Skeptical of Meta-Church Methodology

1. Institutional Ecclesiology, as defined in Chapter 9, is essentially a conceptual problem, not a structural one. While Ralph Neighbour and Carl George have accurately described some of its symptoms, they have not prescribed a cure. Their respective models still reflect the following conceptual evidences of institutionalization:

    a. Infatuation with numerical growth as the primary measure of success for a local church. To both men, bigger is still better.

    b. Institutional credentials still predominate in staffing vocational roles in ministry leadership. Ralph Neighbour readily admits that this factor threatens the viability of cell group oriented churches following transitions in leadership. (RN, p. 87)

    c. Significant personal needs are still addressed primarily by programmed responses rather than by people flowing along the comfortable lines of long-term relationships.

d.   Relationships are fully developed only at a cell level so that few members in a church are known to one another. Without a link being formed at the congregational level, large church worship and cell group involvement alone provide too little connective tissue for the healthy growth and development of the body.

e.   Unity between cells is based on artificial and arbitrary organizational ties.

f.   If newcomers are attracted primarily through the normal "front door" entrance in a small group, spiritual authority will stem from mostly formal positions and a standardized span of control rather than from personal influence. This problem is mitigated when newcomers enter through a small group "side door" into church life. This "side door" dynamic is an extremely rare phenomenon in a large church setting.

g.   Cell group members are still viewed by leaders as "consumers" to be given an array of alternatives as they shop for the religious services they desire. (CG, p. 22)

2.   As an institutional, organizational program, these models are unnecessarily complex. The Meta-Church model, especially, is dominated by superfluous jargon, cumbersome structural schemes and numerous charts of overlapping design. Never before has a small group ministry been made so intricately complicated and ornately designed. Average laymen will

struggle to understand much less operate and replicate this model.

3. With unlimited growth of a single church as a stated goal, these models are endeavoring to make the rare exceptions in church development a general rule. The carrot held before those considering the cell group church or the meta-church model is that following these methods, every pastor can have a church like Cho's! It seems to me that God is not making these large church exceptions His global general rule! The truth is, small churches exist in large numbers in every evangelized cultural setting and are especially predominant when unevangelized cultures are first being penetrated with the gospel.

4. Both authors are building their house on a foundation of sand:

    a. Carl George is betting on his own yet-to-be-fulfilled forecast of a future where "churches will be larger than anything we have imagined. In fact, the next generation of churches will dwarf our current successes — including the great congregation in Seoul, which is rapidly pushing toward a three-quarter million figure!"

    b. Ralph Neighbour sees his model as born of a "recent activity of the Spirit.... The Holy Spirit is the author of this pattern, and it has sprouted up like mushrooms all over the globe.... Innovative cell group churches in America alone (number) in the thousands." The existence of such a great number of these new wineskins is unsubstantiated and attributed merely to an estimate made by an unnamed "Nashville church-watcher." Neighbour himself admits that 95 percent of the world's churches are smaller than 350 members. Where are all these cell church extravaganzas?

5.   In my view, cell groups are not large enough or strong enough to bear the weight of complex needs presented by what Carl George calls "extra grace required" people (EGR's). George admits referrals outside the cell are mandatory to prevent such needy people from killing their cells. Ralph Neighbour maintains that Christian Community is possible with only three people and that, "it is (in the cell group) *and nowhere else*, that Christians can be taught to appreciate, desire and exercise spiritual gifts." (emphasis his) I think congregations (groups of 35-120) are a better setting for community dynamics and that they provide a more complete context for understanding the release of spiritual gifts in the church. They also provide a context for natural relational development among cell group members. When needs within a cell exceed the capacity of the small group to respond, the congregation with which it is already identified is available to bring additional resources to bear. EGR's are not a danger to congregations, they are a divinely appointed opportunity to experience body life.

6.   When "extra grace required" people begin to drain a cell group, the meta-church model relies on institutional fabric (a leadership organizational chart) to mobilize resources impersonally rather than relationally to meet the presenting need. Extended networking of families relationally in a true Christian Community is far more effective, far more responsive and far less artificial in producing similar results. The key is to deliver a response of grace through an interpersonal channel rather than an institutional one.

7.   The unlimited growth potential which is the driving force

and motivation for using these models will, in the long run, mitigate against church multiplication — which remains the most effective approach to evangelizing any target culture. While Carl George maintains the Meta-Church model is in essence a *franchise operation*, it would seem more nearly analogous to a large *retail department store* or at best a *chain store operation*. I prefer *sponsorship* of *small business entrepreneurs* as a market place paradigm for encouraging church planting movements among the unreached and under-evangelized peoples of the earth.

8.   I'm interested to know which of these authors is accurate regarding their assessment of the suitability of their respective small group methodologies as an approach to church renewal. Carl George suggests the Meta-Church is a viable renewal program which can be incorporated readily into existing churches. Ralph Neighbour unequivocally says such a hope for his cell group methodology is an impossible dream. "We must actively abandon the hope that stagnant churches can be renewed by painful restructuring and the tacking on of cell group principles.... After devoting nearly a quarter of a century to the attempt to help 'renew the churches,' I am a total skeptic that it can be done. The only hope for old wineskins is to pour out the wine they contain into new ones and *throw the leaky things away*!" (emphasis his) Neighbour strictly advises against using his cell group approach as a renewal strategy and prophesies certain doom for pastors who dare to try their hand at this endeavor. Which leader is right remains to be seen but Neighbour's warning here is serious enough that potential users should proceed with caution!

Appendix II

Major Paradigm Shifts in World Evangelization

by Bruce K. Camp

*M*omentum is building in the Christian community to evangelize the world by the year 2000. Some suggest that every person should have the opportunity to hear the gospel by the end of the century. Others believe, at the very least, that we can have a church planting movement underway in every unreached people within this time frame. Regardless of the perspective, many assume that the American Church will play a significant role in the evangelization of the world during this decade. But will it?

The mission paradigm as it relates to the local church is changing, and until more congregations recognize the new paradigm and act accordingly, we probably will not be able to evangelize the world during this decade. More critically, if the American Church continues with the attitude of "business as usual," it will have lost a window of opportunity to help evangelize every unreached people group prior to the advent of the 21st century.

A paradigm is a model, a way that individuals view something, the rules of a game or the way people perceive reality (Barker 1992).

Examples of paradigms abound. Some common paradigms in missions circles include the concept that only mission agencies are equipped to send missionaries, or mission leadership is male in gender, or missionary candidates must have 30 hours of formal Bible training.

Paradigms are useful to missions strategists, as they help to explain why something is happening as opposed to what is happening. They do not simply describe the new activity, but provide insight into the reason for the change.

Paradigms do change; they are not static. Local churches are reassessing their role and activities in world missions given the political changes that are occurring around the globe. While the goal of world evangelization has not changed, nor will change, the church's *modus operandi* must change, if it is to play a significant role in starting church planting movements in every unreached people group by the end of this decade.

Generally speaking, local evangelical churches in the United States have experienced a major paradigm shift during the last 20 years with regard to understanding their role in obeying the Great Commission. More specifically, numerous congregations have conducted their global missions activities based upon two paradigms (supporting and sending). Currently, a third, the *synergistic* paradigm is emerging.

It is important that the American Evangelical Church understand those paradigms. Presented in this article is a descriptive analysis and comments to assist both agencies and congregations in thinking through the implications of these mission paradigm shifts.

A major paradigm shift currently occurring with churches is that they increasingly want to assume more active responsibility in world missions. The local church is seen as needing to become a primary participant in the task of global evangelization (Camp 1992). This paper will outline the major paradigms through which many churches have and are evolving. In reality, these paradigms represent a continuum of missions activities. No congregation fits one paradigm entirely and perfectly. A particular church may utilize selected ideas found within each of the three paradigms. For the sake of illustration, however, the paradigms will be presented as if each one is all-inclusive of a particular church's activities. Thus, while these paradigms overlap and complicate reality, examining them independently will enable us to make certain observations.

The Supporting Paradigm

The supporting paradigm is still the predominate model for evangelical churches and can be traced back at least to the 1970s. From this perspective, the role of the local church in world missions is understood largely as a merely supportive one. The prevailing question is: What is their game plan? In other words, churches look to mission agencies to set the missions agenda. Basically, whatever agencies want to do is accepted as correct because they are perceived to be the experts. A descriptive summary word for this model is "dependence" in regard to how the local church conducts its missions activities through the agencies.

From a local church perspective, a number of ideas are used to describe this paradigm. These include a high loyalty to denominational and non-denominational mission agencies. Financial support is given to individuals who may reside outside the geographical region of the congregation. Missionaries travel throughout the country to speak and raise support, rarely staying at one church from one week to the next. Mission education is provided by outsiders (generally visiting missionaries) via speakers, slides and mission conferences. Financial support for a missionary is assumed for the duration of their career. Agencies make most of the decisions.

Churches operating in this paradigm are mainly dependent upon mission agencies. They implicitly trust the agencies to know best, and follow the agencies' programs. Prayer support for missionaries is usually limited, since the congregation is often only superficially involved in the life of the missionary and his or her ministries. Although some churches still operate in this support model, changes in the supporting paradigm began to occur in the early 1980s as local congregations started to think in terms of a more participatory role and model of missions.

The Sending Paradigm

Instead of maintaining a *supporting* role, many churches in the 1980s increasingly began to assume a *sending* role in world missions. The key word became "my," and the key question became: "What is my church's plan?" In this model churches have shifted from a more dependent mode to an independent one in their relationship to mission agencies. Congregations utilize the services of mission agencies when they want to, but churches are no longer dependent on any one agency. Some churches send their own missionaries, bypassing the agencies altogether. (I am not suggesting that churches bypass agencies. I view agencies, both historically and currently, as gifts from God to help churches fulfill their mission mandate.) Nonetheless, direct sending of missionaries from local churches is a trend that will not go away. In many cases, this direct sending is a result of congregations wanting to work in areas beyond existing work. Some local churches believe that agencies have become bogged down into working primarily among reached peoples (AD 2000 Global Monitor 1992:2).

Several factors characterize this second paradigm. The agency to which a church was loyal in the previous decade now becomes one of many. Denominational and/or organizational loyalty is predominately a notion of the past for churches which have accepted the sending paradigm. Financial support is regionalized. No longer are missionaries sent throughout the country to find support partners. Congregations now insist on both quantity and quality time with its missionaries whom it supports and sends. If candidates for support cannot spend significant time with a church, then they are not considered for support. Churches in this paradigm demand relationships with their missionaries that go beyond financial support.

Mission education also changed significantly in this sending paradigm. For example, church members began to speak about doing missions based on their mission training in a Perspectives class or on a short-term missions trip. If an outsider was brought in, the individual had to be an excellent communicator. Expectations for quality presentation rose dramatically during this time. In the process, the goal of the sending church changed to directly recruiting and training its own people to be missionaries for their own local church. Congregations still may work with agencies, but only as equal partners. If an agency does not accept this new role of the church as a partner, then a church may opt to find an agency that cooperates with the church's sending task.

Positive factors for missionaries that have resulted from congregations which have become sending churches include: 1) A stronger emotional tie with their home church; 2) Greater prayer and financial support; 3) More accountability to the local church.

Certainly not everyone agrees that a church should take a more active role in world missions. Some interpret this action as churches beginning to act like mission agencies. Negative factors of churches who do this, according to missions executive Sam Metcalf, include: 1) The potential weeding out of the best candidates who are unwilling to go through the church's pre-field training program; 2) More strings attached to church support which causes candidates to go to individuals for donations thus slowing down the time it takes missionaries to raise support; 3) According to Metcalf's view of history, whenever churches begin to exercise control of the missionary enterprise or seek to become an agency, "the missionary effort is eventually impaired and may even die" (1993:146).

Most churches currently still operate in the supporting paradigm. However, a growing number of influential congregations have transitioned to the sending paradigm. A few congregations are shifting to a third model, the synergistic paradigm which is appearing on the horizon in the 1990s. Larry Walker, a church missions consultant for ACMC, estimates that 90 percent of the mission-active churches in North America fit the supporting paradigm, while 8-9 percent represent the sending paradigm and 1-2 percent fit the synergistic paradigm (Personal communication July 5, 1993).

Synergistic (Owning) Paradigm

The definition of the synergistic paradigm contains the idea of joint action by agents that when taken together, increases the effectiveness of both. Another term for the synergistic paradigm is "owning" since a foundational element to this paradigm is emotional ownership of the activity. The key word of this model is "we." The question a church asks is: "What is our role in obeying the Great Commission?" Instead of trying to accomplish numerous missions activities by themselves, synergistic churches will focus on a few items which they can do well. Synergistic congregations are fellowships which partner with others and combine their efforts to produce greater effectiveness than either party can accomplish independently. This partnership model assumes an inter-dependent (not independent) perspective. The churches realize that they do not have to respond to every need, and realize that they are not able to, and so instead, concentrate their energies and finances on a few needs. Frequently, such concentration of energies and finances is channelled to reach an unreached people group.

In this model, mission education is accomplished by both "high tech" and "high touch" efforts. Missionaries increasingly stay in communication with their supporters by the use of faxes, telephones, electronic mail, and voice mail. Synergistic type churches encourage Baby Boomers and others in their congregation to visit the mission field in order to gain a sense of ownership, and to understand why their church should strive for a strong missions emphasis (Engel and Jones 1989). Short-term trips are encouraged, since they greatly facilitate more prayer for world evangelization and especially focus prayer on the part of the participants (STEM Ministries 1991).

The question of the church's role in world missions is precipitated by several factors. One is the recognition of a global Christian community. The missions-active church, in this paradigm, recognizes that the North American Church does not have sole responsibility for world evangelization. The Great Commission applies to every church throughout the world, and since over two-thirds of the Christian community is now non-Western (Douglas 1990:56), the synergistic church realizes that, at least numerically, the role of the American church is diminishing.

The synergistic church recognizes that the number of non-Western missionaries is increasing dramatically. Whereas in 1991 only 36 percent of the world's Protestant missionary force was from the Two-Thirds World, by AD 2000, it is projected that this number will rise to 55 percent (Pate 1991: 58-59). This increase, coupled with the growing concern about the cost of support for North American missionaries, has encouraged the idea that supporting nationals is more cost effective.

Synergistic churches desire to make a significant impact on the non-Christian world. They will adopt various approaches to missions, including an entrepreneurial one. Congregations utilizing the synergistic paradigm likely will reflect many of the Boomers' values such as a desire for multiple options in ministry, appreciation for diversity among individuals (men and women, lay and professional, ethnic and Anglo), desire for change and a hope for significance in their lives (Barna 1990; Collins and Clinton 1992) as well as the Thirteeners' value of pragmatism (Strauss and Howe 1991). For example, synergistic churches, influenced by the Thirteeners value of pragmatism, will scrutinize agencies and plans based upon actual accomplishments, as opposed to rhetoric. They likely will agree with Andrall Pearson, Professor of Business Administration at Harvard's Business School, who writes: "Successful companies today realize that change is the new order and innovation is the primary driver" (1992:70).

Mission organizations which are likely to flourish during the time frame of this model are those which facilitate a local church's mission plans. Antioch Network is a prime example. Its goal is to network congregations that want to send church planting teams to unreached peoples (Antioch Times 1993:3). The organization called Issachar is another example. This organization partners with local churches to assist them in developing their vision and strategies in reaching their adopted people groups (Moats 1991:5). The Adopt-A-People concept is a strategy which corresponds well with the synergistic paradigm, and should blossom during this decade. The idea of a single people group focus for a given church correlates well with the question of a church's role in owning and obeying the Great Commission. Rather than strategizing to evangelize several thousand unreached people groups, the local church rather focuses on only one people.

Other factors, often influenced by the values of the Boomers and/or Busters, both positively and negatively, which may affect the church are:

1. *The blurring of religious distinction and categories.* Polarizing theological issues such as charismatic/non-charismatic or Protestant vs. Roman Catholic will be less of a concern in this decade of the synergistic paradigm.
2. *The changing missionary role in North America.* As national churches mature, the role of the American missionary must change. They will adopt a *facilitating* role to assist the church in specialized areas. Church-related tasks in which missionaries have traditionally worked will fall to national leaders (Pate 1991:61). However, in areas and people groups where the church has not yet been established, traditional church planters will still be needed.
3. *The recognition that mission is not just overseas.* Numerous language and ethnic groups have come to the United States that must be evangelized and reached. For example, in Los Angeles County alone, people from about 140 different countries are represented. In 1989, only 43 percent of the population was Anglo. By 2010, it is projected that in Los Angeles, there will be more Hispanics than Anglos. In the Los Angeles Unified School District, it is estimated that close to 100 different languages are

spoken by the students (Pearlstone 1990). Synergistic church leaders recognize that demographics are changing in the United States. They realize that their mission fields include ethnic groups who reside within their own communities.

4. *The intertwined growth of evangelism and social programs.* There is a growing perception that the dichotomy between evangelism and social programs is artificial. Ministries like Prison Fellowship which intertwine the two will flourish. Issues like AIDS, refugees, gangs, drugs and starvation will not be dealt with only on the spiritual level.

5. *The recognition to hear God speak through Christians from around the world.* For many years, God used Westerners to set the Christian agenda for the rest of the world. Today, believers want to listen to non-Westerners also.

6. *The perception that changes in the world occur rapidly and require a quick response.* God often grants only brief windows of opportunity for believers to seize. For example, there is no indication of how long some of the new Muslim-dominated countries in the Commonwealth of Independent States will remain open to missionary endeavors. Synergistic churches expect to respond quickly to current opportunities.

Church and Mission Implications

These paradigms are based on historical observation. They are not developmental states. In other words, a church could begin its mission involvement from the synergistic paradigm. While there is no one right approach from which a church should operate, normally churches should strive for interdependence as opposed to dependent or independent paradigms.

Not all churches have changed their mission paradigm, nor should they. Some still fit the paradigm of support, while others have become involved in the sending model. But, some are becoming interdependent-synergistic churches. Agencies need to think through how to work in terms of these paradigms and be able to assist churches operating in the three models.

What are the implications of this synergistic paradigm for mission agencies? How should agencies respond? If the key question for this model is: What is our role in obeying the Great Commission?, then several questions must be considered on the part of agencies. Like: Does our agency offer a pre-packed program, either by attitude or action, of what a church should or should not do in missions? Do we strive to enable churches to fulfill their vision? For example, does our Adopt-A-People program allow for creative and genuine partnership? Do we (the agencies) dictate the game plan for ministry? Do we welcome dialogue with churches in the development of strategies, especially to unreached peoples?

The synergistic paradigm does not mean that the leaders of an agency no longer have the prerogative to set the direction for that agency. However, if an agency agrees with the synergistic paradigm, it will allow others to have input into where and how the agency might minister in the future.

As an example, leaders of the Evangelical Free Church Mission (my mission) recognized that there indeed is a paradigm shift occurring among local churches. Beyond acknowledging this shift, they also considered their response to local churches which may want to originate their own overseas ministries. As a mission, the Evangelical Free Church has stated that there are at least four types of responses which they could give to churches which launch their own initiatives. First, they could respond at the *encouragement level*. Here, they rejoice in what a church is doing and show genuine interest in their ministry. Second, they could respond at a *consultant level*. At this level, the mission meets with the leadership of a church to help them think through the pros and cons of the project and what would be necessary for it to flourish. The mission's expertise and resources come to bear here and would be made available to the church. Third, they could respond at a *partnership level*. The terms of partnership would need to be negotiated as to lines of authority, finances, role of the local church and role of the mission, etc. The fourth response would be the *adoption level*. Adoption means that the mission would ultimately take responsibility for the ministry. Any of these four responses could apply to entering a new country, targeting an unreached people, or evangelizing a world class city.

We need to understand that agencies can still provide a great service to local churches which are operating in terms of the synergistic paradigm. To be effective, however, agencies will need to think creatively about how to work in *true partnership* with local churches. Just as national churches on the mission fields move through various stages of development with a mission agency (Fuller 1980), so like-wise local churches must be allowed to move through stages of mission development and involvement.

Frequently congregations do not realize that there are various paradigms from which they can operate. They need to ask themselves what the pros and cons are of each model. They should also discuss what issues need to be addressed for their church in following one or another paradigms. For example, what global realities do they see that will have a bearing on how a given church should conduct missions in the 1990s? What do they believe is the role of the church in obeying the Great Commission? What is the strategy of their church for this decade? As a church transitions from a supporting mode to a more involvement and partnership model, what changes will need to occur in their church's missions understanding and practice?

The synergistic (owning) paradigm offers local churches meaningful participation in the Great Commission. Yet, it is not a panacea. It will not cure every ailment found in the world mission enterprise. It does, however, address the changing global realities. It recognizes that the North American Church still has a significant role to play in world evangelization. At the same time, it also acknowledges that the American Church is not the only player in this endeavor.

SUMMARY OF PARADIGM SHIFTS IN WORLD EVANGELIZATION

PARADIGMS	SUPPORTING	SENDING	SYNERGISTIC (Owning)
Time Period	1970s and before	1980s	1990s
Key Word	"They"	"My"	"We"
Description	Dependent	Independent	Inter-dependent
Key Question	What is *their* game plan	What is my church's plan?	What is our role in obeying the Great Commission?
Mission Agency	High loyalty to a given agency	Awareness that an agency is one of many	Recognition of a global Christian community
Decision Making	Agency makes decisions	Partnership with the agency	Forming a strategic ministry
Geographic Support	Support outside the region	Support within the region	Support of non-Western missionaries
Philosophical Support	Support American missionaries	Recruit/train/ support our own	Partnership with others (Americans/others)
Congregational Outreach	Non-directive philosophy	Directive philosophy	Empower church constituency philosophy
Relationships	Superficial contacts with missionaries	Quality/quantity time with our missionaries	Make a significant impact on the non-Christian world
Mission Education	Mission education by outsiders	Mission education done by insiders and by quality teachers	High-tech and high-touch mission training
Church Participation	Emphasis on goers	Emphasis on goers and senders	Emphasis on everyone participating in outreach
Focus	Focus on money	Focus is on people	Focus is on opportunity
Strategy	No church strategy	A single church strategy	Multi-pronged strategy
Signs of Success	Bigger budgets for missions, better mission conferences	Bigger budgets and more missionaries sent	Souls saved, churches planted, more members empowered for ministry

Conclusion

Will there be a church planting movement among every unreached people group by the year 2000? The answer is no, unless changes occur in how churches participate in world evangelization! While all three paradigms allow for involvement by churches in evangelizing unreached peoples (Camp 1993), only the synergistic ownership model allows for an aggressive and full-orbed participation by congregations in bringing closure to the final task in the foreseeable future. If indeed our goal is "a church for every people and the gospel for every person by the year 2000," then a myriad of supporting and sending churches must take a more active role and consider becoming synergistic churches.

The paradigm of passive mission involvement characterized by most local churches in the past is not conductive to the accelerated momentum and emphasis needed for world evangelization. More biblically and missiologically informed, as well as Spirit-led action is needed, especially as it relates to evangelizing the remaining unreached peoples. Our prayer is that both churches and mission agencies accept the challenge and blessing of the synergistic (owning) mission model and in the process form strong partnerships to finish the task that remains.

References

ACMC 1988 "Cultivating a Missions-Active Church." (Available from ACMC P.O. Box ACMC, Wheaton, IL 60189).

AD 2000 Global Monitor 1992 New Trends. 23 (Oct.):2.

Antioch Times 1993 Questions & Answers. (Available from Antioch Network 301 West Indian School Road Suite A-119, Phoenix, AZ 85013).

Barker, Joe Arthur 1992 *Future Edge: Discovering the New Paradigms of Success.* New York: William Morrow and Company.

Barna, George 1990 *The Frog in the Kettle.* Ventura, CA: Regal Books.

Camp, Bruce K. 1992 *Scripturally Considered, the Local Church Has Primary Responsibility for World Evangelization.* D. Miss dissertation. School of Intercultural Studies, Biola University.

1993 *Strategies of Adoption.* OUTLOOK. 4(1):1-3. (Available from the Evangelical Free Church Mission 901 East 78ᵗʰ St. Minneapolis, MN 55420).

Collins, Gary R. and Timothy E. Clinton 1992 *Baby Boomer Blues.* Dallas, TX: Word Publishing.

Colson, Charles 1992 *The Body.* Dallas, TX: Word Publishing.

Douglas, J.D., ed. 1990 *Proclaim Christ Until He Comes.* Minneapolis, MN: World Publications.

Engel, James F. and Jerry D. Jones 1989 *Baby Boomers and the Future of World Missions.* Orange, CA: Management Development Associates.

Fuller, W.H. 1980 *Mission-Church Dynamics.* Pasadena, CA: William Carey Library.

Metcalf, Samuel F. 1993 *When Local Churches Act Like Agencies.* Evangelical Missions Quarterly. 29 (2): 142-149.

Moats, Jim 1991 *The Enosis Concept.* Strategic Times Journ. 5(2):1-5.

Pate, Larry D. 1991 *The Changing Balance in Global Mission.* International Bulletin of Missionary Research 16 (2): 56-61.

Pearlstone, Zena 1990 *Ethnic L.A.* Beverly Hills, CA: Hillcrest Press.

Pearson, Andrall E. 1992 *Corporate Redemption and the Seven Deadly Sins.* Harvard Business Review 71 (3): 65-75.

STEM Ministries 1991 *Is Short-Term Mission Really Worth the Time and Money?* (Available from STEM Ministries P.O. Box 290066 Minneapolis, MN 55429).

Strauss, William and Neil Howe 1991 *Generations.* New York: William Morrow and Company.

This appendix as taken in its entirety from the ACMC *Mobilizer*, Winter 1994, pages 1-16 and is used with the author's permission.

Appendix III

The Bosnia Project Agreement

Between the Evangelical Free Church Mission and Northside Community Church in Atlanta

I. VISION:

To call local churches within the Evangelical Free Church of America (EFCA) to facilitate a church planting movement in Bosnia. This goal will be accomplished by encouraging existing national churches to develop a multiplication mentality and by planting new churches which share this vision. The movement will be launched by forming an association of Bosnian local churches into an interdependent relationship with each other that will be united with a common purpose and direction under the Evangelical Church of Bosnia-Herzegovina.

II. INTRODUCTORY EXPLANATION:

Northside Community Church (NCC) is conducting its ministry in Bosnia under the auspices of a separate non-profit corporation, Ministry Resource Network (MRN). This nonprofit umbrella was formed by a Church Initiated Partnership to facilitate fundraising from non-EFCA churches for missionaries requiring long-term support in Bosnia. MRN presently represents a consortium of three EFCA churches in Atlanta, Georgia. These churches include Northside Community Church, East Gate Congregation and Living Hope Community Church. MRN and these churches are also to be viewed as partners to this agreement by virtue of their common involvement in Bosnia. In Bosnia, MRN is operating under a pseudonym, Church Resource Network International (CRNI). CRNI has four full-time staff members working in Bosnia. For purposes of this agreement, references to NCC will be understood to include its Atlanta-based church partners and MRN. It is possible that other U.S. church partners could join this consortium in sending missionaries to Bosnia under MRN in the future.

III. PREREQUISITES, LINES OF AUTHORITY AND COMMUNICATION:

A.   As a prerequisite to implementing this agreement between NCC and the Evangelical Free Church Mission (EFCM), it is understood that:

    (1)   NCC will complete a suitable written partnership agreement with the Evangelical Church of Bosnia-Herzegovina (ECBiH) patterned after similar agreements already utilized by the EFCM and its existing national partners in Europe. In this instance, NCC will, in effect, be in a "National Church Movement" partnership with the ECBiH. The EFCM will be in partnership only with NCC and other EFCA churches who decide to participate in the Bosnia Project.

    (2)   NCC will take the necessary steps to register itself or its non-profit corporate umbrella, MRN, as a legal entity recognized by the Bosnian government as a lawful church planting and humanitarian aid organization operating within the country.

(3)   Should the EFCM's plans for developing a network of Theological Education Extension Sites in the various mission fields of Central Europe come to fruition, the NCC field director or another appropriate individual serving in the leadership of the Bible school already functioning in Mostar, will commit to remaining involved in that EFCM network. This commitment is made in hopes of advancing the training potential for church leaders emerging in the various EFCM fields including Bosnia. NCC is anticipating an ongoing strategic influence in the Mostar Bible school. Since, however, NCC has no proprietary interest in the school, only NCC staff can be bound by this part of our agreement.

B.   The initial responsibility for the EFCM effort in Bosnia under this agreement will be assumed by NCC and its team under the leadership of field director, David Lively. The EFCM's Europe Director will immediately provide counsel with respect to strategy and direction of the EFCM work in Bosnia and will also speak to pastoral care issues as an objective observer. Primary responsibility for pastoral care of individuals on the field, however, will be maintained by the local churches involved in sending workers to Bosnia under NCC auspices, or by the EFCM as it begins to mobilize its own missionaries under this agreement. The key to this arrangement will be developing a good working relationship between local U.S. church partners, their teams on the field, the EFCM leadership in Europe and national leaders in Bosnia.

C.   Under this agreement, David Lively will be the initial EFCM "Country Leader" in Bosnia. All full time missionaries and church planters working under this agreement will be accountable to the Country Leader who will in turn be accountable to a Project Council (PC). The PC will be composed of the EFCM Europe Director, the EFCM Bosnian Country Leader, a representative of the ECBiH, and a representative of the U.S. Joint Mission Team described in section IV D below. The EFCM Europe Director will chair the PC.

D. U.S. church partners will also continue to have ultimate responsibility for financial and prayer support as well as a voice in the direction of their personnel ministering in Bosnia under NCC. Each church's voice regarding direction of their personnel will be expressed in the context of the U.S. Joint Mission Team (JMT). The JMT will be comprised of a pastor and/or a mission leader from each sponsoring church and a U.S.-based representative of the EFCM. The interests of the JMT will be conveyed to the PC by a representative chosen from the JMT to serve on the PC. All U.S. church partners participating in this agreement also acknowledge the important advisory role of the EFCM's Europe Director and the authority the EFCM will maintain over the missionaries it mobilizes to work in Bosnia.

While the EFCM accepts full responsibility for the financial, prayer and pastoral support for missionaries it mobilizes to Bosnia, churches involved in this Bosnia Project Agreement will endeavor to participate in prayer and financial support for EFCM missionaries approved for service in Bosnia.

A change in the individual designated to be the EFCM Country Leader may be required as this partnership progresses. Such a change will be effected by action of the PC in consultation with the JMT as these two groups act together in the best interest of the work in Bosnia. It is our desire from the outset of this agreement to minimize motivations growing out of proprietary interests and to maximize cooperative efforts put forth in good faith.

NCC and each local U.S. church partner, through partnering with the EFCM in Bosnia, will further commit to pursue and preserve the overall goal of starting a church planting movement in Bosnia. The accomplishment of this goal will be measured against twelve important criteria. Six of these criteria characterize the kinds of local churches we hope to develop in Bosnia. They include the following:

1. That the new churches be evangelical.
2. That the new churches be congregational.
3. That the new churches be associated with the emerging Evangelical Church of Bosnia-Herzegovina (i.e. that they be interdependent rather than independent).
4. That the new churches become indigenous in both leadership and financial support.
5. That the new churches be committed to church planting.
6. That the new churches be characterized by clear Bible teaching and joyous corporate worship.

The remaining six criteria describe the kind of church movement we trust this cooperative effort to produce. These distinctives direct our efforts toward a church planting movement which is.

1. Theologically evangelical
2. Culturally indigenous
3. Locally autonomous
4. Regionally interdependent
5. Internationally united
6. Globally focused

E.   In furthering the work of the partnership we are all committing to cooperate in the following areas:

1.   To agree upon an entrance and disengagement strategy for Bosnia to be developed by the PC and implemented by all partners to this agreement.

2.   To agree on the overall strategy of establishing a movement of 20 to 30 churches in key population centers based on a demographic study of Bosnia. These primary church planting targets should be selected in coordination with the existing expansion plans of the Evangelical Church of Bosnia-Herzegovina.

3.   To recruit both long-term and short-term U.S. workers to come to Bosnia and to help mobilize nationals to ministry leadership roles whenever possible.

4.   To encourage other local U.S. churches to consider sharing in this effort by offering opportunities for involvement as an expression of the supporting, sending or synergistic mission paradigms and through sending either long-term workers or short-term teams.

5.   To help meet the financial and physical needs of the sister churches started in Bosnia including, but not limited to:

A. Short-term support for national church planting team members
B. Helping provide equipment
C. Assisting in procuring or building permanent facilities

D. Helping provide materials

E. Helping in provision of humanitarian needs

Note: The PC will establish policy guidelines for physical and financial support of nationals to insure that the developing Bosnian churches are self-supporting as soon as possible.

6.   To involve ourselves in a structured prayer strategy for the entire church planting process.

7.   To communicate regularly with U.S. church partners, the EFCM, the Bosnian church plants and all U.S. missionaries on the field. This goal will be accomplished by allowing Bosnian church leaders and all U.S. church partners to this agreement access to the monthly prayer reports and quarterly concerts of prayer communications coordinated through the office of the EFCM Europe Director.

8.   To encourage Bosnian churches to develop their local assemblies based on the 12 points of distinction appearing earlier in this document. (Lines of Authority and Communication -Section III F)

9.   To provide for maximum communication and coordination between NCC leaders, local American church partners and EFCM leaders. This will be accomplished through regular meetings of the JMT and the PC and through the prayer communication described under # 8 above.

10.   To be available to aid in developing the global EFCM church planting movement strategy by recruiting other EFCA churches to work in Bosnia and by encouraging these other churches to consider the

full range of possible involvements in other existing EFCM mission fields.

11.   To commit all future missionaries to the EFCM prescribed training processes including missionary candidate school, field director's orientation, field director training, church planter's training, and annual regional conferences as deemed appropriate by EFCM leadership. NCC's Training Director, Bill Smith (or another individual later serving in that capacity), will be included in the EFCM training process as such is deemed appropriate. Present NCC staff serving in Bosnia will endeavor to avail themselves of this training as time allows but will not be required to return to the United States to do so as a prerequisite for this agreement.

SPONSORS OF MISSIONARIES SERVING IN BOSNIA UNDER THIS AGREEMENT

A.   MRN missionaries: An MRN missionary is one who meets the normal requirements set by the EFCM but who has not formally applied for candidate status within the EFCM. All existing NCC staff in Bosnia will be considered MRN missionaries. The country leader in Bosnia must personally approve future candidates for service as MRN missionaries prior to their deployment to the field. To the extent allowed by law, NCC will share the MRN missionaries' file with the EFCM. In order to keep the EFCM files up to date on each MRN missionary candidate, routine 1st and 2nd applications with psychological evaluations will be made available to EFCM.

B.   EFCM missionaries: EFCM missionaries are those candidates who have officially applied for ministry in Bosnia as staff members of the EFCM. To the extent permissible by law, the file of all regular EFCM missionaries approved for service in Bosnia will be shared with NCC leaders and mobilization to Bosnia will be implemented only with the approval of the PC on a case by case basis. The country leader in Bosnia must personally approve candidates for missionary service under his leadership prior to their deployment to the field.

Equal Status: Whether having the title EFCM or MRN missionary, all field staff in Bosnia will have equal status under this agreement. To the extent possible, we want to strive to avoid a "we-they" dichotomy between regular EFCM missionaries and MRN missionaries mobilized directly by NCC or other U.S. church partners. It is our expectation that maintaining two sponsors and thus two routes of entree to Bosnia will ultimately increase the number of missionaries mobilized to this field.

NCC may request short-term exposure to the field in Bosnia as a prerequisite to mobilizing any candidate as an EFCM missionary or MRN missionary under this agreement.

V. PARTNERSHIP REVIEW

This Partnership Agreement represents a five year commitment from the date shown below but shall be reviewed annually by leadership representatives from the EFCM and NCC. By its very nature, a cooperative effort like this one rests significantly upon the continued good faith of all partners. At the outset, it is understood that all parties to this agreement anticipate a sustained commitment to establish the desired church planting movement in Bosnia.

VI. ADDITIONAL PARTNERSHIPS

Representatives of the EFCM and NCC will consult with each other prior to entering into any additional partnership in Bosnia.

Appendix IV

Suggestions for Synergistic Partners

A recognizable shift from the traditional supporting and sending paradigms to the synergistic paradigm in world missions methodologies (see Chapter 13, Two Are Better Than One, and Appendix II, Changing Paradigms In World Missions) is creating significant stress for some mission agency leaders. The pressures of the changes we are experiencing can also be a challenge for local church pastors who want to practice what they preach about the Great Commission and God's desire to have the gospel of Christ taken to the nations.

This appendix is intended to provide food for thought for pastors and agency leaders alike who may be motivated by this book and other indications of change to cease striving against the synergistic paradigm. It is hoped that the following "dos and don'ts" will offer insights that may make your steps toward synergistic missions ministry more productive early in the transition.

Thoughts for Local Church Pastors

1. Do resist the institutional pressure to assume that missions ministry belongs in the realm of the mission professional. The path to greater progress in global evangelism begins with pastors assuming that missions ministry is not just a theoretical

responsibility in the local church. Review Acts 13 and begin to interact with your local church leaders about what would need to be changed if they were leading in the Antioch Church and the progress of world missions depended solely upon your local congregation.

2. Do expect that adding this practical responsibility to the priorities of your church will impact the work that you do as a pastor. Especially if you are the senior pastor, your contribution to your church's synergistic effort in missions will require you to labor in the areas of:

    •   **prayer:** If your members are to develop an intercessory burden for your mission target, they will best catch their vision for intercession by observing your own prayer commitment. Praying for your part of the world will need to become a major priority in your own ministry schedule.

    •   **vision:** You will need to be the primary vision caster for your congregation. If you don't "own the vision" personally, neither will the majority of those who follow you.

    •   **visitation:** In this approach to missions, you will likely not be able to point others to a field for which you have no passion. It is best for you to lead the way and beneficial for you to visit the field routinely along the way. After nearly eight years in Bosnia, I still travel there once or twice a year.

    •   **training:** To be successful in the long run, your commitment to training will need to be upgraded. If your church adequately responds to the need to reproduce reproducing leaders, your pastoral skills will likely be needed to help shape your training environment.

    •   **investment:** If you are successful in developing a synergistic effort, you will ultimately invest more money, more energy and more people in the process than you now think possible. Expect to be asked by God, to give your congregation's best efforts in each of these areas.

3. Do develop relationships aggressively along the way. Your personal networking efforts are likely to produce the best partners for your long-term work. Focus especially on building strong personal relationships with nationals. In the final analysis, they will be giving you leadership on the field. Make sure you find people you can trust implicitly.

4. Do learn to be a good "synergistic partner." Approach missions as you would other aspects of relationships in the body of Christ, applying the principles of selflessness offered in Phil. 2:3-5. Your purposes will be best served if your partners are all prospering with your sacrificial support.

5. Do practice at home what you are preaching for the mission field. If prayer, evangelism, training, church multiplication and release of laborers are priorities among the unreached peoples of the world, these ought also to be priorities in your ministry at home.

6. Don't expect to become an expert in missions methodology without investing time to gain necessary experience yourself. Only considerable effort will allow a pastor to achieve the exposure and training required to lead a missions effort first-hand. You can apply what you are learning as you journey along the way but you must be a committed learner or you will not successfully lead others in missions ministry.

7. Don't get frustrated with agency leaders who doubt your potential for success or who keep calling you back to other paradigms. Persevere in relationship with them and help them gain confidence that you can be effective in developing your own global outreach potential. Agency leaders will need to be convinced that pastors can be as committed as they are to staying at the missions task for the long haul.

8. Don't view the necessary commitment of funds and energy to your world missions strategy as a competitive ministry that deprives the work of your church in the local area. As people learn to give, to go, to pray, to minister, to reproduce and to

follow God's will for their lives in missions, they will be better laborers at home as well.

9. Don't hesitate when you stand before an open door that represents enhanced opportunity. Lots of lost momentum in missions has been sacrificed on the altar of undue timidity and caution. If you err at all, err on the side of being bold for the kingdom.

10. Don't adopt the synergistic paradigm if you hope to delegate all the hard work to others. This model for missions will revolutionize your church if you will allow it first to revolutionize you. Roll up your sleeves and expect God to do the impossible as you join others in doing the possible.

Thoughts for Mission Agency Leaders

1. Do eliminate your "general partner" presumption and prepare yourself and your staff to become enablers for the vision of national leaders and local church pastors. Your enthusiastic service of others will ensure an ongoing strategic role for your mission in the future.

2. Do raise your appreciation for the potential of synergistic partnerships and promote this model aggressively – especially among smaller congregations. This approach will permit you to do more to inspire, mobilize and release small churches in missions than the supporting and sending paradigms ever hoped to allow.

3. Do creatively expand your capacity to enable others in the mission community to lead. The increasingly obvious potential of local churches and national leaders is a testimony to your effectiveness to date. Learn how to come alongside and even to labor under the capable leadership of your traditional partners as they have labored under your guidance over the years. Barnabus' work with Paul along this line could offer helpful insights.

Potential enabling roles in a retooled "synergistic environment" might include:

- **A Networking Function**
  — link synergistic churches deliberately
  — look for mentoring churches that can help others develop
  — encourage church-based initiatives and focus your promotional efforts on maximizing local church mission potential instead of strictly marketing your own agency's vision

- **A Conferencing Function**
  — create a "show case" forum for local church success stories
  — encourage small churches to think big and to keep growing in the synergistic paradigm

- **A Promotional Function**
  — infect your church networks with a contagious spirit of enthusiasm

- **A Referral/Consultation Function**
  — use qualified church leaders as unpaid "field staff" (see number 8 below)

- **An Investment Function**
  — where possible give financial support to local church initiatives you believe in
  — offer services, training, materials and administrative support with no fee or with minimal fees
  — Don't let your partners out give you

4. Do try to improve your strategic decision making methodology so that you can be more immediately responsive when

opportunity knocks at the door. Rapid response time has been a key factor in our success to date in a synergistic environment. Communication and travel technology is cooperating with this priority – make sure your decision-making models are as well.

5. Do offer your expertise and experience to protect your church and national partners from the ravages of learning only in the school of hard knocks. Willingly re-enlist in God's global army even if He chooses to promote others over you from time to time. In all the armies of the world, inexperienced officers give formal leadership to sage master sergeants whose experience far exceeds their own. They do this with little difficulty and with great appreciation for the seasoned perspective that non-commissioned leaders bring to the war effort. Why should the armies of God be different?

6. Don't allow yourself the luxury of remaining in a competitive posture with other church and mission leaders on the field. Market share is of little concern to soldiers in the midst of a pitched battle. Stop selling and instead stretch your capacity to serve. Aggressively promote a kingdom mindset whenever possible.

7. Don't ignore the value of the synergistic paradigm just because it is less familiar to you. Start today and find some one you trust to test this method. In your broad circle of supporting and sending church partners, find a church you respect enough to recruit as a partner in the synergistic paradigm. If such a church has history with your agency, their capacity to lead is likely a direct fruit of your ministry. Be blessed and promote their efforts to initiate a vision which you can be excited about serving!

8. Don't keep trying to stretch your financial base and your staff to make sure you can maintain control of the momentum your mission generates worldwide. Learn how to affirm, release and rely on "non-staff" partners to your own advantage and for the benefit of global evangelism. Applying this sugges-

tion could allow you to use local church and national partners of proven worth as unpaid "field staff" for your mission. As a result it is possible that you could:

- Increase personal service to your constituents without increasing payroll or administrative costs
- Increase field visits for your mission without increasing your travel costs
- Increase training and potential partner/candidate development without drawing on limited headquarters staff time
- Increase a regional sense of presence without opening branch offices. As our work in Bosnia progresses for example, local church partners are emerging in Pennsylvania, Indiana and Arizona as well as in Georgia. Pastors and missions leaders in these churches can represent our denomination's work in Bosnia just as effectively as the EFCM headquarters' staff can. Through these partners, we already have "regional offices" in place that operate at no cost to our mission!

9. Don't keep trying to defend your traditional place on the playing field. God cares more about getting His global mandate accomplished than He does about preserving any of our traditions.

10. Don't keep thinking of small churches as irrelevant to the cause of world missions. You will likely keep defining them out of the ball game if you are unwilling to accept the suggestions this book makes regarding the need to embrace a change in ecclesiology, a change in missions paradigm, a change in a sense of responsibility for missions and a change in your agency's particular role in partnership with local churches and with nationals. It really is time for you and your colleagues to learn to see as God sees so that modern-day Davids can begin to fight Goliath again.

Reconciliation in Eastern Europe

by Peter Kuzmic[***]

Peter Kuzmic's passion is the suffering in his country. He and others have organized a non-profit, non-denominational organization called Agape, which was founded in 1991. An excerpt from their newsletter reads, "The word Agape is used by many groups around the world, but in the former Yugoslavia its meaning is particularly appropriate. In a place where killing your neighbor because of his difference has become a way of life, offering help and hope to people of all nationalities and religions grabs attention. We find that feeding Serbs, Muslims and Croatians in the same room makes people ask why. And there we

---

[***]Peter Kuzmic is a native of Slovenia and a citizen of Croatia in former Yugoslavia. He is the foremost evangelical scholar in Eastern Europe and is considered an authority on the subject of Christian Response to Marxism and on Christian Ministry in post-Communist contexts. A former pastor of two churches, he is a founder and director of the Evangelical Theological Seminary in Osijek, Croatia. An award-winning speaker and writer, Dr. Kuzmic is the Paul E. Toms Distinguished Professor of World Missions and European Studies at Gordon-Conwell Theological Seminary in South Hampton, Massachusetts.

seize the chance to share how our Christian God is different and why He tells us to do good to all people. "

For many of us as we look at what is going on in that part of the world, we can feel very hopeless. But we serve a God of the impossible. And I believe that here is a man who God has prepared and has strategically placed for just such a moment in time as this. Dr. Kuzmic is a man of tremendous energy, of strong faith, of commitment to the gospel of Jesus Christ and of a deep compassion for his people. He is a true ambassador of reconciliation.

— Joanna Mockler,
Friend of World Vision

Europe has been a divided continent for the greater part of this century. Eastern and western Europe are not just geographical designations; they are also ideological designations. They speak of two irreconcilable enemies, two opposing blocs. Western Europe has been free. Eastern Europe has been under totalitarian communist regimes.

In eastern Europe, the Marxists claimed a monopoly on both power and truth. We recognize now how they abused power and distorted truth. Their ultimate goal was not just a classless society, but a religionless society. They considered all religion, especially Christianity, to be a remnant of the old order: pre-scientific, superstitious, obscure, irrational, outdated, totally irrelevant, and a harmful way of thinking that had to go.

During the Lausanne Congress on World Evangelization in Manila in 1989, one of the delegates said it looked like the Christian Church was losing the battle against it's most powerful enemy of the 20th century and the most powerful enemy of the Christian faith in history: Marxist communism.

At the end of that year, however, history picked up pace in an amazing way. The Berlin wall was down by November and there was great euphoria all over the world. People believed we had arrived, that East and West were reconciled.

There was great celebration among Christians because we could now evangelize, plant new churches, and train for ministry. Thousands from the West moved into the spiritual vacuum where there was an unprecedented freedom and a large scale search for spiritual reality. However, the freedom was more due to anarchy than to design. The new design would come into existence and the freedom would be restricted again. We are witnessing that today.

A Painful Transition

Eastern Europe is presently going through a very painful, three-fold transition which is causing conflict, growing tension, violence, and even greater threats for the future.

Political Transition – Countries are moving away from one party totalitarian regimes toward multi-party democracies. However, democracy does not happen overnight because, in many of those countries, there are no democratic traditions or instruments. The people have to learn the ABCs of democracy.

Moreover, since communists had a monopoly on power, they were the only people schooled and trained for political decision making. Many former leaders have changed the names of their parties from communist to Socialist in order to become more palatable, yet they possess the old mind set; and many of these leaders are in power again. We have a saying in our country: "they changed from red to pink."

Economic Transition – Countries are moving away from centrally-planned command economies to free-market or mixed-market economies. The transition is painful not only because of the huge, paralyzed bureaucracies that have not been dismantled in many places, but because of state-subsidized industries. Without state subsidies, hundreds of thousands of people become unemployed. This results in social unrest, a dangerous opportunity for political manipulation or military take-overs.

Communism also killed or at least stifled creativity and initiative, two basic prerequisites for a free market. One of the "missionary" needs is for businessmen and politicians who will promote value-based understanding of the world of economy and politics.

Meanwhile, economic crime is on the rise. Some of my friends from Moscow tell me the city is ruled by Mafia. There are all kinds of conflicts and painful divisions nearing the boiling point and, in some places, exploding. Some people, tired of anarchy and poverty, are expressing nostalgia for the old ordered socialist times.

Religious Transition – Under communism, atheism functioned like a state-supported substitute religion. When communism collapsed, whatever communism suppressed began exploding. The two prime examples are nationalism and religion.

Communists suppressed nationalism in their attempts to build a new proletarian internationalism. Many ethnic groups had their cultures, even their languages, suppressed.

Religion was suppressed because the communists set out to build a scientifically based and ideologically controlled atheistic society. They did everything they could to make sure that history was moving in the direction where religion would wither away and disappear.

The explosions of nationalism and religion go hand in hand because the former national churches see themselves as preservers of national culture, identity, and sense of nationhood. They want to reclaim a monopoly on the religious life and activity of their nations. This powerful synthesis of nationality, religion and culture is very dangerous because it will hinder the free development of democracy and the growth of a genuinely free pluralistic society.

The talk now is: if you are Russian, you are Orthodox. If you are Romanian or Serbian you are Orthodox. If you are Polish or Croatian you are Catholic. If you are anything else you are not a good citizen, not a good patriot. Christian faith is frequently defined along ethnic lines and citizenship rather than in terms of a commitment to Jesus Christ and His teaching.

I recently read a statement by the Russian Orthodox bishop in which he said that Protestantism is an imported western religion and that it threatens the sense of unity of the Russian people because "the Russian soul is Orthodox." As such, it is an intrusion and is a threat to national-religious unity. The day may not be far away when evangelicals will be the new dissidents of these societies.

A Nation in Pain

Let us look at Yugoslavia, for this country is in the midst of all three painful transitions. The situation is further complicated because of its violent break-up and war in Bosnia. Yugoslavia has been called the India of Europe: six republics, two autonomous regions, a number of strong national minorities in addition to Slovenians, Croats, Serbs, Bosnians, and Macedonians. So public education was taught in 12 or 13 languages. University level education in six languages. Add to that, two alphabets and three main religions. Serbs are Orthodox; Croats and Slovenians are Roman Catholic, and the majority of Bosnians and Albanians in Kosovo are, at least culturally, Muslims.

Yugoslavia was created in 1918, first as a kingdom of Serbs, Croats and Slovenes with a Serbian monarch. In 1945 Tito came to power, leading a small communist party prior to WWII, but successfully organizing a popular liberation movement against the German occupation.

Tito died in 1980, and in 1990 the country had its first elections. Of the six republics, Slovenia, Croatia, Bosnia, and Macedonia elected strong anti-communist governments, while Serbia — the biggest — and Montenegro — the smallest — retained the same communist leadership.

When army generals, who are mostly Serbian and the staunchest of all the communists, saw that the Federal Communist Party was dissolving, they founded the new communist party: the League of Communists-Movement for Yugoslavia. They tried to preserve the old socialist federal structures with their privileges within that system. When it became obvious that the movements for democratic changes and the right of self-determination for suppressed national groups could no longer tolerate these artificially created Socialist Federations, they changed their tactics and their goals.

A strategic military alliance between the federal army generals — mostly Serbs — and the Serbian communist oligarchy in Belgrade was created. The slogan became "Wherever there are Serbs, it is Serbia." Under the guise of protecting Serbian minorities in other republics, they went out to create "Greater Serbia," which resulted in the war in Slovenia. Consequently, one third of Croatia was occupied. Later, in a brutal war coupled with ethnic cleansing, seventy percent of Bosnia came under Serbian control.

Bosnian Myths

There are three myths about the conflict in Bosnia. One is that the war is an ethnic or tribal war — an eruption of old, uncontrolled, large-scale, ancient, ethnic hatreds. If this were true, how does one explain thousands of inter-marriages in Bosnian cities if there was so much animosity? How does one explain so many Bosnian Serbs, including high ranking commanders, fighting in the Bosnian Army against the Serb aggression? This is an imported hatred, an ideological clash coupled with territorial cleansing and expansionists plans of the Belgrade architects for "Greater Serbia."

The second myth is that it is a civil war. In reality, the war was engineered and supported by Belgrade. The concept of "Greater Serbia" is still their concept, so it certainly did not begin as a civil war.

The third myth speaks of "the defense of the Christian West against the onslaught of fundamentalist Islam" in Europe. It is very unfortunate that the Bosnians are generally labeled Muslims because for most of them it is not primarily a religious designation. It is the way they identify themselves culturally. There are many Muslims who are atheists, who don't have any religious convictions. It is certainly inaccurate and unfair to describe Bosnian Muslims as "militant fundamentalists" who are a threat to "Christian Europe."

So the genesis of the war was ideological and territorial, not ethnic or religious. Those elements came in later as they were manipulated by the political leaders who had sick ambitions to enlarge their empires regardless of the human cost.

Yugoslavia had one of the best-equipped armies on the continent of Europe—built by Tito in order to keep the Russians from unhindered access to the Mediterranean basin. When the war began, the international community imposed an arms embargo on all of Yugoslavia. Serbs controlling the Yugoslavian Army had a monopoly on arms and thus had a distinct military advantage.

In the very beginning of the democratic process, when they thought they were losing elections in some of the republics, they collected all of the arms, even from the national guard. Slovenes, especially Croats and Bosnians, had no arms to defend themselves. That is why in a very short time one third of Croatia was occupied; why more than 70 percent of Bosnia is under Serbian control; why more than 200,000 people have been killed; why there are more than 3 million refugees.

The Reconciliation Commission

I was a pastor of an inter-ethnic church in the city of Osijek where every fourth citizen was a Serbian. At the beginning of 1991 I was asked by our Prime Minister if I would serve on an inter-ethnic reconciliation commission. I was writing at that time for a secular journal and had considerable media exposure, in which I was pleading for understanding and tolerance and for cultivation of a culture of dialogue. So, of course, I agreed.

In one instance, the members of the commission were among those called upon to go into a town where the night before Serbs had blown up the house of a Croat leader. A parliament member, the vice president of our city, another distinguished leader, and I were to go in and participate in a public meeting, which included speeches on reconciliation and forgiveness.

I was away on ministry in another part of Croatia and was unable to join them, but the others went in. The Croat had a machine gun and when he saw them coming, he said, "Revenge! No reconciliation," and he machine gunned them. They were all killed.

Several days later my wife and I were at the funeral of the vice president of our city. It was a gathering of several thousand people. We were holding hands, and she pressed my hand more and more, our tears flowing as we watched the heart-broken pregnant widow and her four year-old child. Suddenly I felt her nails in my palm and she said, "Peter, you are resigning from that commission." I said "I can't. What do I tell people who have trusted me? How do I explain I am a Christian, and Christians are bridge builders. We are to be peacemakers, Jesus calls us to be reconcilers." She started crying. She blurted out, "Tell the prime minister and tell everyone that if they want a clergyman on the reconciliation commission, let them find a celibate. You've got our three daughters, and you've got me!" I'm not sure I'm qualified to speak on reconciliation because I resigned from that commission.

In the meantime, they started shelling our city. In eight months, over 150,000 shells fell. We had to evacuate. In my last sermon before we left, I preached on the 2nd chapter of Ephesians. I emphasized how Christ the Reconciler had "made the two one" by destroying the enmity. I even said He would make Serbs and Croats one if they would just respond to His loving, redemptive initiative. He destroyed the barrier, the dividing wall of hostility, and He wants to reconcile enemies through the cross.

God does not kill the enemy, but the enmity. There is no concept of class struggle or hate of the enemy. There is a conflict of love. The enemies are candidates for salvation. They are loved by God. I emphasized how God actually killed the enmity, the power of sin that was between them and God, and focused on the redemptive and reconciling power of the cross.

Witnessing a Parable

When we speak about reconciliation as Christians, I don't think we can speak about it without speaking of the cross. That was my difficulty in participating in a reconciliation commission that was more or less secular. How do I translate the most central Christian concepts — concepts which motivate me and give me reason to participate in these attempts — to those who do not accept these concepts, who do not acknowledge Christ as Lord of their lives?

As I was speaking on Ephesians 2, suddenly the air sirens went off and there was warning of an impending air attack. There were a couple hundred people who started screaming, "Let's run for the basements."

I said, "Please don't run. Stay. How do you know you will not be hit out there? Let us pray. Let's trust the Lord."

We prayed for a long time and finally when I opened my eyes I saw a parable, which became strong and vivid. I saw a Croatian family and a Serbian family embracing each other. I saw a Hungarian family embracing a Serbian family, although Hungarians were fleeing Serbian aggression in Hungary. Then I saw people looking for people from other ethnic groups to ask for forgiveness on behalf of their nations or their people, although they personally had done no wrong.

There were tears and there was reconciliation. I said, "Oh Lord, outside they kill each other. They hate each other. Here they love each other. Outside there is revenge. Here is reconciliation. There is hate. Here is love."

What is the difference? The cross of Christ. They worship the one holy and yet loving God who would not shed the blood of his enemies, but would in his divine redemptive plan allow the blood of his righteous son to be shed so that we, enemies of Him and of each other, may be forgiven and reconciled.

Our Role in Reconciliation

As followers of Christ, we need to bathe in prayer all our concerns about our broken world. Under communism in Eastern Europe we have learned about the power of prayer. In the post-communist ethnic conflicts we are learning that reconciliation is more a question of spirituality than strategy. Reconciliation is not brought about simply by a technical problem-solving rationality, but by a response to God's reconciling initiative in Christ.

In our churches we need to develop a biblically based non-sectarian understanding of the church, knowing that the Kingdom of God is bigger than our denominations and our organizational agendas. We must remove the "scandal of division" by praying and working for unity so that the world may recognize that we love each other (John 17). We must compliment each other's ministries rather than compete for souls, income and turf. We must also learn how to evangelize without proselytizing, especially to alleviate the fears of our Orthodox friends in post-communist eastern Europe.

We are called to work for justice in society. In international relations, we need to promote social order and cultural climates in which no one feels threatened. We must recognize that often there are social, racial, economic, and even religious obstacles to reconciliation. We must work systematically and persistently against all discrimination and inequality, especially in areas of education and employment. We need to unite in coordinated, intelligent action, being both the *proclaimers* and the *instruments* of peace and reconciliation.

We as leaders must think strategically, globally, and politically. Instead of narrowing our focus to small conflicts here and there, we need a long range preventative strategy: a comprehensive global agenda in this ministry of reconciliation. We need to contribute to the climate of dialogue and development of democracy and peace as we want to be instruments of reconciliation in our world.

One of the problems in our world at this critical juncture of human history is the lack of leadership globally — leadership marked by clarity of vision, moral conviction, and the will to act appropriately. Many conflicts in our world will not be resolved and the cry of the suffering and oppressed will not be effectively heard without such leadership.

We are called to be co-workers with Christ; to be ambassadors of peace, instruments of reconciliation. What a privilege we have. Our God, since the cross and resurrection, is in the process of creating a new humanity, a new creation. Let us never give up hope, for hope will energize us for action today.

Let me conclude with two statements of hope. St Augustine said, "Hope has two daughters: anger and courage. Anger with the way things are and courage to change them." The ministry of reconciliation calls us to have holy indignation and to take creative and courageous action. An Episcopalian bishop recently said, "Hope is the ability to listen to the music of the future. Faith is the courage to dance to it in the present." In the light of the biblical vision of the Kingdom of God, this is what our present ministry of reconciliation is about.

This article is taken from *Reconciliation in Difficult Places*, a publication prepared for the Washington Forum and edited by World Vision's Office of Advocacy and Education, Monrovia, Cal., 1994. It is used with the permission of the author.

$n\eth note s$

Chapter 1

[1] John Bartlett, Justin Kaplan, General Editor, *Bartlett's Familiar Quotations,* (Boston, MA: Little, Brown and Company), p. 57:20.

[2] Bruce Camp, "Major Paradigm Shifts in World Evangelization," *International Journal of Frontier Missions,* Vol. 11:3 July/Aug. 1994 (See a summary description of these paradigm distinctions in Chapter 9, Reshaping the Role of Missions Agencies).

[3] Ambassadors for Christ, 1355 Terrell Mill Road, Building 1484, Marietta, Georgia, 30067, (770) 956-8144.

[4] Partners International, 2302 Zanker Road, San Jose, Cal., 95131, (408) 453-3800.

[5] By 1996, Joshua Project 2000 had narrowed the list to just 1739 unadopted people groups. Each of these groups represents at least 10,000 people which are believed to be less than two percent evangelical and less than five percent composed of "Christian adherents." Because of the emphasis being steadfastly placed on reaching the unreached by Joshua Project 2000 and others, the remaining task of world evangelization is getting smaller every day!

Chapter 2

[1] Patrick Johnstone, *Operation World,* (Grand Rapids, MI: Zondervan Publishing House, 1993).

[2] Robert D. Kaplan, *Balkan Ghosts* (New York, NY: St. Martins Press, 1993), p. 7.

[3.] Ibid. p. 7.

[4.] David Manuel, *Bosnia Hope In the Ashes* (Brewster, MA: Paraclete Press, 1996), p. 167.

Chapter 4

[1.] David Manuel, *Bosnia Hope in the Ashes*, (Brewster, MA: Paraclete Press, 1996) p. 122.

[2.] *Mission Frontiers*, U.S. Center for World Mission, March-April 1996, p. 5.

[3.] John Bartlett, Justin Kaplan, General Editor, *Bartlett's Familiar Quotations*, (Boston, MA: Little, Brown and Company) p. 338:9.

Chapter 5

[1.] Fred R. Barnard as quoted in *Bartlett's Familiar Quotations*, Justin Kaplan, editor, (Boston, MA: Little, Brown & Company, 1992).

[2.] Donald A. Jensen, *Excelling In Global Giving* (Wheaton, IL: Conservative Baptist Foreign Mission Society, 1991).

Chapter 6

[1.] C. Peter Wagner, *Your Church Can Grow* (Ventura, CA: Regal Books, 1976), p. 135.

Chapter 7

[1.] Gerard Kelly & Lowell Sheppard, *Miracle In Mostar* (Oxford, England: Lion Publishing, 1995) p. 27-28.

[2.] Ibid. p. 26.

[3.] Ibid. p. 40.

[4.] Ibid. p. 48.

[5.] Ibid. p. 156.

[6] Henry T. Blackaby & Claude V. King, *Experiencing God* (Nashville, TN: LifeWay Press, 1990) p. 15.

Introduction to Part 2

[1] Hadden W. Robinson, *Biblical Preaching* (Grand Rapids, Michigan: Baker Books), p. 5.

Chapter 8

[1] Donald A. McGavran, *Understanding Church Growth* (Grand Rapids, Michigan: William B. Eerdmans Publishing Co.), p. 43.

[2] Ibid., p. 41.

[3] Ibid., p. 45.

[4] Ibid., p. 311.

[5] Jim Montgomery, *DAWN 2000* (Pasadena, CA: William Carey Library, 1989) p. 47.

[6] Ibid., p. 69.

[7] Carl George, *Prepare Your Church for the Future* (Old Tappan, NJ: Fleming H. Revell Co. 1991).

[8] Ralph W. Neighbour, Jr., *Where do We Go From Here?* (Houston, TX: Touch Publications, Inc., 1990).

[9] George, op. cit., p. 22.

[10] Bill M. Sullivan, *Ten Steps to Breaking the 200 Barrier* (Kansas City, MO: Beacon Hill Press 1988).

[11] Ibid., p. 12.

[12] Neighbour, op. cit., p. 14.

Chapter 9

[1] Ralph Winter, "Part II: Crucial Issues in Missions: Working Toward the Year 2000," *Mission Frontiers*, November 1990, p. 19.

[2] Proponents of the meta-church and cell group church context claim that the small group systems which comprise these expansive models can adequately provide for quality congregational care. In Appendix I, I offer eight reasons why I am skeptical of this claim.

[3] Carl George, *Prepare Your Church for the Future* (Old Tappan, NJ: Fleming H. Revell Co. 1991) p. 105.

[4] George Barna, *The Frog in the Kettle* (Ventura, CA: Regal Books, 1990), p. 142-143.

[5] Ralph Winter, "The Two Structures of God's Redemptive Mission," *Missiology: An International Review*, January 1974, p. 135.

[6] Richard C. Halverson, *How I Changed My Thinking About the Church*, (Grand Rapids: Zondervan Publishing House, 1972), p. 73, 74.

[7] C. Peter Wagner, *Leading Your Church to Growth* (Ventura, CA: Regal Books, 1984) p. 103-104.

[8] Barna, op. cit., p. 150.

[9] Howard A. Snyder, *The Community of the King* (Downers Grove, IL: Inter-Varsity Press, 1977), p. 65.

Chapter 10

[1] George Otis, Jr., *The Last of the Giants* (Terrytown, NY: Flemming H. Revell Co., 1991), p. 52.

[2] Lyle Schaller, *The Small Church Is Different* (Nashville, TN: Abingdon Press, 1982).

3. Kent and Barbara Hughes, *Liberating the Ministry from the Success Syndrome* (Wheaton, IL: Tyndale House Publishers, Inc., 1988), p. 29.

4. George Barna, *The Frog In the Kettle* (Ventura, CA: Regal Books, 1990), p. 79.

5. Ibid, p. 126.

6. Ibid., p. 121.

7. Ralph Winter, "An Inside View of MacGavran," *Mission Frontiers*, June-October 1990, p. 8-9.

8. Leith Anderson, *Dying for Change* (Minneapolis, MN: Bethany House Publishers, 1990), p. 85.

Chapter 12

1. Ralph Winter, *Mission Frontiers*, Vol. 20 No. 3-4, March-April 1998, p. 2-5 "Editorial Comments."

2. Peter Wagner, *Leading Your Church to Growth.*

3. Jeff Reed, Presented to North American Professors of Christian Education, "Church-Based Theological Education: Creating a New Paradigm," Oct. 17, 1992.

4. Jonathan Chao, "Education and Leadership," Chapter 11 in *The New Face of Evangelicalism: An International Symposium on the Lausanne Covenant*, edited by Rene Padilla (IVP, 1976).

5. Robert W. Ferris, *Renewal In Theological Education*, Billy Graham Center, Wheaton College, 1990, p. 16.

6. James F. Engle, *A Clouded Future? Advancing North American World Missions* (Milwaukee, WI: Christian Stewardship Association, 1996) p. 25.

[7] Ralph Winter, op. cit. p. 2.

[8] Ibid. p. 2-3.

[9] Ibid. p. 4.

[10] *Mission Frontiers*, Vol. 20 No. 3-4, March-April 1998, "Mission Training File: Next Step Launched," p. 69.

[11] Ferris, op. cit. p. 20.

[12] Ibid. Appendix A, p. 139-146.

[13] William Taylor, Editor, *Internationalizing Missionary Training*, p. 5.

[14] Edgar J. Elliston, *Home Grown Leaders* (Pasadena: CA: William Carey Library, 1992) p. 76-77.

[15] Ibid. p. 56.

[16] Taylor, op. cit. p. 8.

[17] Ibid. p. 231.

[18] Ibid. p. 234.

[19] Ibid. p. 195.

[20] Elliston, op. cit. p. 132.

[21] Taylor, op. cit. p. 195.

[22] Elliston, op. cit. p. 3-4.

[23] Taylor, op. cit. p. 5.

[24] Ibid. p. 6.

25. Ibid. p. 33-35.

26. Elliston, op. cit. p.134 –135.

Chapter 13

1. Henry Kissinger, *Diplomacy* (New York, New York: Simon & Schuster,1994) p. 161.

2. Bruce Camp.

3. Engle p. 21.

4. Ibid., p. 6.

5. Ibid., p. 4.

6. Chuck Bennett, "Six Spheres of Mission Overseas," *Mission Frontiers,* Vol. 20, Number 3-4, March-April 1998, p. 40.

7. Phill Butler fax to Dr. Paul Cedar 1/17/96.

8. Engle, op. cit., p. 11.

9. Ibid., p. 12-13.

10. Ibid., p. 13.

11. Ibid., p. 5-6.

12. Bruce Camp's article articulating this change in agency church relationships is entitled, "Paradigm Shift In World Evangelism." It is reproduced in its entirety in Appendix II and recommended for any reader serious about understanding this trend.

13. Engle, op. cit. p. 17.

14. Chuck Bennett, "Trouble In Paradox," 1996 *MISSION TODAY*, p. 27-29.

15. Camp, op. cit. p. 5.

[16.] Samuel F. Metcalf, "When Local Churches Act Like Agencies," *Missions Frontier Bulletin*, U.S. Center for World Mission, July/August 1993, p. 28.

[17.] Ibid., p. 27-28.

[18.] Ibid., p. 26.

[19.] Gary Cowin, "Here Come the Missiomega Churches," *Evangelical Missions Quarterly*, Vol. 33, No. 2, April 1997, p. 143.

[20.] Ibid., p. 142.

[21.] Jeff Reed, "Church-Based Missions: Creating a New Paradigm," presentation to BILD Annual Conference, October 23, 1992.

[22.] Camp, op. cit. p. 136.

[23.] Antioch Network, 5060 North 19th Ave., Suite 312, Phoenix, AZ 85015, (602) 242-4414.

[24.] Because neither pastoral leaders nor the professionals guiding most mission agencies have had experience in formulating mutually beneficial partnerships under this new paradigm, I offer in Appendix IV some suggestions as to how these leaders' respective concerns can be resolved. I hope that reviewing these suggestions will stimulate further creative thinking about synergistic partnerships so that the full potential of all mission partners can be realized to the glory of God.

Chapter 14

[1.] Ralph Winter, "Two Structures of God's Redemptive Mission," an address given to the All-Asian Mission Consultation, Soul, Korea, August 1973.

[2.] Kenneth S. Wuest, *Wuest's Word Studies from the Greek New Testament*, Vol. One (Grand Rapids, MI: Wm. B. Eerdmans Publishing Company, 1973) p. 89.

[3.] The full text of an article reflecting Dr. Kuzmic's views on the war in Bosnia is contained in Appendix V. My readers are encouraged to read the article in its entirety to gain perspective on this war from a national's perspective. This quote is taken from the portion of the article found on page 4 of that appendix.

Scripture Index

General Index

Possible Agency Partners for Your Own Church-Based Mission Effort:

ACMC
P.O. Box 3929
Peachtree City, GA 30269-7929
770-631-9900
Atlanta@ACMC.org

AD 2000 & Beyond Movement
2860 S Circle #2112
Colorado Springs, CO 80906
719-576-2000
Web: http://www.ad2000.org/

Alliance for Saturation Church Planting
P.O. Box 668767
Charlotte, NC 28266-8767
704-357-3355

Ambassadors for Christ
1355 Terrell Mill Road #1484
Marietta, GA 30067
770-980-2020
73440.127@compuserve.com

Antioch Network
5060 North 19th Ave. Suite 312
Phoenix, AZ 850-15
602-242-4414

BILD International
P.O. Box 1507
Ames, IA 50014-1507
515-292-7012
BILD@AMES.NET

Caleb Project
#10 W. Dry Creek Circle
Littleton, CO 80120
303-730-4170
Info@cproject.com

EFCM
901 E. 78th Street
Minneapolis, MN 55420-1300
612-854-1300
72220.2577@compuserve.com

Frontiers
325 N. Stapley Drive
Mesa, AZ 85203
602-834-1500
http://www.us.frontiers.org/

INTERDEV
P.O. Box 3883
Seattle, WA 98124
425-775-8330
INTERDEV-US@xc.org

Jesus Film Project
P.O. Box 72007
San Clemente, CA 92674-9207
1-800-432-1997
Postmaster@ccci.org

Joshua Project 2000
c/o AD2000 & Beyond
Movement (see above)
719-593-9340

Mission America
901 East 78th Street
Minneapolis, MN 55420
612-853-1762

Ministry Resource Network
5185 Peachtree-Dunwoody Rd.
Atlanta, GA 30342
404-256-5700
74222.2507@compuserve.com

OC International
P.O. Box 36900
Colorado Springs, CO 80936
719-592-9292
103130.3660@compuserve.com

Operation Mobilization
P.O. Box 444
Tyrone, GA 30290
770-631-0432
Info@omusa.om.org

Partners International
2302 Zanker Road Suite 100
San Jose, CA 95131
408-453-3800

U.S. Center for World Mission
1605 E Elizabeth Street
Pasadena, CA 91104
626-797-1111
Firstname.Lastname@uscwm.org

United World Missions
P.O. Box 668767
Charlotte, NC 28266-8767
704-357-3355

World Relief
P.O. Box WRC
Wheaton, IL 60189
630-665-0235
WorldRelief@xc.org

Want Further Information?

For further information on Bosnia, church-based missions, or ministry in the small church, contact us:

At our web site: www.northsidecommunity.org

At our e-mail address: 74222.2507@compuserve.com

At our toll-free number: 1-877-CHURCH5

Or write us at   Northside Community Church
                    5185 Peachtree Dunwoody Road NE
                    Atlanta, GA 30342

The book is also available from Amazon.com and Spring Arbor

For credit card orders call 1-800-931-BOOK